TOTAL
IMMERSION

TOTAL IMMERSION

A *Mikvah* Anthology

edited by
Rivkah Slonim

Liz Rosenberg
consulting and contributing editor

JASON ARONSON INC.
Northvale, New Jersey
London

This book was set in 10 pt. Times by AeroType, Inc.

Acknowledgments for permission to reprint previously published material appear on pp. 249–251.

10 9 8 7 6 5 4 3 2 1

Library of Congress Cataloging-in-Publication Data

Total immersion : a mikvah anthology / edited by Rivkah Slonim.
    p.   cm.
  Includes bibliographical references and index.
  ISBN 1-56821-534-7 (alk. paper)
  1. Mikveh.   2. Jewish women—religious life.   I. Slonim, Rivkah.
  BM703.T68   1996
  296.7—dc20   95-21766

Manufactured in the United States of America. Jason Aronson Inc. offers books and cassettes. For information and catalog write to Jason Aronson Inc., 230 Livingston Street, Northvale, New Jersey 07647.

To the eternal life and spirit of
the Lubavitcher Rebbe,
Rabbi Menachem Mendel Schneerson

Contents

PART II
VOICES

PART III
MEMORIES AND TALES

Preface

No one talks much about *Mikvah,* and why would they? People either joke or whisper about it, but few address it seriously.

In Jewish homes committed to observance, it is a fact of life closely associated with the sexual rhythm of a couple. The inherent modesty of a religious lifestyle precludes *Mikvah* from becoming a household word.

For the vast majority of Jews, though, *Mikvah* is simply irrelevant, a nonissue. To be sure, many have heard some horror story—real or imagined—about a *mikvah* experience of their grandmother or even someone closer to their own ages. They may know some observant woman who still practices the rite. And then there are all those funny stories about religious Jews and sex and *Mikvah.* . . .

But *Mikvah* is rarely, if ever, the theme of public discourses or the subject of editorials. It is not something even sisterhoods include in their realm of programming. It is not what "the girls" or mothers and daughters talk about. And so it is that one of the most central and beautiful rites in Judaism has been lost to many.

This anthology grew out of my desire to bring the ritual of *Mikvah* out of the shadow and into the light.

Twelve years ago, young and probably blushing, I—like all other self-respecting observant wives-to-be—attended "*kallah* classes," the time-honored euphemism for study sessions in which the laws of Jewish married life are taught to brides. It was in that venue that I officially learned the rudiments of an observance called *Mikvah,* or Family Purity. I say "officially" for I had read literature on the subject before: first as a youngster who had stumbled on something bordering the forbidden and later, over the years, as I amassed a general knowledge of the laws that delineated the holy institution of marriage. But then it had all been theoretical, and now it was my life.

Once a week, for six weeks straight, I would forget the hassles of school, job, and pre-wedding preparations and ride over to a neighborhood school where these classes were held. I remember those two hours as being inviolable. No matter what else had to be done—gown, menu, flowers, apartment hunting—*kallah* classes came first. Stepping into the class, I could see the same feeling of intensity on the other faces. We were in a sorority of sorts, and we were determined to fulfill our pledge.

In a systematic, matter-of-fact, decidedly unsentimental fashion, the instructor impressed upon me and the dozen or so young women in the room the importance of the laws governing the intimate life of a Jew. And she taught us the details. The simple classroom we sat in became the epicenter of all that is right, holy, pure. I began to see my body and my menstrual cycle as being very significant, very powerful, very important. I began to see how I could and would, through *Mikvah,* impact my husband, my family, my people.

But I don't remember thinking much about how this would affect me—that is, us. I don't remember considering if I would enjoy the ritual or not. I was an observant Jew, and this was part of how I lived. My preoccupation was with the nuances of the observance itself.

But all this quickly changed. After a few months of marriage my anxiety about the details of *Mikvah* gave way to an understanding and appreciation of the concept. As a newly married woman, all kinds of new emotions welled up in me. There were the delicious sensations of loving and being loved, of being a woman—somebody's special woman—and there were thoughts about our future, the family we hoped to create together. And always there was the *mikvah,* at the very crux of all that was important to me.

I loved counting down to that special night—I felt like I had a secret, a precious gift. And indeed I had.

I loved knowing that my husband was counting too. Here were two people— just two more in the huge universe—but we shared something no one else did.

I loved the night of reunion. It was a major holiday that no one else knew of.

I loved the way *Mikvah* gave me the chance to bring God into my life in a very real, palpable way. The kosher diet brought God into my kitchen. Candle-lighting on *Shabbat* and holidays brought God into my home. But *Mikvah*—as I felt the rush of waters around and within—brought God into *me*.

I loved the feeling of connection to the generations of women who had preceded me in their adherence of this rite. I began to understand how special it must have been for my mother when she accompanied me to the *mikvah* on the eve of my wedding. And I remember my grandparents kissing me lovingly when I returned home that night, their hands fingering my hair still wet with *mikvah* waters.

Mikvah wasn't always easy. But my appreciation for what this two week on, two week off rhythm did for my marriage increased over time. I marveled at the brilliance of the divine law. I reveled in the tradition I had inherited.

Especially when *Mikvah* presented difficulties, I thought about its spiritual significance. At its core was consecration, the renewal of my holy covenant with God—and with my husband. In this rite I heard the resonance of the holy words with which I was wed: "Behold you are sanctified to me according to the laws of Moses and Israel."

The birth of my first child showed me yet another dimension. Like a typical first-time mother, I read every piece of material in the doctor's office. Each of these books, pamphlets, magazines included a chapter on the inevitable changes and tensions that befall one's sex life after birthing. My experience, however, was radically different.

Adherence to the laws of *Mikvah* meant waiting for the reinstatement of our physical relationship until I had completely stopped bleeding; not even a hint of residual staining could remain. Up until that time and for seven days thereafter, when I would immerse in the *mikvah,* we couldn't as much as hold hands. It was then I learned the meaning of anticipation. When *mikvah* night finally came, I was ready—body, mind, and soul. *Mikvah*'s power swept over me like a tidal wave. Without even knowing it, I had adopted *Mikvah* as my very own favorite *mitzvah.*

Some time later, living in Binghamton, New York, where my husband and I direct the Chabad House Jewish Student Center, my enthusiasm for the *mikvah* took on a new—more public—form. It happened quite accidentally. My husband was scheduled to leave for New York for a weekend conference, and I was staying home alone. Just as I had resigned myself to a quiet, even lonely, *Shabbat,* something inside me prompted me to make it special. I decided to host a Friday-night dinner for women only and feature a discussion on love and marriage the Jewish way. After the food and drinks, laughter and songs, and kibitzing—as the *Shabbat* flames burned low—the young women looked at me expectantly, and we settled down to discuss the matter at hand. Drawing on a host of Jewish sources, I presented them with a different—to them radically new—perspective on themes that figure prominently in collegiate life: love and sex. But my new twist included words like commitment, restraint, consecration, and, of course, *Mikvah.*

Instead of vehement opposition or—worse yet—polite, condescending silence, rolling eyes, and sympathetic glances, my presentation was met with
genuine interest and receptivity. There were no quick conversions in lifestyle or
promises of change on the part of these thoroughly modern young women. But
they were intrigued by the millennium-old outlook I had shared with them. It
wasn't just the glow of the candles or the blush of the red *Kiddush* wine. Beyond
the "hole in the sheet" myth, they had never heard much about what traditional
Judaism has to say on these subjects. They found it relevant to their lives; they
were impressed with their tradition and thankful for the newfound knowledge.
This was not what one would expect from heiresses of the sexual revolution.

The discussion lasted far into that night. The discussion continues today.
That memorable evening was the beginning of a decade of conversations and
speaking engagements that have taken me around the country and beyond.

Everywhere I go things are the same. *Mikvah* is a concept shrouded in
obscurity and more often than not projected and perceived in a disparaging
light. It seems as if Jewish women of the last two or three generations have
inherited a legacy of disdain towards this ritual. There is repulsion, anger, and
more than a little confusion. *Mikvah* is deemed arcane, sexist, and misogynist.
There is little understanding of the central role it plays in Jewish life, its
possibilities for feminist expression, or how it can enhance marriage.

And yet in spite of all the negative press and stereotypes, there is great
interest. The people who comprise the audiences I speak to prove that. They are
generally not committed to religious observance. But they are turning to their
Jewish roots in search of meaning, stability, and lasting values with which to
infuse their lives. When they learn about *Mikvah,* most are shocked to find that
they have stumbled—quite accidentally—upon beauty and wisdom, direction
and strength.

Many are angry that they were never taught or told about *Mikvah,* even by
the rabbis who officiated at their weddings. And this happens to some, even
after specifically asking about everything they should or could do to start their
lives off right.

Many are surprised to hear of *Mikvah*'s importance—on a par with *Shabbat,
Kashrut,* and, yes, Yom Kippur and circumcision.

Others are compelled by the power *Mikvah* vests in their femininity. They
are intrigued by what *Mikvah* can do for their sense of womanhood.

"Why didn't anyone tell me?" became a litany, a cry I heard echoed one time
too many. It was what started me thinking about making a contribution—as
simple as it might be—toward righting this wrong. I wanted to help bring
Mikvah out of the closet.

During the many generations of persecution, Jews built *mikvahs* in hiding—in
underground tunnels, in cellars, under tables, and, yes, often literally in closets.

Then came the modern age of emancipation and assimilation. This time Jews dug deeper, burying the *mikvah* in the darkest, farthest recesses of their collective mind and conscience.

Obscured by misinformation, caught in an intricate web of stigma and innuendo, *Mikvah* still lies hidden under a cover of silence. But I am convinced this can be changed. I have seen the power of education at work. And I know that the time is ripe to bring *Mikvah* back to its rightful and honored place in our lives.

Our great grandmothers used the *mikvah* monthly. Most of our grandmothers visited the *mikvah* before they married. Many of our mothers did, too. What of ourselves, our daughters, and their daughters? Jewish women of today and tomorrow deserve at the very least to make an informed choice.

And so in these pages are recorded the echoes of times past and the sounds of *Mikvah* waters splashing today. Part I, In Theory and Practice, contains various essays that discuss *Mikvah* and the consequences of its use from the theological, philosophical, mystical, practical, and historical perspectives. Part II, Voices, offers a collection of writings that capture the attitudes and responses of women (and some men) to this rite. It presents some of the earliest prayers, speeches, and writings on the subject as well as an eclectic gathering of testimonials by contemporary women. Part III, Memories and Tales, offers an extensive collection of *Mikvah* stories from the Warsaw Ghetto to Aruba, from Communist Russia to Alaska. What emerges is a beauty and depth found only in the complexity of multiplicity.

I took a gift I was given and wrapped it—in many layers of various patterns, shades, and hues—to give to you, my soul sister. Because all Jewish women should know of their right to experience total immersion.

Rivkah Slonim

Acknowledgments

As a child I always felt lucky. For as long as I can remember—far before I realized its value or scarcity—I've been blessed with a deep sense of good fortune. With the passage of time—with maturity and experience—that feeling is strengthened as is my appreciation for those who are at its source. There is also profound recognition of how deeply these individuals have effected every facet of my life and thus brought me such abundant opportunity and joy. It is with great humility and immeasurable gratitude that I acknowledge, at least partially, my debts.

No child could ever hope for or dream of receiving more love, support, and inspiration than I have from my parents, Rabbi Nochum and Mrs. Esther Sternberg. They, along with my grandparents, Rabbi Schnejer Zalman and Rebbetzin Chava Gurary and Rabbi Mordechai (of blessed memory) and Rebbetzin Gitel Sternberg, provided me with majestic examples of what it means to live and learn Judaism and imbued me with a love and devotion I can only hope to pass on.

No student could ever hope to be educated in a more stimulating, wholesome, and nurturing environment than I enjoyed in the Bais Rivkah educational system. My principals and teachers were inspiring role models, and their lessons—both in and out of the classroom—remain with me to this day.

No woman could ever hope for more in a life partner than I have in mine, Rabbi Aaron Slonim.

And no Jew could ever hope for a greater privilege than serving as a *shliach,* an emissary, of the Lubavitcher Rebbe. In that capacity I have been challenged and infinitely enriched—intellectually and spiritually—by the thousands of individuals who have been and continue to be part of my life at the Chabad House in Binghamton, New York.

This volume is in no small measure the result of these combined influences. I will never know what I did to be deserving. And so I offer endless thanks to the one above, the source of all. I pray that I be worthy in some small measure of all the good he has bestowed upon me and of his continued benevolence.

Like many books this one began with a germ of an idea. I thank the hundreds of women (and men) who asked me to recommend reading on the subject of *Mikvah.* It is they who served as the catalyst for my work on this collection. I am thankful, too, to Mrs. Chana Gorowitz, Mrs. Leah Klein, and Ms. Martha Jean Schechter for their encouragement and for their belief in my ability to follow through on my inspiration. Special appreciation goes to Arthur Kurzweil, my publisher, for his enthusiasm and the careful attention he gave the book from start to finish, and to Jean Pease, my editor, for her assistance and warm support.

The many contributors to this volume added depth and vibrant complexity to my already passionate feelings on the subject of *Mikvah.* It was a pleasure working with them all. I thank them for their work and devotion to this project and for the rich texture and multiple dimensions they have lent this collection.

When I began work on this project, I could not foresee the great amount of time and energy it would demand. My husband, Aaron, encouraged and supported me through every phase of the project, offering generously of his wisdom, eternal optimism, and practical assistance. His belief in the project and its success was integral to the process and took me through my many moments of doubt and frustration. For all of this and much more than I can ever express, I thank him.

The individual to whom I am most thankful for her help in bringing this book to fruition is Liz Rosenberg. Only God could have brought Liz and me together (see page 154 for her account) and with her came many blessings. Liz spent hours working on the manuscript—many more than I could ask for (even with substantial *chutzpah*) and she knew she possessed—reviewing, analyzing, and revising. An award-winning poet and author, editor, and teacher of creative writing and English, Liz has left her mark on every one of the contributions in this book. Her gifted pen is matched only by the beauty of her soul, whose imprint is found on the pages of this volume. And in our work together, I have gained a very special friend. May God bless her and her family with all material and spiritual goodness.

For his kindness in taking of his precious time to review the manuscript and for his invaluable suggestions and insight, I am deeply indebted to Rabbi J.

Immanuel Schochet. Needless to say, all of the book's shortcomings and failings are my responsibility alone.

For their recommendations and feedback at various stages of work on this book, I thank my friends and colleagues Michla Schanowitz, Hinda Leah Sharfstein, and Chana Silberstein and my sisters and sister-in-law, Sarah Raskin, Malkah Dubov, Chanah Diskind, and Mariashah Sternberg. For providing that sense of calm amidst the chaos, for going that extra mile (make that a few thousand miles) always with a smile, I thank Carol Seidel, a very special friend and part of our family. For their kind assistance in proofreading the manuscript, I thank Marlene Serkin, Marlene Wolsh, and Gila Zamir.

Lastly, I thank my children, Levi Yitzchok, Chanah, Yehudah Leib, Shmuel, and Chayah Muskah (whose conception, gestation, and birth coincided with the various stages of this book), for their patience and good humor—despite the endless phone calls and my preoccupation with the computer—and above all for being such a source of light and joy, otherwise known as *nachas*. One day they will understand this acknowledgment and just how much they mean to me.

In closing, I pray: "Our Father, merciful Father who is compassionate, have mercy on us, and grant our heart understanding to comprehend and to discern, to perceive, to learn and to teach, to observe, to practice and to fulfill all the teachings of Your Torah with love."

Introduction
Understanding *Mikvah* and the Laws of Family Purity

Rivkah Slonim

I

The world's natural bodies of water—its oceans, rivers, wells, and spring-fed lakes—are *mikvahs* in their most primal form. They contain waters of divine source and thus, tradition teaches, the power to purify. Created even before the earth took shape, these bodies of water offer a quintessential route to consecration. But they pose difficulties as well. These waters may be inaccessible or dangerous, not to mention the problems of inclement weather and lack of privacy. Jewish life therefore necessitates the construction of *mikvahs* (*mikvah* pools), and indeed this has been done by Jews in every age and circumstance.

To the uninitiated, a modern-day *mikvah* looks like a miniature swimming pool. In a religion rich with detail, beauty, and ornamentation—against the backdrop of the ancient temple or even modern-day synagogues—the *mikvah* is surprisingly nondescript, a humble structure.

Its ordinary appearance, however, belies its primary place in Jewish life and law. The *mikvah* offers the individual, the community, and the nation of Israel the remarkable gift of purity and holiness. No other religious establishment, structure, or rite can affect the Jew in this way and, indeed, on such an essential level. Its extraordinary power, however, is contingent on its construction in accordance with the numerous and complex specifications as outlined in *Halachah,* Jewish Law.

Briefly: A *mikvah* must be built into the ground or built as an essential part of a building. Portable receptacles, such as bathtubs, whirlpools, or Jacuzzis, can therefore never function as *mikvahs.* The *mikvah* must contain a minimum of two hundred gallons of rainwater that was gathered and siphoned into the *mikvah* pool in accordance with a highly specific set of regulations. In extreme cases where the acquisition of rainwater is impossible, ice or snow originating from a natural source may be used to fill the *mikvah.* As with the rainwater, an intricate set of laws surrounds its transport and handling.

The casual observer will often see only one pool—the one used for immersion. In reality, most *mikvahs* are comprised of two, sometimes three, adjoining pools. While the accumulated rainwater is kept in one pool, the adjacent immersion pool is drained and refilled regularly with tap water. The pools share a common wall that has a hole at least two inches in diameter.

The free flow, or "kissing," of waters between the two pools makes the waters of the immersion pool an extension of the natural rainwater, thus conferring upon the immersion pool the legal status of a *mikvah.* (The above description is one of two methods sanctioned by *Halachah* to achieve this goal.)

Modern-day *mikvah* pools are equipped with filtration and water-purification systems. The *mikvah* waters are commonly chest high and kept at a comfortable temperature. Access to the pool is achieved via stairs. (*Mikvahs* accessible to the handicapped or infirm are equipped with lifts; see pages 239–240 for a partial listing of these *mikvahs.*)

The *mikvah* as an institution is the victim of a popular misconception. Immersion in water is naturally associated with cleansing. To further complicate the issue, Jews historically were often barred by the authorities from using rivers in their cities for bathing. In response they built bathhouses, many with *mikvahs* in or near them. Together, these factors forged an inextricable link between the idea of *Mikvah* and physical hygiene. But the *mikvah* never was a monthly substitute for a bath or shower. In fact, the *Halachah* stipulates that one must be scrupulously clean *before* immersing. To facilitate this requirement, preparation areas—with baths and showers, shampoos, soaps, and other cleansing and beauty aids—are a staple of the modern *mikvah.*

Many *mikvahs* are located in synagogues, always in a discreet part of the building and usually with their own entrance. Larger *mikvahs* are generally housed in freestanding buildings. Until a relatively short time ago, most *mikvahs* could best be described as utilitarian: function, not comfort, dictated their style. A new awareness among modern Jewish women, the rabbinate, and community leaders over the last few decades has sparked a new trend in *mikvah* construction. Beautiful, even lavish, *mikvahs*—complete with elegant foyers and waiting rooms, fully equipped preparation areas, and well-designed *mikvah* pools—are being built across this country and around the world. Some *mikvahs* rival luxurious European spas and offer patrons more amenities than they could enjoy at home.

In communities with large populations of *mikvah* users, the building may house as many as twenty or thirty preparation areas and two to four immersion pools. In these facilities, an intercom system linking each of the rooms to a central desk and an attendant ensures the privacy of the many *mikvah* users. Some of the larger *mikvah* buildings include conference rooms used for tours and educational programming.

Today it is not just a Jewish metropolis that can boast a *mikvah*. In remote, even exotic, locations—Argentina and Brazil, Tasmania and Austria; Anchorage, Alaska, and Bogota, Colombia; Yerres, France, and Ladispoli, Italy; Agadir, Morocco, and Asuncion in Paraguay; Lima, Peru, and Cape Town, South Africa; Bangkok, Thailand, and Zarzis, Tunisia; and almost every city in the C.I.S. (former Soviet Union)—there are kosher and comfortable *mikvahs* and rabbis and rebbetzins willing and able to assist any woman in their use.

In many communities a tour of the *mikvah* is available on request. Upon arrival in a new city or when traveling, information about *mikvahs* in the region can be obtained by phoning the local *mikvah* office, the Orthodox synagogue, or the Chabad House.

II

Immersion in the *mikvah* has offered a gateway to purity ever since the creation of man. The *Midrash* relates that after being banished from Eden, Adam sat in a river that flowed from the garden. This was an integral part of his *teshuvah* (repentance) process, of his attempt at return to his original perfection.

Before the revelation at Sinai, all Jews were commanded to immerse themselves in preparation for coming face to face with God.

In the desert, the famed "well of Miriam" served as a *mikvah*. And Aaron and his sons' induction into the priesthood was marked by immersion in the *mikvah*.

In Temple times, the priests as well as each Jew who wished entry into the House of God had first to immerse in a *mikvah*.

On Yom Kippur, the holiest of all days, the High Priest was allowed entrance into the Holy of Holies, the innermost chamber of the Temple, into which no other mortal could enter. This was the zenith of a day that involved an ascending order of services, each of which was preceded by immersion in the *mikvah*.

The primary uses of *Mikvah* today are delineated in Jewish Law and date back to the dawn of Jewish history. They cover many elements of Jewish life. *Mikvah* is an integral part of conversion to Judaism. *Mikvah* is used, though less widely known, for the immersion of new pots, dishes, and utensils (purchased or obtained from a non-Jew) before they are used by a Jew. The *Mikvah* concept is also the focal point of the *Taharah,* the purification rite of a Jew before the person is laid to rest and the soul ascends on high. The manual pouring of water – in a highly specific manner – over the entire body of the deceased serves this purpose. *Mikvah* is also used by men on various occasions; with the exception of conversion, they are all customary. The most widely practiced are immersion by a groom on his wedding day and by every man before Yom Kippur. Many chasidic men use the *mikvah* before each *Shabbat* and holiday, some even making use of *mikvah* each day before morning prayer (in cities with large populations of observant Jews, special *mikvahs* for men facilitate these customs). But the most important and general usage of *mikvah* is for purification by the menstruant woman.

For the menstruant woman, immersion in a *mikvah* is part of a larger framework best known as *Taharat Hamishpachah* (Family Purity).

As with every area of Jewish practice, Family Purity involves a set of detailed laws; namely, the "when," "what," and "how" of observance. Studying with a woman who is experienced in this field is the time-honored way of gaining familiarity and comfort with the practice. In cities or communities with large Jewish populations, there may be classes one can join. The majority of women, however, come by this knowledge through a more personal one-on-one encounter.

While books are a poor substitute for a knowledgeable teacher, select titles can be used as a guide to this ritual or for quick reference (see suggested book list on pages 235–236). Those with a serious interest in observing this ritual may want to follow up their reading with discussion and/or further study. On occasion, medical conditions or other factors might necessitate rabbinic counsel. Wherever you are, you can count on one thing: there is always someone available and eager to help you, in person or by phone (see pages 236–237 for contact sources).

What follows is only a brief overview of these laws. It is not, and was not intended to be, a substitute for proper study of this subject.

Family purity is a system predicated on the woman's monthly cycle. From the onset of menstruation and for seven days after its end, until the woman immerses in the *mikvah,* husband and wife may not engage in sexual relations. To avoid violation of this law, the couple should curtail their indulgence in actions they find arousing. They should put a check on direct physical contact and refrain from manifestations of affection such as petting, necking, caressing, and the like. The technical term for a woman in this state is *Niddah* (literal meaning: to be separated).

The seven-day transition period, known as the "clean" or "white" days, begins only after the woman has determined the complete cessation of her menses by means of a simple internal examination. The examination should be carried out before sunset of the day her period ends, provided there has been a minimum of five days from the onset of menstruation. (Even if a woman's period lasts less than five days she must still wait a minimum of five days from its onset before examining herself.) If her bleeding ceases after nightfall, she waits for the afternoon of the next day to examine herself and begin her week-long count.

During the seven day "white" period, the woman should examine herself regularly to ensure that there is no further issue of menstrual blood. In addition, white underclothes are worn during this period so that the woman can be sure to sight any bloody discharge.

Exactly a week from when the woman has established the cessation of her flow, barring any staining or spotting, she visits the *mikvah* (i.e., if she examined herself before sunset on Monday, she will visit the *mikvah* the following Monday evening). Hence, there is a minimum of twelve days during which conjugal life is suspended.

Immersion takes place after nightfall of the seventh day and is preceded by a requisite cleansing. The immersion is valid only when the waters of the *mikvah* envelop each and every part of the body and, indeed, each hair. To this end, the woman bathes, shampoos, combs her hair, and removes from her body anything that might impede her total immersion.

A female attendant, known as a *shomeret,* is present at immersion. She assists in ensuring that there are no intervening substances or objects (makeup, loose hair or jewelry, etcetera) on the woman's body and that her whole body is submerged all at once during immersion. In keeping with the biblical injunction against placing oneself in danger, the attendant is also there to assist the woman as necessary.

Immersion in the *mikvah* is the culmination of the *Taharat Hamishpachah* discipline. It is a special moment for the woman who has adhered to the many nuances of the *mitzvah* and has anticipated this night. Sometimes, however, the woman may be feeling rushed or anxious for reasons related or unrelated to this rite. At this point, she should relax, spend a few moments contemplating the importance of the immersion, and in an unhurried fashion, lower herself into the *mikvah* waters. After immersing once, while standing in the waters of the *mikvah,* the woman recites the blessing for ritual purification and then, in accordance with widespread custom, immerses twice more. Many women use this auspicious time for personal prayer and communication with God. After immersion, woman and husband may resume marital relations.

III

Before exploring the deeper dimensions of this ritual, we must briefly examine the centrality of *Mikvah* to Jewish life.

Most Jews, even those who deem themselves secular, are familiar, at least conceptually, with religious observances such as the Sabbath, the dietary laws, Yom Kippur and a number of other Torah laws. *Mikvah* and Family Purity, on the other hand, are shrouded in obscurity—pages torn out of the book, as it were.

The observance of Family Purity is a biblical injunction of the highest order. The infraction of this law is equated with major transgressions such as eating *chametz* (leavened foods) on Passover, intentional violation of the fast on the holy day of Yom Kippur, and not entering into the covenant through ritual circumcision, *brit milah*.

Most Jews see the synagogue as the central institution in Jewish life. But Jewish Law states that constructing a *mikvah* takes precedence even over building a house of worship. Both a synagogue and a Torah Scroll, Judaism's most venerated treasure, may be sold to raise funds for the building of a *mikvah*. In fact, in the eyes of Jewish law, a group of Jewish families living together do not attain the status of a community if they do not have a communal *mikvah*.

This is so for a simple reason: private and even communal prayer can be held in virtually any location, and venues for the social functions of the synagogue can be found elsewhere. But Jewish married life, and therefore the birth of future generations in accordance with *Halachah,* is possible only where there is accessibility to a *mikvah*. It is no exaggeration to state that the *mikvah* is the touchstone of Jewish life and the portal to a Jewish future.

IV

We have already determined that the function of *Mikvah* is not to enhance physical hygiene. The concept of *Mikvah* is rooted in the spiritual.

Jewish life is marked by the notion of *Havdalah*—separation or distinction. On Saturday night, as the *Shabbat* departs and the new week begins, Jews are reminded of the borders that delineate every aspect of life. Over a cup of sanctified wine, the Jew blesses God who "separates between the holy and the mundane, between light and darkness, between Israel and the nations, between the seventh day and six days of labor. . . ."

In fact, the literal definition of the Hebrew word *kodesh*—most often translated as "holy"—is that which is separated; segregated from the rest for a unique purpose, for consecration.

In many ways *Mikvah* is the threshold separating the unholy from the holy, but it is even more. Simply put, immersion in a *mikvah* signals a change in status—more correctly, an elevation in status. Its unparalleled function lies in its power of transformation, its ability to effect metamorphosis.

Utensils that could heretofore not be used can, after immersion, be utilized in the holy act of eating as a Jew. A woman, who from the onset of her menses was in a state of *Niddut,* separated from her husband, may after immersion be reunited with him in the ultimate holiness of married intimacy. Men or women in Temple times, who were precluded from services because of ritual defilement, could, after immersion, alight the Temple mount, enter the house of God and involve themselves in sacrificial offerings and the like. The case of the convert is most dramatic. The individual who descends into the *mikvah* as a gentile emerges from beneath its waters as a Jew.

God's commandments, the 613 injunctions known as *mitzvot,* are divided into three distinct categories:

Mishpatim are those laws governing the civil and moral fabric of life; they are logical, readily understood, and widely appreciated as pivotal to the foundation and maintenance of a healthy society. Examples are the proscription against murder, theft, and adultery.

Eidut are those rituals and rites best described as testimonials. This category includes the many religious acts that remind Jews of historic moments in their history and serve as testament to cardinal beliefs of the Jewish faith, such as the observance of the Sabbath, the celebration of Passover, and the affixing of a *mezuzah* on the doorpost.

The third category, *chukkim,* are suprarational principles; they are Divine decrees about which the human mind can form no judgment. *Chukkim* completely defy human intellect and understanding. From time immemorial they have been a source of amusement, a target of scorn, and an uncomfortable and shameful presence to the detractors of Jewish observance. For the observant Jew, they personify a *mitzvah* at its best; a pure, unadulterated avenue of connection with God. These *mitzvot* are recognized as the greatest, the ones capable of affecting the soul on the deepest level. Unimpeded by the limitations of the human mind, these statutes are practiced for one reason only: the fulfillment of God's word. Examples are the laws of *Kashrut,* the prohibition against wearing *shatnez* (clothes containing a combination of wool and linen), and the laws of ritual purity and *Mikvah.*

When all is said and done, an understanding of the ultimate reason for the framework of Family Purity and its culminating point—immersion in the *mikvah*—is impossible. We observe simply because God so ordained it. Still there are insights that can help add dimension and meaning to our *Mikvah* experience.

In the beginning there was only water. A miraculous compound, it is the primary source and vivifying factor of all sustenance and, by extension, all life as we know it. But Judaism teaches it is more. For these very same attributes—water as source and sustaining energy—are mirrored in the spiritual. Water has the power to purify: to restore and replenish life to our essential, spiritual selves.

The *mikvah* personifies both the womb and the grave; the portals to life and afterlife. In both, the person is stripped of all power and prowess. In both there is a mode of total reliance, complete abdication of control. Immersion in the *mikvah* can be understood as a symbolic act of self-abnegation, the conscious suspension of the self as an autonomous force. In so doing, the immersing Jew signals a desire to achieve oneness with the source of all life, to return to a primeval unity with God. Immersion indicates the abandonment of one form of existence to embrace one infinitely higher. In keeping with this theme, immersion in the *mikvah* is described not only in terms of purification, revitalization, and rejuvenation but also—and perhaps primarily—as rebirth.

V

In years gone by, menstruating women were a grave source of consternation and fear. At best they were avoided, at worst they were shunned and cast aside. Often, menstruating women were blamed for tragedy and mishap, as if they had polluted the environment with their breath or gaze. This was a simplistic, if not misguided, response to a complex phenomenon whose rhyme and reason eluded the primitive mind. In those societies, peace could be made with menstruation only by ascribing it to evil and demonic spirits and by the adaptation of a social structure that facilitated its avoidance.

Viewed against this backdrop, the Jewish rhythm in marriage is perceived by many as a throwback to archaic taboos, a system rooted in antiquated attitudes and a ubiquitous form of misogyny. In truth, Family Purity is a celebration of life and our most precious human relationships. It can be understood most fully only within a deeper notion of purity and impurity.

Judaism teaches that the source of all *Taharah,* "purity," is life itself. Conversely, death is the harbinger of *Tumah,* "impurity." All types of ritual impurity, and the Torah describes many, are rooted in the absence of life or some measure—even a whisper—of death.

When stripped to its essence, a woman's menses signals the death of potential life. Each month a woman's body prepares for the possibility of conception. The uterine lining is built up—rich and replete, ready to serve as a cradle for life—in anticipation of a fertilized ovum. Menstruation is the shedding of the lining, the end of this possibility. The presence of potential life within fills a woman's body with holiness and purity. With the departure of this potential, impurity sets in, conferring upon the woman a state of impurity or, more specifically, *Niddut.* Impurity is neither evil nor dangerous and it is not something tangible. Impurity is a spiritual state of being, the absence of purity, much as darkness is the absence of light. Only immersion in the *mikvah,* following the requisite preparation, has the power to change the status of the woman.

The concept of purity and impurity as mandated by the Torah and applied within Jewish life is unique; it has no parallel or equivalent in this postmodern age. Perhaps that is why it is difficult for the contemporary mind to relate to the notion and view it as relevant.

In ancient times, however, *Tumah* and *Taharah* were central and determining factors. The status of a Jew—whether he or she was ritually pure or impure—was at the very core of Jewish living; it dictated and regulated a person's involvement in all areas of ritual. Most notably, *Tumah* made entrance into the Holy Temple impossible and thus sacrificial offering inaccessible.

There were numerous types of impurities that affected Jews—regarding both their life and Temple service—and a commensurate number of purification processes. *Mikvah* immersion was the culmination of the purification rite in every case. Even for the ritually pure, ascending to a higher level of spiritual involvement or holiness necessitated immersion in a *mikvah.* As such, the institution of *Mikvah* took center stage in Jewish life.

VI

In our day, in this post-Temple period, the power and interplay of ritual status has all but vanished, relegating this dynamic to obscurity. There is, however, one arena in which purity and impurity continue to be pivotal. In this connection only is there a biblical mandate for *mikvah* immersion—and that is regarding human sexuality. To understand why this is so, we must first understand how the Torah views sexuality.

The alleged incompatibility of sexuality and spirituality—more precisely, their antithetical nature—is a notion that, while foreign to Torah thought, is attributed by many to Judaic philosophy under the larger and completely mythical rubric of a "Judeo-Christian" creed. Few concepts have done more harm than this widespread misapprehension.

In stark contrast to Christian dogma—where marriage is seen as a concession to the weakness of the flesh, and celibacy is extolled as a virtue—the Torah accords matrimony an exalted and holy position.

Within that consecrated union, the expression of human sexuality is a mandate, a *mitzvah*. In fact, it is the first *mitzvah* in the Torah and one of the holiest of all human endeavors.

Moreover, human lovemaking signals the possibility and potential for new life, the formation of a new body and the descent from heaven of a new soul. In their fusing and meshing, man and woman become part of something larger; in their transcendence of the self, they draw on, and even touch, the Divine. They enter into a partnership with God; they come closest to taking on the godly attribute of creator. In fact, the sacredness of the intimate union remains unmitigated even when the possibility of conception does not exist. In the metaphysical sense, the act and its potential remain linked.

Human sexuality is a primary force in the lives of a married couple; it is the unique language and expression of the love they share. A strong relationship between husband and wife is not only the backbone of their own family unit but is integral to the world at large. For the blessings of trust, stability, continuity, and, ultimately, community, all flow from the commitment they have to each other and to a joint future.

In reaffirming their commitment, in their intimacy, the couple adds to the vibrancy and health of their society, of humanity, and ultimately to the fruition of the Divine plan: a world perfected by man. In their private, personal togetherness, they are creators of peace, harmony, and healing—on a micro-cosmic scale but with macrocosmic reverberations—and as such are engaged in the most sacred of pursuits.

In this light it becomes clear why marital relations are often referred to as the Holy Temple of human endeavor. And entrance to the Holy always was, and continues to be, contingent on ritual purity.

While we can not presently serve God in a physical Temple in Jerusalem, we can erect a sacred shrine within our lives. Immersion in the *mikvah* is the gateway to the Holy ground of conjugality.

VII

The laws of Family Purity are a divine ordinance. There is no better, more legitimate, more logical, or essential reason for their observance. It is a difficult commandment, a discipline that makes demands on our time, our psyche, and our emotions. It is a force at odds with the flesh, a way of life that the average person would not likely choose or devise. It calls for willful suspension of self-determination, the subservience of our most intimate desires to the bidding of a higher authority. And therein lies the *mitzvah*'s potency. The knowledge that it is sourced in something larger than the self—that it is not based on the emotions or subjective decision of one or the other—allows *Taharat Hamishpachah* to work for the mutual benefit of woman and husband.

Ironically, this "unfathomable" *mitzvah* reveals its blessings to us more than almost any other, in daily, palpable ways. Its rewards are commensurate with the challenge of observance.

At first glance, the *Mikvah* system speaks of limitations and constraints—a loss of freedom. In truth, emancipation is born of restriction. Secure, confident, well-adjusted children (and adults) are disciplined children; they understand restraint and ultimately learn self-control. Safe, stable countries are those pieces of land surrounded by definite, well-guarded borders. The drawing of parameters creates terra firma amid chaos and confusion and allows for traversing of the plain we call "life" in a progressive and productive manner. In no area of life is this more necessary than in our most intimate relationships.

"From every tree of the garden you may indeed eat but from the Tree of Knowledge of Good and Evil you must not eat. . . ." So God commanded Adam and Eve on the day of their creation. But they indulged on that fateful Friday afternoon, and the history of mankind was altered forever.

The complicated nature of human sexuality has its genesis in this tale. For the Tree of Knowledge contained a mixture of good and bad, and indulgence of this "knowledge" by primeval man introduced a new world order: a world where good and bad intermingled, a world of confusion and challenge, multiple choices, and endless potential.

No longer would intimate relations—one among many human biological functions—be as natural and uncomplicated as the others. Banishment from the Garden of Eden meant the introduction of a new sexuality: one pregnant with possibility and fraught with tension. It would hold the key to great ecstacy and excruciating pain, the most tantalizing fulfillment and most devastating sensation of void. A meaningful union would necessitate unequivocal commitment and constant nurturing by man and woman. But even the maximum effort put forth by man would need to be augmented by help from above. The blessing would flow from a reservoir called *Mikvah,* and Eden as it was before the sin would be attainable.

Trite as it may sound, *Mikvah* offers couples the possibility of repeated "honeymoons" during the course of their marriage. Boredom, a seemingly innocuous state of affairs, can beleaguer any relationship and chip away at its foundation. The mandatory monthly separation fosters feelings of longing and desire—at the very least, a sense of appreciation—which is followed by the excitement of reunion.

Over the course of a lifetime, open-ended sexual availability may well lead to a waning of excitement and even interest. The monthly hiatus teaches couples to treasure the time they have together and gives them something to look forward to when they are apart. Every month they are separated—not always when convenient or easy—but they wait for one another. They think about each other and how it is when they can be physical—all the while counting the days until their togetherness—and each time there is a new quality to their reunion. In this regard the Talmud states: "So that she will be as beloved as on the day of her marriage."

The man–woman relationship thrives on a model of withdrawal and return. The Torah teaches that Adam and Eve in their original form were created as an androgenous being. Subsequently, God separated them, thus granting them independence on the one hand and the possibility for a chosen union on the other. Men and women have been pulling apart and coming together ever since. The *Mikvah* system grants the married couple this necessary dynamic. Within their commitment to live together and be loyal to each other forever, within their monogamy and security, there is still this springlike mechanism at work.

God wanted man and woman to find each other on their own and to work at that quest—not merely once but constantly—in an ongoing process of becoming "one flesh."

Human beings share a nearly universal intuitive tendency for the forbidden. Solomon, the wisest of all men, spoke of "stolen waters which are sweeter." How many otherwise intelligent, calculated individuals have jeopardized their marriages and families in pursuit of the illicit because of its seeming promise of the romantic and the new? *Mikvah* introduces a novel scenario: one's spouse—one's partner in life, day after day, for better and for worse—becomes temporarily inaccessible, forbidden, off limits. Often this gives couples reason and opportunity to consider each other anew. In this "removed" span of time, from this new vantage point, they view and approach each other with enhanced appreciation.

The *Taharat Hamishpachah* discipline is helpful in other ways as well: fluctuation and disparity in sexual desire can never be completely alleviated. Yet the regulation in the *Mikvah* system serves to assuage tensions that arise from this source. For couples who must abstain for a minimum of twelve days a month, the time they have together is peak time for both, a time they cherish and savor.

While a physical distancing is mandated, emotional intimacy is encouraged and indeed nurtured. Meaningful communication—that precious and increasingly rare form of art—is given full expression as couples must learn to embrace and hug, comfort and rejoice, all without touching skins. A new strata is uncovered in their relationship, a new possibility emerges: friendship.

Jewish mysticism speaks of two types of love. There is *ahavah shel eish,* love that is compared to fire. This love is hot and passionate; it abates and flares up cyclically in its quest to rise ever higher. This flaming emotion must be guarded lest it sputter and die.

Then there is *ahavah shel mayim,* love that is like water. This love is cool, deep, and ever present; it is not extinguishable, there is no fear of an eclipse.

Love between a man and woman must be twice blessed; it must contain the miraculous combination of fire and water. *Mikvah* — with its two weeks on, two weeks off schedule — lends venue to the development of both; it brings fruition to the blessing conferred upon every Jewish couple under the *chuppah:* that of love *and* harmony, peace *and* friendship.

For many women, their time as a *niddah* also offers them a measure of solitude and introspection. There is, additionally, an empowering feeling of autonomy over their bodies and, indeed, over the sexual relationship they share with their spouses. There is strength and comfort in the knowledge that human beings can neither have their every whim nor be had at whim.

The benefits brought to married life by the practice of Family Purity have been recognized by numerous experts, Jew and gentile alike. To be sure, this type of analysis, as any other, is subject to argument and critique. Ultimately, however, *Mikvah*'s powerful hold on the Jewish people — its promise of hope and redemption — is rooted in the Torah and flows from a belief in God and His perfect wisdom.

VIII

Judaism calls for the consecration of human sexuality. It is not enough that intimacy be born of commitment and sworn to exclusivity, it must be sacred. As such, the first mandated time for immersion in the *mikvah* is at the threshold of marriage.

Mikvah before marriage, strictly speaking, is not contingent upon a commitment to regular observance of Family Purity. Even so, it should not be understood as unrelated to this larger framework. It is simply the first time a Jewish woman is commanded to purify herself in this way. And it is an awesome and auspicious way to start a new life together with one's beloved.

After learning of the details and giving them due consideration, *Mikvah* is a ritual that can be easily incorporated in the prewedding preparations by every Jewish bride and groom. The wedding date should be planned around the bride's monthly cycle, thus allowing for her immersion before the nuptial.

Tremendous amounts of time and energy are expended in planning a wedding. There is an innate human hope that a perfect wedding equals a perfect start in life. Yet all thinking individuals recognize human limitations. That which we most need and want — health, good fortune, and children — are beyond our control. As we voice the age-old greeting of *mazel tov,* we are offering up a prayer to the one above, asking that He bless the new couple with abundant goodness. Immersion in the *mikvah* is an important way of drawing God and His blessing into the marriage.

For as long as a woman menstruates, her monthly cycle dictates the rhythm of conjugal relations within the marriage, and each month it is a *mitzvah* for husband and wife to draw renewal from the waters of the *mikvah.* For those who have not made a lifelong commitment at the onset of married life, it is never too late to begin following the laws of Family Purity. Similarly, while observance should ideally be continuous, one should not allow a lapse of any length to deter further commitment. Nor is this practice contingent on the observance of other precepts in the Torah. *Mikvah* is not, as is often thought, the exclusive domain of the strictly observant.

Even if they are not ready for adherence to these laws at all times, women and their husbands should give particular consideration to this *mitzvah* before the conception of their children. *Mikvah,* we are taught, is the conduit for drawing down an exalted (a pure) soul vested in a receptive and healthy body.

For the postmenopausal woman, one final immersion in the *mikvah* offers purity for the rest of her life. Even a woman who has never used the *mikvah* before should make a special effort to immerse after menopause (it is never too late for a woman to do this even if many years have elapsed since her menopause), thus allowing for all subsequent intimacies to be divinely blessed.

The single greatest gift granted by God to humankind is *teshuvah*—the possibility of return—to start anew and wash away the past. *Teshuvah* allows man to rise above the limitations imposed by time and makes it possible to affect our life retroactively. A single immersion in the *mikvah* late in life may appear insignificant to some, a quick and puny act. Yet coupled with dedication and awe, it is a monumental feat; it brings purity and its regenerative power not only to the present and future but even to one's past.*

In this way, each woman can link herself to an ongoing tradition that has spanned the generations. Through *Mikvah* she brings herself in immediate contact with the source of life, purity, and holiness—with the God who surrounds her and is within her always.

---

*See "Going to the *Mikvah* (at My Age!)," page 149, and "A Mother's Gift," page 210.

I

In Theory and Practice

1
Loving Jewishly

Gila Berkowitz

Buried deep beneath the rubble of assimilation, shrouded by the dry language of legalism, lies an extraordinary secret of Judaism: the treasure of Jewish sexuality.

Those who would explore this mine with discipline, discretion, and wisdom will find the opportunity to express the most exquisite sweetness of their physical, emotional and spiritual selves. In the union of man and woman, they will become a metaphor for divine union; in their love for one another, they will achieve the most perfect evocation of the commandment to "Love your friend as yourself."

Judaism seeks to make of the marital bed an altar.

Despite the blushing nomenclature of "Family Purity," the focus of the *Mikvah* laws is on establishing strong marriages by providing lifelong sexual satisfaction and excitement within the wedded union. Spiritually, the system is even more ambitious. It seeks to elevate every sexual act to the realm of holiness. There is a sexual ménage à trois at the heart of Judaism: husband, wife, and God.

At first glance, the restrictive aspects of the laws seem prohibitive and puritanical, but even a single month's experience of loving Jewishly can open new vistas in a marriage. Researchers at the world-renowned Kinsey Institute have shown that couples observing the sexual laws of Judaism, compared to

3

similar subject populations, not only tended to be more satisfied with sex in general, but actually enjoyed a greater *number* of sexual episodes. In fact, of all American groups studied by Alfred Kinsey in his landmark *Sexual Behavior in the Human Male* (Indiana University Press, 1949), observant Jews had the most sexual experiences over the course of a lifetime.

Most people are nothing less than astonished to hear of Judaism's enthusiastic support of a vibrant sexual life for adult, married members of the community. After all, we are used to seeing "religion" and "sex" as diametrically opposed, and marriage as the anticlimax of sexual adventure. Christianity and Islam view sexual desire as a human weakness, and Eastern thought sees the marital act as an impediment to the pursuit of full enlightenment. On the other hand, Western, materialistic society is opposed to religion in direct correlation to the extent to which it is fixated on sex.

Judaism takes an entirely different approach from any of these philosophies. It rejects the notions that sex is a necessary sin, an essential defect, or a distraction from the spiritual. It also vehemently denies that sex is a mindless pleasure, a value-free diversion. Instead it models human sexuality on a divine template: the consummation of the relationship between Israel the Bride and God the Bridegroom. Sanctified by the Torah, the union between man and woman exalts each spiritually and makes their bond a common bond with God.

For Jewish thinkers, particularly the mystics, sex is a high—perhaps the highest—form of worship. According to tradition (*Yoma* 54a–b) the golden cherubim that adorned the Ark of the Law, situated in the Holy of Holies of the Temple in Jerusalem, were male and female. When the Children of Israel found grace with the Lord, the cherubim were locked in coitus. When the Israelites sinned, the cherubim turned their backs to each other like a quarrelling couple.

Throughout rabbinic literature, sex sanctified by the *Mikvah* laws, while always veiled in modesty, is exuberantly positive. One dictum (*Taanit* 8b) declares that sex is one of the three hints of Paradise that humans can experience during their lifetime (the others are the Sabbath and sunshine).

Like other forms of worship (and the Sabbath and sunshine, for that matter), sex requires physical parameters to define its spirituality. These parameters include defining the sexual *partner* as exclusive and sacred, and defining the *time* of sexual activity and sexual rest in the *Mikvah* laws. Judaism promises that within those borders, each partner in a marriage can find not only satisfaction and comfort but an inner truth.

On a mundane level the laws enhance performance and pleasure, increasing the mutual- and self-esteem of each of the partners. In the spiritual scheme of things, Family Purity invests the act of physical union with holiness and purpose. The historical result has been better and more stable marriages, the key to the survival and flourishing of the Jewish people.

The tenacity with which Jews throughout the ages and everywhere in the world have clung to this tradition is powerful testimony to its efficacy. In Ethiopia, a parched land, the Jews were known as "the people who stink of water." In Afghanistan, mountain women proudly took their axes with them to chop holes in frozen rivers so that they might immerse. In the Soviet Union, Jewish engineers built illegal, ingenious *mikvahs* in the closets of tiny apartments. At Massada, the Jewish rebels left behind the marvel of ritually and aesthetically perfect *mikvahs*. In martyrdom, as in life, they acted not as individual heroes but as eternally unified families.

But what can Family Purity do for couples in the posttechnological era?

It can, and almost always does, transform a marriage. While sex the Jewish way cannot save a bad marriage, it can make a good one transcendent. It does so in immediate and dramatic ways, as well as by subtle means whose effects become manifest only after years or even decades.

The most direct result of observing the cycle of separation/immersion/consummation is an intensification of the couple's sexuality.

Since the dawn of time, humans have sought to sharpen the sexual experience, to recapture the ardor of youth and courtship. But aphrodisiacs of every sort work temporarily, if at all. Because sexuality is such a strong component of identity, with the ebbing of desire many individuals see the loss of their own vitality and worth.

All humans face a paradox: sex is a complex feeling involving body, mind, and spirit, but while mind and spirit love best when loving long, the body reaches a point of exhaustion relatively soon. This dip in ardor is often mistaken for a loss of interest in one's partner or a failure in oneself. When the event occurs—as a seven-year itch, in the second-year slump, or even on the honeymoon—the results can be catastrophic. Either husband or wife, or both, may seek out other partners, conclude that the marriage has failed, and/or take desperate, humiliating, or even dangerous measures in the attempt to rekindle the flame.

The monthly separation of the purity cycle is a simple but highly effective means to keep the fire burning. On a regular basis absence makes the heart grow fonder—and the hormones surge with more vigor. Caresses and physical endearments that can otherwise become clichéd are newly appreciated after a refreshing pause.

A frequent comment about the *mikvah* night is: "We feel like a bride and groom each time." Physical memory is short, so each postimmersion encounter has the giddy excitement and expectant thrill reminiscent of the wedding night.

Yet there is more to the experience than simple separation. Wife and husband continue without pause to be lovers in mind and spirit. All the experiences that nourish and enrich the partnership continue. Only their bodies take a hiatus to recharge.

The predictability of the cycle promotes cooperation, mutual interests, and expressions of affection other than the sexual, which are vital to any marriage.

In the early part of a relationship, while everything is bathed in the glow of sexual desire, it is easy to overlook differences in favor of the shared passion and convenient to settle disputes by the kiss-and-make-up technique.

Once the glow fades, unpleasant reality can set in. Rarely do personalities mesh as neatly as sexual organs. The partner's faults come to the fore.

"He is not the person I married." "All she ever wants to do is . . . [something that bores me to tears]." "He never wants to talk." "All she ever wants to do is blab." "I've grown, but my partner hasn't." "We have nothing in common." The pair concludes that the end of the sizzle means the end of the steak. Divorce, all too often, seems the only recourse.

But the practice of the Family Purity cycle underscores—early in the relationship, while there are still large reserves of good will—the necessity of working together for mutual goals, developing shared interests that don't require physical intimacy, facing up to differences, and solving disagreements in a civil way.

These skills become useful throughout the cycle and leave sex as a preserve of mutual love and enjoyment, rather than forcing it to meet all the challenges and carry all the burdens of a marriage.

Although the system takes the pressure off the couple's sexuality to act as a cure-all, it actually emphasizes the importance of sex in marriage.

Ironically, our sex-obsessed culture, which uses this basic instinct to swing elections and sell trucks, downplays sexuality within marriage. Most people recognize the social advantages of a legal union but concede that sexually it is the end of exploration and growth. For many, marriage is a sexual compromise; the era of sexual adventure is the single years of adolescence and adulthood that are remembered with wistful nostalgia.

The arts and popular culture collude in downgrading the sexuality of married people. While young lovers' excitement garners sympathetic winks, people who have been married for a while are expected to "grow up." In other words, they are supposed to concentrate on supposedly more important things: work, mortgages, children, and other responsibilities.

Judaism maintains that one's sexual potential can *only* be reached within marriage. The wedding is not the end of the fairy tale, but its possibility-rich beginning.

What's more, sexuality is not bait to keep adults toeing the line of responsibility. A rich sexuality is central to the functioning of adult life. For the tuned-in Jewish couple, at least once a month, on the night of immersion in the *mikvah*, all other responsibilities are put on hold. With the exception of medical emergencies and very few religious obligations (such as Yom Kippur), nothing keeps a couple from reconsummating their marriage. The needs and wants of other people—even their own children—are secondary to those of husband and wife.

The Family Purity system augments and supports other sexual laws, particularly the commandment of *onah,* the husband's obligation to sexually satisfy his wife. While a woman is enjoined from denying her mate sexual access out of spite, a man is obligated by the positive Torah precept to "delight his wife" and the negative one, "her marital rights he shall not withhold." Within the allotted period, the husband is better able to sensitize himself to what may be obliquely expressed overtures from his wife. Thus the notorious communication gap between the sexes can be breached.

While observing the sexual laws does not put all of life's disappointments and responsibilities on a neat schedule, it guides a couple's reactions to the challenges of intimacy by pacing intimate episodes.

It is a rueful fact of life that lovers' desires do not always coincide. *He* may be bright-eyed and bushy tailed on the very evening of the day she lost an important account, got an irate call from Junior's math teacher, and ran out of gas on the highway. *She* may lay out her red satin nightgown and douse herself with perfume only to hear him say, "Oh, I forgot to tell you, honey, I asked the accountant over tonight to do our taxes."

In the former case, for example, the frazzled wife, if she is in the *niddah* period, can insist on talking out her bad day and receiving sympathy and advice, after which she can get some rest. If the bad day happens during the active cycle, she may decide to shelve the disasters for the night and release her tensions sexually.

In the second case, if it takes place during the *niddah* period, the couple may decide to share in the task of tax preparation, or the wife might allot the time for herself by taking a long bath or reading a novel. If it occurs in the ritually pure period, the husband might reschedule his appointment or limit the session to business at hand, rather than linger into the wee hours with refreshments and social conversation.

The natural pacing of Family Purity becomes especially helpful during pregnancy and the postpartum period. Intercourse and other physical expressions of intimacy are encouraged during a healthy pregnancy. This helps to relax the parents-to-be, who are apt to be quite anxious, and bond them in a united love for their child.

After childbirth, immersion in the *mikvah* is delayed until seven days after the mother has stopped all bleeding—that is, is completely healed. The onus of a sexual relationship is taken from the parents, who are likely to be overwhelmed with caring for the newborn. The woman is not asked to please her husband at the expense of her own well-being, nor is she required to "choose" between her man and her baby. The husband, having to put his sexual desires on a longish hiatus, does not risk hurting his wife, being put in the humiliating position of competing for her caresses, or having to take her sexual disinterest as personal rejection.

Another way in which Family Purity promotes a better marriage is by legitimizing personal and shared "space."

One of the pervasive fears of marriage is that one's spouse will devour one's individuality. Both men and women are terrified that they will lose all sense of themselves in the marital "we." But attempts to assert individuality by pursuing interests and friendships without the partner can be seen as extremely threatening to the relationship.

The halachic sexual system defines separate physical and emotional space during the nonsexual phase. One has, at the very least, a bed of one's own. Yet this separation is not a criticism of the partner, but a prescription of the law. During the physically active phase of the cycle, the partners will naturally try to maximize their mutual activities, in and out of bed, affirming their basic commitment to each other.

One of the ways the feminist movement has affected modern sensibility is by making us aware of the extent to which sex is used to wield power, to manipulate, coerce, and oppress. This awareness makes one particularly appreciative of how effectively Family Purity curtails sexual power plays.

The power of sex, and the sexiness of power, are hauntingly universal. Yet the stability of the human race—embodied in marriage—depends on overcoming conquest, subjugation, and force as part of eroticism.

Sexual coercion, however, remains an ugly constant in modern marriage, in forms as crude as rape or as subtle as the threat to withhold money for household necessities.

Sex as a tool of oppression is mostly used by men. Their superior physical and economic strength gives them a decisive edge in violence and harassment. The ability to *limit* a partner's sexual satisfaction, on the other hand, is a sexual weapon that many women wield.

The Family Purity laws make it difficult for either partner to take control of when or whether sex will take place. Compliance with the laws puts control in the system, defusing the jockeying for supremacy. It also severely limits the use of sex as a reward or its withdrawal as a punishment.

Another universal problem that is tackled by the *Mikvah* system is the uneven distribution of sexual experience through life. That is, in an unregulated life, sexual activity will be concentrated in youth. But sexual needs are often greater in middle age and persist into old age. Family Purity regulates and maintains sexual frequency throughout adult life.

When Alfred Kinsey surveyed American sexual practices in the late forties, he studied many social and ethnic groups, including Orthodox Jewish men (of whom a substantial proportion could be expected to maintain the Family Purity laws). In the youngest age group studied, the Orthodox men had far fewer sexual episodes than other ethnic cohorts. This can be explained by the supposition that Orthodox men have fewer premarital sexual experiences, and that, among married men, ritual separation forced them to curtail the frequency of sex that is natural to young men. However, in subsequent age groups, the Orthodox men equaled and then exceeded other cohorts in frequency of sexual episodes. Calculating total sexual experiences in the course of a lifetime, Kinsey found that the Orthodox men scored highest of any group studied.

The practice of the sexual laws paces sexual experiences but does not diminish them. Although a cap is placed on youthful passion, that energy is apparently preserved, for there is little diminution in sexual activity during middle age—as there is in the general population. Upon entering old age, when the practice of the laws becomes largely moot, the couple still maintains an active sex life, fueled by the rhythms learned in youth.

There is a growing body of scientific evidence that the practice of Family Purity shields against gynecologic disease, enhances fertility, and promotes genetic health.

For centuries young Jews were warned against the ills that would befall them—specifically, painful, embarrassing sicknesses and defective children—should they violate the laws. The enlightened generally dismissed these as old wives' tales. Now biologists such as MacArthur scholar Margie Profet of UC Berkeley posit that during menstruation the uterus cleanses itself of semen-borne pathogens.[1] This theory has special immediacy in light of epidemiological evidence that menstrual blood is a highly efficient conduit of the HIV virus, as well as viruses responsible for Hepatitis B and Hepatitis C.[2]

But the Jewish sexual laws go beyond abstaining from sex during menstruation, and this difference accounts for some interesting aspects of women's and infants' health. It should be noted that the majority of cultures have taboos against menstrual intercourse, and many individuals feel naturally squeamish about it. Moreover, prior to modern disposable tampons, barrier devices, and laundering, such sex meant hours of labor cleaning up after the act.

Yet differences definitely exist between populations that adhere to the Torah laws and those that merely abstain from coitus during the period. For example, it has long been noted that Jewish women have a lesser incidence of cervical cancer than non-Jews. Since this difference holds true among the contemporary Jewish population, the great majority of which does not practice Family Purity, it has been assumed that the benefit is conferred by male circumcision (almost universal, even among nonreligious Jews). But a historical overview suggests otherwise.

Hiram M. Vineberg, chief gynecologist at New York's Mount Sinai Hospital, analyzed records of the incidence of the disease between 1893–1918. The study included over 50,000 women. Between 1893–1906, Jewish women were twenty times less likely to have cervical cancer than gentile women. Between 1906–1911, Jewish women were fifteen times less likely to suffer the disease; between 1911–1918, ten times less likely. The drop in protection parallels the drop in *mikvah* use among New York's Jewish population during that time.[3] Protective advantage against cancer of the cervix drops to five percent or less among contemporary Jewish women who do not observe *Mikvah* law. Dr. A Shechter of Beilinson Hospital in Petah Tikvah, Israel, believes it is negligible.[4]

In 1930, Dr. Howard Kelly at Johns Hopkins University studied deliveries to Orthodox Jewish women in Baltimore. He found they had a smaller percentage of forceps deliveries, a lesser incidence of trauma during such deliveries, and fewer cesarean births than in the general population. Kelly noted the similarities to the Jewish women of the Book of Exodus who were "notorious as being more lively on the birth stool than the Egyptian women, so that midwives found it hard to get to the mothers before the babies were born." He also noted that while the rate of noncervical cancer of the uterus was equivalent to that of the general population, the mortality rate was lower.

He attributed the results of his study to the Jews' "better regulated sex life, more restraint in intimate relationships, less promiscuity [which lead to] less liability to persistent congestions."[5]

The Family Purity laws are geared to maximize the chances of advantageous conception. While technological advances lull us into thinking we have great control over human fertility, the fact is that rates of infertility have been climbing steadily for a generation. Today, one in five American couples have difficulty in conceiving.

The time of *Mikvah* immersion usually coincides with ovulation, thus insuring the best chance for insemination. At this time the ovum has been freshly released into the fallopian tubes and has not yet begun the process of rapid decay that can result in miscarriage or birth defects.

Male fertility is also at its peak on the *Mikvah* night. Immediately after the period of continence, the ejaculate is rich with active sperm; their number as a percentage of the semen decreases with frequent ejaculation. Also, healthy sperm are highly motile, so they are most likely to beat out defective sperm in the race to fertilize the ovum.

When intercourse takes place considerably before ovulation, the most active sperm die out while the slower ones linger, already deteriorating genetically, to inseminate the ovum. When intercourse is delayed considerably past the time of ovulation, the ovum has begun this process of deterioration.

Medical surveys among ultra-Orthodox Jews in Israel indicate a markedly lower incidence of genetic problems such as Down's Syndrome, although, of course, such ills do occur even among those who scrupulously observe Family Purity.[6]

There is new evidence regarding the increased immunological strength of the female body during ovulation and the period following it. Those women who have breast cancer surgery during the ten days following ovulation have two to four times the chance of being cancer-free ten years later than women having surgery at other times during their cycles.[7] Other types of surgery, it is indicated, also tend to be more successful at this time, so many surgeons are timing elective surgery for this period for all premenopausal patients.

God created all the cures, says the Talmud, before he created the diseases.

The Jewish sexual system promotes more than physical health. A return to the salubrious practices of Judaism can help Jews overcome the psychological ravages of the Diaspora on a Jew's sense of self, which is so deeply grounded in sexuality.

So much of Jewish humor, literature, and other aspects of popular culture present the Jew as a sexual misfit. The Jewish man is seen as sexually inadequate, the Jewish woman as frigid and bitter.

It is obvious that these images, largely created by Jews themselves, are a reaction to anti-Semitic images of the Jews as sexual monsters. While Nazi-era depictions of hook-nosed, fiendishly powerful polluters of the Aryan gene pool are thankfully absent from the mainstream, many Americans continue to believe that Jews have too much economic and political power. Jews have succeeded in mollifying jealousy by promoting an image of themselves as losers in the one area where even the disenfranchised can affirm their basic worth: in bed.

But this deflection of resentment has come at a high price: Jews have convinced themselves that they are unattractive, undesirable, and sexually incapable. Because sexual self-image is integral to self-definition, failure of the sexual self turns all other successes to dust.

The Jewish lover, lame and halt, worthy of nothing but laughter, is now what most Jews see in the mirror. It is what they think of themselves when they think of themselves as Jews. Often the shame of this image is unbearable. Many seek to free themselves of it by disposing of their Jewishness entirely.

What is to be done? How can the American Jew—"crushed in the privy parts"—be healed?

The solution lies in reclaiming Judaism's sexual roots. In returning to the way of Family Purity, Jewish men and women can realize a potent and dynamic sexual identity. The very word *"mikvah"* comes from the root "to hope." *"Mikvah* Israel," the Hope of Israel, is one of God's names. This God has provided for the survival of His people through a special strength and joy embodied in the Law.

The benefits of Family Purity extend even to those who do not practice it. The peace it promotes extends to the young, the unmarried, the widowed. The strength and the joy radiate outward, to the family, to the community, to the Jewish people, and, ultimately, to all humanity in the great prophetic vision of redemption.

"The Lord will give strength to His people; the Lord will bless His people with peace."

Notes

1. *Quarterly Review of Biology* (September 1993).

2. DeWitt W. Brown, *Journal of the American Medical Association* (January 26, 1990).

3. Jacob Smithline, *Scientific Aspects of Sexual Hygiene* (New York: United Jewish Women, 1967). (Smithline was consulting gynecologist to the White House during the Truman Administration.)

4. Michael Kaufman, *Love, Marriage, and Family in Jewish Law* (Northvale, NJ: Jason Aronson, 1992), p. 208.

5. Smithline, *Scientific Aspects of Sexual Hygiene.*

6. Richard M. Goodman, *Genetic Disorders Among the Jewish People* (Philadelphia: Johns Hopkins University Press, 1979).

7. William Hrushesky, Veterans Administration Medical Center, Albany, NY, reported in *McCall's* (July 1993), p. 42.

2

To Number Our Days

Tamar Frankiel

Teach us to number our days, that we may acquire a heart of wisdom.
— Psalm 90

Many regard the rituals of *Taharat Hamishpachah,* "Family Purity," as obsolete today. Yet we find more and more young women taking them on. What leads women to choose a practice that involves a period of sexual abstinence? What are we to make of a system that seems to give women no choice about their sexuality? The *Halachah,* Jewish law, stipulates that each month, for the duration of our menstrual period plus seven more days, we must practice abstinence from sexual relations. So, of course, must our husbands. But why should we be coerced by our biology? Although our breasts give milk, we do not necessarily become chief cook and table setter in the household. Why, then, because of our periods must we follow a sexual schedule?

From another perspective, however, the "schedule" suggested here is not an external discipline. It comes from the rhythms of our own bodies. Unfortunately, modern Western society has taught us to ignore the signals of these rhythms. If we are aware of a heightened emotionality, sexual arousal, or irritability at regular intervals, we are taught to hide or belittle these variations. Tribal and ancient cultures set up a variety of rituals of seclusion for women, but we are expected to perform on a nine-to-five, fifty-weeks-a-year job, or

13

cook and keep house day in and day out for our families, accomplishing our tasks with equanimity every day. Any oversights during "that time of the month" are considered weaknesses rather than signs that we might do better redirecting our energy in some other way.

In this light we can see that our culture, despite its supposedly liberal attitudes, is actually intolerant of menstruation. These attitudes reveal that despite our intentions to be positive, open, and honest about our physiology, we still prefer to make menstruation invisible. We no longer view the menstruating woman as actually dangerous, one who pollutes all she touches and who must be segregated. But we have no positive vision of this time. Our culture has offered instead the sexless—or at least hormoneless—woman: she who never falters or shows extremes no matter what her body is doing.

Jewish tradition suggests a different path, neither the tribal way of radical seclusion nor modern culture's path of ignoring feminine rhythms. The Torah defines precisely what is at issue. Variable moods, inclinations, or abilities are only the superficial symptoms of something deeper. Even the obviously physical purposes of ovulation and menstruation—repeatedly preparing the body for pregnancy—lie on the surface. The process is something else: a scale drawing, so to speak, of the creativity of the universe. The pivotal point of that creativity is the union of male and female. Its rhythm in time is rooted in the feminine body, and it is cyclical, like the moon.

In other cultures women not only used the moon's phases to count their cycles, they also connected femininity with the moon in religious symbolism. In the Torah, women's connection with the moon was honored through *Rosh Chodesh,* the New Moon, a half holiday for women.[1] Moreover, following the Torah, we count our "moon-days": the days until we immerse in the *mikvah* and reunite with our husband. Yet we can be sure that this was not given to us merely as a convenient calendar. What comes from the Torah must have a deeper spiritual significance.

To elucidate this, it is helpful to look to the findings of certain scholars of comparative religion, who have suggested that the lunar and the feminine are connected because they are closely related archetypes, or basic structures, of our psyches.[2] The lunar–feminine structures lead us to experience relationships and similarities, to see things in a unified way, and to trust intuition and feeling. Moreover, both moon and woman go through phases: the moon waxes and wanes, women have menstrual cycles. Both represent openness to change and the possibility of regeneration. This is in contrast to the solar–masculine archetypes, which represent separation, differentiation, logical organization, and the quest for permanence.

Masculine and feminine principles are present in every human being; but the lunar–feminine archetypes are more decisive in most women's conscious lives, whereas solar–masculine ones serve as the unconscious "assistant" or "adviser" to her principal direction in life. When they are both operating together, one has harmony within oneself. In Hebrew, "complete" and "perfect" can both be signified by the same word, *shalem,* and their root is the same as the word for peace, *shalom.* This suggests what psychology also tells us: when the two perspectives, masculine and feminine, are integrated, we achieve unity within ourselves and with the fundamental creative principles of the cosmos.

Women's connection with *Rosh Chodesh,* with the moon, thus has a message for us. To bring into being the world we were meant to have, it is primarily women's responsibility to activate the lunar–feminine ways of knowing. This does not mean just discussing archetypes as intellectually interesting ideas. For us, unconscious archetypes must be accessed through actions of the whole person. Our practices surrounding menstruation actually do this by relating women directly to the rhythms of their own bodies.

In ancient times, women may have been able to synchronize their menstrual periods with the dark and new moons. Even today when technology has distanced us from natural influences, statistics confirm that there is still a tendency for more women to menstruate at the dark of the moon. This suggests that our connection to our menstrual cycles is part of a universal rhythm through which we can connect to deeper levels of ourselves. Studies show that our ability to relate to the lunar rhythms through our menstrual cycles can actually improve our overall mental health. Women who suffer from premenstrual tension or cramps can benefit by synchronizing their cycles with the moon, and by acknowledging and relating to the rhythmic, lunar aspect of their own being.[3]

The rites of *Taharat Hamishpachah* specified by the Torah are direct and, as we will see, amazingly powerful. We count our days, like women from ancient times. The counting marks two phases: we count from the beginning of one menstrual period to the next so that we can know when our next menstrual flow will likely begin and when we will begin abstaining from sexual relationships, and we count from the end of our flow seven "white days," to know when we can go to immerse in the *mikvah* and then reunite with our husbands. These two countings mark, approximately, the two poles of a woman's cycle, ovulation and menstruation.

If we look at these two poles briefly, we find that physiologically they are very different. Both poles are associated with higher-than-average sexual desire, yet women commonly report significant differences in the nature of their desire. For example, many women around the time of ovulation tend toward a receptive mode, wanting initiatives from their husbands, while at the other pole, before menstruation, many experience a desire to be more active and initiating themselves. Some researchers have suggested that following a drop in sexual desire immediately after ovulation, during the last ten days or so of the typical cycle, women often show a level of interest in sexuality that sometimes leads men to regard their partners as "oversexed."[4] Jewish tradition has prescribed the ten to fourteen days before menstruation as the time for husband and wife to enjoy sexual relations, and this seems to be the period when most women desire more sexual activity.

But sexual interest is not the only thing that changes as our bodies move from one pole to the other. At ovulation, one's external senses are heightened, particularly the sense of smell. With the onset of menstruation, the senses of hearing, smell, sight, and color vision are all diminished; but interior sensations increase. Many women sleep more at the menstrual pole; the Sages observed that the neck muscles of a menstruating woman are weaker, so that she frequently dozes off. As many women know, irritability often increases in the days preceding menstruation: PMS is one of the most commonly reported disturbances among women. Unfortunately, PMS can become quite severe and has even been associated with extreme depression and violence against oneself or others.[5]

Our traditional practices require that at the menstrual pole, we separate from our husbands and practice a strict sexual abstinence. In modern times, some women have compared this to customs of menstrual seclusion and have claimed that the whole idea is a patriarchal and mysogynist invention: men, fearing menstrual blood, created the idea that women are unclean during their periods. This ignores the fact that women have often valued the separation. More importantly, it denies the possibility that there may be benefits of separation or seclusion of which we are unaware and indeed cannot be directly aware because they operate in the realm of the unconscious. For example, clinicians have suggested women need more sleep because we need to dream at this time, and the most likely reason for the almost universal practice of women secluding themselves during their menstrual period is our need to rest, meditate, and dream.[6] If we accept separation and solitude, then we may use that time to connect with our inner selves, with the "moon knowledge" of meditations and dreams, with intuition and feeling.[7] We may need to be in touch with these to activate some of our deeper, often more powerful, levels of knowledge through which we intuit the rhythms and interrelations of things.

One aspect, then, of the Torah's insistence on sexual abstinence is to guard women's own inner creativity. Folk wisdom has taught that new insights often come to birth with the new moon, the presumed time of a woman's monthly flow. Harding, from a psychological point of view, writes that "ideas formed under the moon . . . have a power and compelling quality that ideas originating in the head rarely have. They are like the moon in that they grow of themselves." The common roots of the words "moon," "menstruation," and "mind" suggest this relationship: the deeper Mind is connected to the lunar aspect of ourselves. Similarly, in Hebrew, *yare'ach* (moon) and *ruach* (spirit) share a like root. The other Hebrew word for moon, *levanah,* is usually associated with the word for "white," *lavan,* conveying not only the white of the moon but also the "whitening" effect that moonlight has on other colors. But this word, too, has another significance: with changes in the vowels, it can also be read *levinah:* "to wisdom."

A biblical verse hints at this when it says, in one of the Psalms, "Teach us to number our days, that we may acquire a heart of wisdom" (Psalm 90).[8] "Heart of wisdom," *lev chochmah,* seems at first a strange phrase. The heart is usually considered the seat of feeling, subject to the struggle of good and evil, the *yetzer hatov* and the *yetzer hara,* or alternatively with *binah,* "development of understanding." In this phrase, however, the heart is connected to *chochmah,* "the source of spiritual wisdom." The "wise heart" is actually associated in the Torah with the spiritual creativity of the artist, the creator of beauty. Among artists, the Torah specifically mentions "wise-hearted women," those "whose heart stirred them up in wisdom" (Exodus 35:25–26) to spin the yarn, linen, and goats' hair for curtains and coverings of the Tabernacle, the place of worship in the wilderness.[9] By mentioning specifically women, it suggests that this creativity can be associated with the feminine. In classical terms, this was the Muse, the feminine inspiration of all artists. This creativity comes from opening to the feminine, the inspiration of the moon, our own inner rhythms. We are directly connected to it even though this connection may remain unconscious. Rituals of separation during the appropriate times enable us to bring this awareness into lived reality, and by this means we become conduits, enabling our husbands and others around us to be connected to it as well.

On the other hand, the Torah's strictness about being separate from our husbands may seem to have a negative tone. The penalty prescribed for having sexual relations during a woman's time of menstruation is quite severe: *kareit,* or being "cut off," meaning spiritually cut off from one's Divine source. Very few sins have such a severe punishment.[10] Nor do the commandments suggest that the separation is to protect the woman. On the contrary, they indicate that, from the Torah point of view, the state of the woman who is menstruating (in Hebrew, *niddah*) is somehow deficient. She is *tameh,* usually translated as "impure." When applied to a person, the term generally means that the person is ritually unfit to bring offerings in the Temple.

We have shown how in light of deeper understanding of women's cycles we can interpret the state of *Niddah* more positively, focusing on the potential it offers a woman of being connected with her inner self. But from the point of view of *kedushah* or "holiness"—holiness being the state that is associated with the highest service of God (as in bringing offerings to the Holy Temple, for example)—the state of *Niddah* is undesirable. Marital relations are to be conducted in an atmosphere of *kedushah;* so the state of *Niddah,* when a woman is *tameh,* or "impure," is inferior to the state of *Taharah,* or "purity," when one can have intimacy with one's husband again. But now we seem to be veering back toward the category of menstrual "pollution." If separation is desirable from the woman's point of view, why should it be hedged about with absolute prohibitions? Doesn't this imply that there is something wrong with a woman's natural state?

A state of being that is "impure" is not sinful.[11] However, as Rabbi Aryeh Kaplan points out, it does signify something awry in human existence, something that is not aligned with the perfection for which we were created in the beginning. Although there is nothing wrong, morally or physically, with being in the state of *Niddah,* and we can even experience benefit to our health from being able to withdraw into ourselves, it is still not the highest level of our existence. In other words, the Torah establishes these strict prohibitions for us to become aware of the difference between lower and higher states of being. That does not make *us* personally inferior when we are in the lower state; indeed, it turns out that this period of separation is good for us. But there is something more: the highest state of men and women is to be together: "He shall cleave to his wife, and they shall be one flesh" (Genesis 2:24).

At the menstrual pole of our monthly cycle, we tend to be—even have to be—self-absorbed; there is a subtle but indubitable psychological barrier between husband and wife. The higher state of being is to be related to another in love, to transcend one's ego in a higher union. *Niddah* signifies an archetype of separation (in this case between male and female) and, on the deeper psychological levels, it represents all the separations and barriers we experience including, ultimately, humanity's separation from God. Conversely, the practice of immersion and the return to a state of "purity," *Taharah,* signify the archetype of union, *yachdut,* intimating that the aim of all life is reunion, epitomized in the spiritual striving of human beings to be at one with God.[12] Like male and female, so the duality of separation and union are integral to creation itself and, the Torah tells us, must be respected. Just as separation is a *mitzvah* at the onset of menstruation, so is it commanded that husband and wife must join together after she immerses in a *mikvah.*

This brings us to the other aspect of "counting our days," the counting toward *Mikvah,* which ends separation and abstinence and initiates the period of reunion. Immersion in the *mikvah* itself is crucial, and again we see the significance of this in comparative religion and psychology as well as in Jewish tradition. The archetype of water as it manifests in many cultures communicates renewal and a new creation. Water is primordial substance—as in Genesis, with "God's Spirit fluttering *on the face of the water.*"[13] Water is also the physical base sustaining existence—as we thank God every morning for "spreading the earth above the waters." Because of the original potentiality and sustaining force of water, contact with water brings regeneration. Immersion, as Eliade writes, "fertilizes, increases the potential of life and of creation." It is equivalent on the personal level to the *Mabul,* the Flood that once destroyed the earth because it had become corrupt: immersion does away with the past and starts creation over again.[14]

The *mikvah* has all these special qualities: it erases the past, regenerates, renews, and sustains our connection to the primordial forces of creation. It symbolizes rebirth; as Rabbi Aryeh Kaplan has stated, it is the spiritual equivalent of the womb. The *mikvah* has this power because it is connected to the primal waters of the Garden of Eden. The waters of our planet were originally formed by a "gathering," or *mikvah,* on the fourth day of creation. Then, the story in Genesis tells us, four rivers flowed out of Eden, and these four became the source of water for all the rivers, lakes, streams, and oceans of the world. A *mikvah* that can be used for our immersions is either a natural body of water or a pool that has a special connection to natural water. The *mikvah* is an urn into which the waters of the first creation continually flow, into our own time. Since the *mikvah* is spiritually connected to the Garden, when we use the *mikvah,* we reinvigorate ourselves with the power of the beginnings of creation, the energy in which Adam and Chava lived and breathed.

Mikvah is often referred to as purifying. We now understand, however, that this kind of purification is not mere cleanliness. Spiritually, we are erasing the past to have a new beginning. "When a person immerses in the *Mikvah,*" writes Kaplan, "he is placing himself in the state of the world yet unborn, subjecting himself totally to God's creative power."[15] The ego, the ordinary self, becomes as nothing so that the person can begin anew.

All our uses of the *mikvah* involve this idea of renewal. The Jews about to stand at Sinai immersed themselves, for they had to forget their past as Egyptian slaves and begin a new life under the Torah. A new convert to Judaism immerses in a *mikvah:* he or she is literally becoming a new person, and the past is no longer significant. Before Yom Kippur we go to the *mikvah,* as one of many ways in which we put the past behind us and begin anew. New dishes bought from a non-Jew must be immersed; as the vessels that will be used on the "altar," which is the dinner table in a Jewish home, they have to acquire a new status as well. Many men have the custom of going to the *mikvah* before morning prayers, to begin the day truly fresh and new.

Likewise, when a woman goes to the *mikvah* she is putting the state of separation behind her and beginning anew. The focus is not on erasing sins or changing outward identity, but rather on moving from the state of individuality to another, higher, identity. We dissolve our egos in the "womb," returning to the original waters. We prepare to unite with our husbands by symbolically reentering the Garden of Eden, when Adam and Chava were freshly created, as "one flesh." This makes it possible for a married couple to be in a state of *kedushah*. In this way we come as close as we can to Godliness, for we were created in God's image together: "male and female He created them."

Godliness is potentially within us also because we are able at this time to join in making new life. Physically, with *mikvah* coming approximately at the time of ovulation, we have the potential to be mothers, and to bring out the potential of fatherhood in our husbands.[16] We open ourselves to begin again the cycle of life. The potential to create a family or, as the marriage blessings say, a *binyan adei ad,* an "everlasting edifice," raises the unity between husband and wife to an even higher level. If conception does not occur or is not intended, the unity of husband and wife is still a deep, profound, and holy one. The mystics say that when we unite in purity, we still bring new souls into the world; they simply do not take on bodies. Love brings forth fruit, whether tangible or not.

This is why the union between husband and wife is compared to the sanctity of the Holy Temple. Just as the Temple was the visual representation of the creation, and channeled blessings to the world, so the marital relationship is the physical, emotional, and social representation of the pinnacle of creation. On one level, material blessings of children and sustenance come from the united efforts of husband and wife, and the world is thereby sustained. On the spiritual level, blessings come from the mutual surrender of husband and wife, for this act reflects God's love for us and ours for God.

We count our days, as our bodies and our psyches move naturally between two aspects of femininity. The rhythm of this *mitzvah* highlights new dimensions in our own experience of ourselves, and in our relationships, through the dynamic of withdrawal and joining, separation and union. We move from inwardness to transformation and renewal, then to the willingness to give ourselves to another in a coming together that mirrors the union of the world with its source. Individuality and independence are balanced, at a deep level, with interdependence and mutual surrender. The rites and practices of *Taharat Hamishpachah* make for a demanding path in some ways, while in other respects nothing could be more natural. They ensure that the structure of intimacy in a family is founded on the woman's inner rhythms, an anchor to the inner psychic life of the family and the people, a ground of holiness in our relationships.

Notes

1. On *Rosh Chodesh,* in addition to the special prayers that everyone says, women are to refrain from heavy labor, and many women have the custom of wearing festive

dress or cooking a special dish for the day. Jewish women obtained that special honor through their devotion to God. In the desert, while Moses was up on the mountain speaking with God, many of the Israelites despaired of ever seeing him again and decided to make a golden calf to celebrate their redemption from Egypt. But the women refused to give their gold jewelry to be melted down for the calf. The calf was a common fertility symbol, expressing pagan beliefs in new life and renewal. In refusing to contribute to its worship, the women were affirming that we must depend for our life only on the one God who is beyond heaven and earth.

2. An archetype is an unconscious structure through which experience is filtered in a certain distinctive way. None of our experience comes to us pure and simple; we never know an object or event in and of itself. Rather, many "filters" color our perception. Most of us are aware that our language, our culture, our family upbringing each contribute their own filters. Archetypes are even more basic structurings of experience. Their source is probably either genetic or etched into our psyches by events far back in human history, beyond recorded memory. In either case, evidence of these structures appears so often, cross-culturally and in dreams, that they appear to be, so far as we know, common to all human beings.

3. Some of the relevant research is discussed in Penelope Shuttle and Peter Redgrove, *The Wise Wound: Myths, Realities, and Meanings of Menstruation,* rev. ed (New York: Bantam Books, 1986). There is a slight rise in incidence of menstruation at the full moon as well but not as great as at the new moon.

4. Ibid., 94, citing the work of Dr. Mary Jane Sherfey on the nature of female sexuality.

5. Ibid., 36–56.

6. Ibid., 79, 107.

7. Although no one is sure why dreaming seems to be healing, some research suggests that dreams are feelings and inner experiences converted into visual images, perhaps by the pineal gland. Of course, analytical psychology since Freud has recognized that interpreting dreams can help a person become aware of feelings that have been "repressed" and have remained inaccessible to the conscious mind.

8. The translation of this verse is difficult. A more literal rendering is, "To the count of our days thus make known, that we may bring a heart of wisdom." Many commentators understand this to mean, in the context of the whole psalm, that Moses is praying that we have a stronger revelation because we have such short lives in which to come to know God. My interpretation follows a different strand, implying that when we recognize the importance of each and every day by "counting," then the divine will be revealed to us more and more.

9. Refer to the Book of Exodus, where Moses was given a vision of the *mishkan* or tabernacle, and the precise instructions for building it. After naming Bezalel, and Oholiab as his assistant, God continues, "and in the heart of all that are wise-hearted I have put wisdom" (Exodus 31:6), that is, to make all the beautiful items for the *mishkan*. Moses follows by commanding "all the wise-hearted" (*chacham lev,* Exodus 35:10) to come and make all that God commanded.

10. Violating Yom Kippur, *Shabbat,* or Pesach, as well as sexual sins, make one liable to the punishment of *kareit.* See Aryeh Kaplan, *Waters of Eden* (New York: Jewish Pride, 1984), p. 44.

11. Sinfulness in the Torah is tied to an act, not a state of being. If people sinned, intentionally or unintentionally, they had to bring a sacrifice at the Holy Temple. No such practice was associated with the period of *Niddah.* Immersion in the *mikvah* is a purification, but not from sin or uncleanness in any moral sense; it has a wholly different orientation.

12. This description depends on a mystical understanding of creation, and of human beings' relation to God, which is beyond the scope of this paper. The reader is referred to Rabbi Adin Steinsaltz, *The Thirteen Petalled Rose,* and the three-volume work by Rabbi Immanuel Shochet, *The Mystical Dimension,* for a deeper understanding.

13. Kaplan, *Waters of Eden,* 14.

14. Eliade, *Patterns,* 189, 194.

15. Kaplan, *Waters of Eden,* 13.

16. Mentioning motherhood frequently brings forth from critics of *Taharat Hamishpachah* the suggestion that returning to sexual relationships at the time of ovulation was another patriarchal plot designed to ensure that women would keep having babies. This is dubious on physiological and historical grounds: physiological, because most women's ovulation would not be so precisely timed; historical, because in ancient times midcycle was not believed to be the most fertile time for women. Archetypal psychology rather than physiological knowledge dictated that women could best return to union with their husbands at this time. The time of ovulation was the time in which psychologically we could become more open, fully related to another in an intimate way, and in which our biological concern for future generations would be most alive. That aspect of the feminine archetype called "the Mother" awakens in us concern for the life of the ovum, oriented toward the potential for a new child.

3

Tumah and Taharah: Mystical Insights

Susan Handelman

Two of the most widely misunderstood concepts in the Torah are contained in the words *Tumah* and *Taharah*. Translated as "unclean" and "clean," or "impure" and "pure," *Tumah* and *Taharah*—and by extension the laws of *Niddah* and Family Purity—often evoke a negative response. Why, it is asked, must a woman be stigmatized as *tameh,* "impure"? Why should she be made to feel inferior about the natural process of her body?

It might be said that, at bottom, these objections arise from a fundamental misunderstanding. *Tumah* and *Taharah* are, above all, spiritual and not physical concepts.

The laws of *Tumah, Niddah,* and *Mikvah* belong to the category of commandments in the Torah known as *chukkim:* statutes, or Divine decrees, for which no reason is given. They are not logically comprehensible, like the laws against robbery or murder, or those commandments that serve as memorials to events in our national past such as Passover and Sukkot. The laws of *Tumah* and *Taharah* are suprarational, "above" reason. And it is precisely because they are of such high spiritual level, beyond what intellect can comprehend, that they affect an elevated part of the soul, a part of the soul that transcends reason entirely.[1]

Even if the human mind can't understand these Divine decrees logically, we can nevertheless try to understand them spiritually and search for their inner meaning and significance. In this endeavor, the teachings of chasidic philosophy are of invaluable aid, for the study of *Chasidut* reveals the inner aspect of Torah, its "soul," and can guide us through realms where unaided human intellect cannot reach. *Chasidut* strives for the direct perception of Godliness underlying everything, and illuminates the spiritual sources of all physical phenomena.

Tumah As the Absence of Holiness

Chasidut explains that, in essence, *Tumah*, "spiritual impurity," is definable as the "absence of holiness." Holiness is called "life," "vitality": it is that which is united with and emanates from the source of all life, the Creator. Chasidic philosophy further elucidates that true cleaving, true holiness, means to be *Bottul;* that is, one's own independent existence is "nullified" to God.[2] On the other hand, that which is distant or separated from its source is called "death," "impurity." According to Jewish law, death is the principal cause of all *Tumah;* the highest magnitude of *Tumah* comes from contact with a dead body.

The forces of evil are, in chasidic terminology, the *Sitra Achra,* the "other side." They are what is "outside," what is far from God's presence and holiness. They flourish in the realm where He is most concealed and least felt, where there is least holiness. In a place where God is least felt, there is naturally more room for "opposition" to Him. And hence, spiritually speaking, what is most evil and most impure in a person is, above all, the assertion of self: one pushes God's presence away and creates a void, a vacuum where His presence should be. That is the deeper meaning, according to *Chasidut* for the phrase to cause a *chilul Hashem,* to desecrate God's name: one should not make a *chalal* (void), a place empty of His presence. Holiness is synonymous with *Bittul:* it has no sense of any true existence independent of God. That is why, our Sages tell us, arrogance is equivalent to idolatry, for idolatry, in essence, means that something is regarded as independent of the Creator and asserts itself in place of Him.

Hence, if we strip the words "pure" and "impure" of their physical connotations, and perceive their true spiritual meaning, we see that what they really signify is the presence or absence of holiness.

An Important Distinction between Two Types of *Tumah*

At this point we must distinguish between the various types of *Tumah* and ask: Why must *Tumah* exist at all? What purpose can it have in God's creation? "The Almighty has created one thing opposite the other," the Book of Ecclesiastes tells us, and as *Chasidut* interprets it, everything in the realm of holiness has its counterpart in the realm of unholiness. On the one hand, these opposing realms are created so that we may have "free choice" in our behavior. On a deeper level, as *Chasidut* explains, when we reject the evil and choose the good and, moreover, when we further transform the evil itself into good, we effect an elevation not only in ourselves but in the entire world, bringing it closer to its ultimate perfection. Hence, the ultimate purpose of *Tumah,* the "other side," is for us to achieve higher levels. As the well known chasidic saying has it: "Every descent is for the purpose of a greater ascent," and all concealments of God make way for a greater revelation. When the soul comes down to this world, for example, to be vested in a material body, it undergoes an incomparable descent from its previous purely spiritual existence. The purpose of this descent, though, is that the soul may rise even higher in its apprehension of God and attain a more elevated rank than it had before it descended to this world. It can attain this elevation only through the vehicle of the body, through serving God in this lower physical world. On the one hand there is concealment and impurity in this lowly material world; on the other hand, only through its struggles here can the soul rise higher.

We must distinguish, then, between two types of *Tumah,* two types of "descent." There is the *Tumah* that we ourselves create when we intentionally push God's presence away and create a void, and there is the *Tumah* that God creates as part of nature. This distinction is crucial to our understanding of *Niddah.* The *Tumah,* the impurity that attaches to a sin, is a void we create and by which we degrade ourselves. The *Tumah* of *Niddah,* however, is a built-in part of a woman's natural monthly cycle: her "descent" from a peak level of potential holiness (i.e., where a life is possible) does not mean that she is, God forbid, "sinful" or "degraded," "inferior" or "stigmatized." On the contrary, precisely because there is such holiness involved in a woman's possession of the godly power to create, as if ex nihilo, a new life within her body, there is the possibility for greater *Tumah* — but also a great elevation.

Let us try to understand further the idea that the more holiness, the more opportunity there is for the forces of impurity to enter. This is no contradiction to what was stated earlier — that the forces of the "other side" can flourish in the absence of holiness. The forces of evil are also called *Klippot,* "husks" or "shells," not only because they cover over and conceal the inner sparks of holiness that gives life to all things, but also because — like the husks or peels of a fruit — they can only derive whatever life they have from this inner spark, the truly living part. When separated from the inner part, they have no more sustenance and "die."

Hence, an excess of *kedushah* can provide "room" for the extraneous forces to derive sustenance, just as, for example, if a barrel is filled to the top, some water will spill over and water weeds as well.

In this light we can further understand the explanation of the Kotzker Rebbe[3] that *Tumah* can set in only where holiness has been and gone. We can connect this with our understanding of the kind of *Tumah* that is part of *Niddah*. The Torah says that when a woman gives birth, she is in a state of *Niddah* for a variable amount of time: If the child is male, she will be *tameh* for seven days and if female, fourteen days. Why should there be *Tumah* at childbirth? The Kotzker Rebbe explains that *Tumah* can set in only when holiness departs. As the Talmud tells us, God is directly involved with every childbirth and does not delegate any powers to His "messengers." Thus, there is a very great level of holiness at birth; the birth of a child involves one of the most sublime powers of God, the ability to create ex nihilo—something from nothing. After birth, this intense holiness, this powerful force of God, "departs" and there is greater potential for *Tumah*. One might conjecture further that the reason the birth of a female involves a longer period of *Niddah* is that a female contains within her the godly power to create yet another new life from "nothing." Because of this higher potential for holiness, there can be more *Tumah*.

The same is true of a woman's monthly cycle: every month, this great potential for holiness, for a woman to engage in the sublime power of creation, reaches a peak in her body (an "ascent"). When the potential is not fulfilled and the holiness departs, the now-lifeless remnants are removed from the body. And therefore this "descent" is susceptible to *Tumah*. It is precisely because of the high level of godliness involved in the procreative process that *Tumah* can occur at all.

But here again this "descent" into *Niddah* is for the purpose of a higher ascent, through purification in the *mikvah* and a new cycle of building up to a higher level of holiness the next month. The *mikvah*—as will be explained later—enables one to ascend even higher than the previous month. In this sense the *mikvah* and the monthly cycle of a woman may be compared to *Shabbat* and the weekly cycle of every Jew. The alternation of the holy day of *Shabbat* with the mundane days of the week is the same cycle of ascent and descent— reenacted every seven days. The six mundane days lead up to Shabbat, on which the world becomes elevated, purified, ascends to its source. And every Jew then receives an "extra soul," which he again loses as the *Shabbat* departs, and he must "go down" again into the struggles of the coming week. Nevertheless, it is these very struggles to purify ourselves and the world that we confront during the six days that become elevated on the *Shabbat* and enable us to ascend higher and higher every week, in constant progression.

Or, let us take another cycle: the daily alternation of sleeping and waking. According to Jewish law, every person upon awakening should wash his hands, to remove the "impure spirit" that adheres to them during sleep. In sleep, there is a "departure of holiness" from the body—the soul, it is said, "ascends to its source" above. Again, this "natural law" allows for impurity to set in. Our hands are *tameh* upon awakening, to be sure, but they are not "evil." The same is true of *Tumah* during a woman's monthly "natural low." It is the result of a departure of holiness but not a state of degradation, inferiority, or shame.

Rabbi Menachem Mendel Schneerson, the Lubavitcher Rebbe, offers an even more profound understanding of the inner nature of these "lows," these descents. Since, he says, the descent is in fact a necessary preparation for the ascent, and its ultimate purpose is the ascent, the descent is nothing other than a part of the ascent itself. The Rebbe explains[4] why the Torah, in speaking of all the journeys of the Jews in the desert, also describes the places where they only rested as "journeys." Since the resting was a preparation for the journey that followed, the resting places are in fact part of the journey onward. Or as in our previous example: sleep gives strength to elevate oneself even more the following day, and is thus part of that ascent itself—though it appears to be a lower state for the body.

And on a broader level, the same is true, the Rebbe explains,[5] of the exile of the Jewish people among the nations. If the exile were only for the purpose of punishing us for our sins, it should have lessened with time. Instead, it grows worse from day to day. (The concealment and darkness, however, are a preparation for—and their ultimate purpose is—a great revelation, the great light that will come in the era of Moshiach—and so the closer we approach that great light, the thicker the darkness becomes.) The inner purpose of the exile is that through refining ourselves and the world, we will ultimately attain a higher level of holiness and unity with God than existed even during the times of the First Temple.

A Comparison with the Moon

In essence, these "natural lows"—absences of holiness that God has created within the monthly cycle of a woman, of the weekly cycle of *Shabbat,* the nightly cycle of sleep, or the entire life cycle of the Jewish people as a whole— are, in their innermost sense, all parts of the process of spiritual ascent. Nor is the connection between these different cycles artificial. The Talmud compares the Jewish people to the moon, for just as the moon waxes and wanes every month, so, too, do the Jews undergo phases of concealment and renewal in exile and redemption. The appearance of the new moon, *Rosh Chodesh,* is a minor holiday, marking the beginning of a new month. And this day is also a special holiday for women, given to them as a reward for not participating in the making and worship of the Golden Calf. A woman's body, of course, also follows a monthly cycle, and *Chasidut* illumines a deeper correspondence between the cycle of *Niddah* and the new moon.

The third Lubavitcher Rebbe, R. Menachem Mendel, the Tzemach Tzedek, explains[6] that on *Rosh Chodesh,* the moon is renewed, "purified," and again "unites" with the sun; it again receives its reflection. This union of the sun and the moon on *Rosh Chodesh* corresponds to the union of man and woman after the days of *Niddah* are over. And in the same way that a woman is renewed monthly, so will the Jewish people be renewed at the time of their redemption, which will culminate in their higher union with God. As the Talmud states, when the Jews were exiled, the *Shechinah,* the "indwelling presence" of God, went into exile with them. And as the Tzemach Tzedek points out, the Hebrew letters of the word *Niddah* also mean *Nod Heh* — "God wanders;" He is in exile with the Jews. Hence the reunion of the sun and the moon on *Rosh Chodesh* reflects the union of man and woman and of God and the Jewish people, whose relationship is compared to that of husband and wife.

Understanding *Mikvah*

We have understood that these natural descents are aspects of ascent. Why, however, must this process be accompanied by immersion in a *mikvah,* and what has water to do with changing one's status from *tameh,* "impure," to *tahor,* "pure"?

Chasidut explains[7] that in progressing from one level to another, there has to be a period of "nothingness in between." For example, when a seed is planted in the ground, it must first disintegrate, lose its first existence, in order to be able to flower. To reach a higher state, one must first lose or nullify his previous state. This is the inner purpose of the *mikvah,* to enable one to attain this state of *Bittul,* "nullification," the "nothingness in between" the two progressive levels. As *Chasidut* points out[8], the letters of the Hebrew word for *bittul* when rearranged spell *tevilah* — "immersion" — a further indication of their spiritual interconnection.

To fulfill the *mitzvah* of *Mikvah,* one must immerse completely, be entirely enveloped by the waters. This total immersion of self means losing one's independent existence, going out from oneself, elevating oneself by becoming a vessel for holiness. Maimonides writes in his code of Jewish Law, the *Mishneh Torah,* that this immersion requires the intent of the heart, the intent to purify oneself spiritually from all wrongful thoughts and bad traits, to bring one's soul into "the waters of pure understanding."

Chasidut makes a further illuminating connection between this concept of *Mikvah* and the nature of the great flood that occurred in the days of Noah[9]. Why, the question is asked, was water the chosen instrument for removing the wicked from the world, and why did the flood have to last for such a long time, forty days and forty nights? Surely if God had wanted to punish the sinners, He could have done so immediately. The answer, *Chasidut* explains, is that the flood was not a punishment, but a purification for the world. It completely enveloped the earth and its forty days and forty nights correspond to the measure of forty *seah* of water required to make a ritually fit *mikvah.* The waters of Noah cleansed the world by immersion in the same way one is purified by immersion in the waters of the *mikvah.* This separation and removal of all extraneous and undesirable elements has the ultimate purpose of bringing the world (and a person) to a higher level.

And this brings us back to the beginning: the ultimate cause of *Tumah* is separation from God; and to be united means to be *Bottul* to Him, to lose the sense of one's independent existence and be attached to one's source. According to Jewish Law, however,[10] one is purified only upon leaving the *mikvah,* not while inside it. As the Rebbe explains[11], this means that the ultimate purpose of our elevated spiritual states, our "ascents," is not to be removed from the world; the purpose of creation is "to make a dwelling place for God in the lower worlds." That is, we must affect the "outside"—bring holiness into the very lowest levels. Despite one's high spiritual state, one is not purified until "going out"—until affecting the "outside." In practical terms, this means that "the essential thing is the deed"—action in the world, in the refinement of one's inner self, and also one's particular "share" of the world, to make a "dwelling place for God." Just as the elevated state of *Shabbat* is called the "source of blessing" for the entire week, and *Rosh Chodesh* that for the entire month, so, too, the purification of oneself in the *mikvah* should permeate all one's thoughts, words, and actions when one leaves the *mikvah.*

Chasidut explains[12] that the performance of *mitzvot* provides "garments" for the soul. The moment of conception is particularly crucial, for the frame of mind and purity of the parents determines, to a great extent, what manner of "garments" that soul will have. In sum, not only do the laws of Family Purity have a deep spiritual meaning, but as the Lubavitcher Rebbe explains[13] the fulfillment of this *mitzvah* has a profound, direct influence on both the spiritual and physical health of one's children—and by extension, on all Jewish generations to eternity.

Notes

1. *Likutei Sichos* of the Lubavitcher Rebbe, vol. 8, pp. 72, 85.

2. *Tanya,* chapter 6: "So, too, are all the utterances and thoughts which are not directed towards God and His will and service. For this is the meaning of *sitra achra*— "the other side," i.e., not the side of holiness. For the holy side is nothing but the

indwelling and extension of the holiness of the Holy One, blessed be He, and He dwells only on such thing that abnegates itself *(Bottul)* completely to Him. . . ."

3. *Sefer Halikutim* — Dach "Tzemach Tzedek," vol. 6, s.v. *Niddah*.

4. *Likutei Sichos*, vol. 6, "Pekudei."

5. *Likutei Sichos*, vol. 2, pp. 358,360-363.

6. *Sefer Halikutim* — Dach "Tzemach Tzedek," vol. 6, s.v. *Niddah*, pp. 38-40.

7. *Yom Tov shel Rosh Hashanah*, 5666, *ma'amor* II, s.v. *'Zeh Hayom."*

8. *Likutei Sichos*, vol. 1, pp. 4-5; *Siddur, Kavannos Hamikvah*, end.

9. *Likutei Sichos*, vol. 1, pp. 4-5; *Torah Or*, s.s. *"Mayim Rabim."*

10. Maimonides, *Hilchos Avos Hatumah* 6:16.

11. *Likutei Sichos*, vol. 1, pp. 14-15.

12. *Tanya*, end of chapter 2; *Iggeres Hakodesk*, section 3.

13. *Likutei Sichos*, vol. 13, pp. 258-262, and see references there.

4

We Will Do and We Will Listen

Janet Shmaryahu

These may be, at once, the easiest of times and the hardest of times to be an observant Jewish woman. We, like Jewish men, are born into the obligation cemented by our forebears three millennia ago: to observe Jewish law. Our loyalty is certainly supplemented by a belief that the maintenance of Jewish law improves our individual, familial, and communal lives in ways we think we can discern and surely in ways we only dimly trace. But the feminist sensitivity of our times presents us Jewish women with a complicated challenge: we need to simultaneously reassert our place in the Jewish community by increasing our knowledge and assuming a greater number and range of Jewish laws, especially those like the laws of *Niddah,* the "menstruant woman," which are practiced by women, and break new ground by finding ways to talk about this observance in terms of the interests of women. We need to find our way between radical feminist claims that the established religions are patriarchal and perpetuate male authority and power at the expense of women, and the traditional Jewish discourses by both men and women which frequently call up an amorphous notion of feminine mystique and privilege and disregard the more problematic aspects of Jewish observance for women.

The laws of *Niddah* are especially susceptible to charges of excessive interference in the private lives of women, in the strict regulation of sexual relations within marriage, and in the impingement on women of such acts as the requisite internal self-examinations and the immersions in the *mikvah.* Some Jewish women (and men, too) are uncomfortable with the primitivity or the uncouthness of a religious ritual in our time based on menstruation. In the last several decades, critiques and defenses of the laws of Family Purity have centered on the persistent claims that the laws operate on an association of menstruation and impurity or contamination, even that these laws may veil an unacknowledged abhorrence of the woman's body.

When we are talking about women in our time consciously deciding to take on the obligations of Jewish law, however, we are presupposing a firm belief by Jewish women that they are, and always have been, Jews in good standing subject to the obligations and promises prescribed by our texts. With this confidence in the rightness of both their intentions and their religion, women would not feel they had to produce the kinds of explanations of the Family Purity laws that largely suppress the latter's unseemliness, strangeness, and inconvenience, and that have not satisfied women of a more feminist or even contestatory ilk. Neither should they let charges of omnipresent patriarchal designs come between them and their religion by birthright. Women do not need to choose between discounting their newly honed sensitivities and pledging their commitment to Jewish observance.

Dissatisfaction with the modern woman's relative estrangement from Judaism has prompted in many circles a determination to take ourselves more seriously as Jews and to believe that our actions count considerably. The Family Purity laws are the place of greatest intersection between ourselves as women and as Jews because of the way they govern our bodies, our sexuality and reproduction, and our most precious and significant relationships with our husbands and our children. By their very constitution, the Family Purity laws can only be maintained by women; Jewish men are commanded to withdraw from their wives in menstruation, but beyond that their compliance with this law is entirely dependent upon their wives' observance in good faith.

I will admit that I have not always been helped in my own complicated thinking about these issues by some of the writings of men and women on their observance of the laws of Family Purity. These writings, too hastily, I feel, assume the self-evidence of the rightness, wisdom, and universal benefit of these laws and assume also that the interests of Jewish women and the laws of Judaism must perfectly correspond. I have been surprised to note the persistently affirmative tone in which they explain and justify their commitment, the near-total repression of the less comfortable aspects of practice, the uniformity of these discussions that are uncomfortably lacking in independent thought, and the lack of distinction between the defenses of men and of women, who are affected in significantly different ways by these issues. These untroubled essays seem strangely designed to avow commitment to the laws of Family Purity by those and to those who are already securely committed and should not seem to need them.

For example, in one jubilant account of *mikvah* use the writer likened the *mikvah* to a luxurious spa with pampering attendants, and wondered sincerely and incredulously why every Jewish woman does not choose to use this service. But the analogy is faulty because it does not acknowledge any of the differences between *mikvah* visitation and the spa. *Mikvah* use is commanded by Jewish law; using a spa is obviously voluntary. The frequency and the times of *mikvah* visitation are regulated; one visits a spa when one chooses. Immersion is preceded by a mandated set of preparations; no particular acts are required before entering a spa. Family Purity laws come inextricably bound with a complex set of ideological assumptions that wed the Jewish individual, the Jewish community, and Judaism and which the individual observer of these laws subscribes to, consciously or not; the use of a spa has no weight or significance whatsoever. In other words, not only does the analogy terribly trivialize, without intending to, the entire enterprise of *mikvah* use, it also erases the fact that no clause of the laws of Family Purity is alterable or elective, except for the vital initial choice to observe or not.

I do not know why we (and I don't know if I mean Jews in general or Jewish women) are reluctant to talk about the difficulty of halachic observance, in general or for ourselves. I believe that a person can at one and the same time unconditionally affirm the necessity of observing *Halachah* and harbor sober, responsible questions about it. I have consistently observed the laws of Family Purity, have never considered doing otherwise, and yet I could not say that my practice has never been (a little) resentful or anxious, and I have no reason to believe that I am entirely unrepresentative. I worry that we, Jewish women, are censoring ourselves too extensively and thereby squandering the opportunity to do something other than perpetuate the tone of rabbinic writing that detailed the laws and, not presuming to speak for women, assumed the uncomplicated attitude of women toward them. I think we need to ask ourselves why we are writing about these issues and to whom. We run the risk of alienating women who are considering committing themselves to the laws of Family Purity or who are observing them tentatively and might be looking for evidence that a woman's utter commitment to *Halachah* can go hand in hand with an acknowledgment that certain aspects of practice are trying and may evade our particular understanding.

We can say, for example, that observance of the *mitzvah* of Family Purity is not always easy precisely because observance must be consistent and comprehensive, whether we feel like it or not. *Mikvah* visitation takes precedence over every other scheduled activity, and, as such, it might engender an amount of occasional (perhaps unconscious) resentment, as do most activities mandated by life's exigencies, such as jobs, home and communal responsibilities, and obligations to all others (children, spouses, parents). In addition, while the requirement to physically separate from the onset of menstruation applies to both men and women, the work of maintaining observance of this *mitzvah* – announcing the separation, counting the days, preparing for the *mikvah,* immersion – lies entirely with the woman. This is the only *mitzvah* I can think of that is required of a couple but whose details are the sole responsibility of one of them; if a couple jointly decides that observance of an aspect of Jewish life, such as *Shabbat, Kashrut,* or Jewish education for children, is important to them, the work of carrying out that decision can be shared by the couple using some formula of division.

The mechanics of *mikvah* use may also be trying: the preparations prior to immersion; getting to the *mikvah,* including negotiating the nighttime dangers, where this applies; the wait, if there is one; accounting for the need for a *mikvah* when traveling; anxiety over immersion itself; reluctance to be seen nude and looked over by another woman as *Halachah* mandates. The knowledge that sexual relations will resume shortly after immersion can also produce a certain amount of tension. There may be unhappiness and resentment with Judaism's use of menstruation as an index; having an already "intrusive" religion so severely regulate and legislate even this, the most private, aspect of our lives; proscribing sexual relations during nearly half of our childbearing years; being told not only when not to have sexual relations but also, more surprisingly, when we should.

But at the same time, we should allow ourselves an interrogation of the current feminist worldview, which presupposes an abyssal division of the genders and an irreconcilable warring of interests and, relatedly, the uncomplicated assumption that the dominant group will exclusively promote its self-serving interests. In fact, when Family Purity laws are practiced, it is the woman who largely controls the timing of sexual relations. The woman informs her husband that she has begun to menstruate, that all physical contact should cease, and when she will go to the *mikvah,* which is when contact and sexual relations will resume. The system fosters a sense in women and men of the power of the woman's body. Outside of this unique Jewish system, the onset of menstruation in the Western world has little regular and significant effect, but for the observant couple it immediately initiates a shift from sexual license and possibility to sexual prohibition. It is not menstruation itself that effects this change, of course, but rather the Jewish law positing that the onset of menstruation must signal a cessation of physical contact. However, the fact that the laws of Family Purity are set into motion by menstruation focuses attention on and invests considerable significance in a regular function of the woman's body. The husband is encouraged by the system to attend to his wife, both to her physical condition (for good or ill) and to her announcement that there are to be no sexual relations, and this attention to his wife's state is unceasing. A man would be as constantly aware of when his wife is available to him as he would be of when she is not. He is aware, too, that she — not he — determines accessibility.

The timing of sexual relations, then, is calculated and announced by the woman because it is synchronized to the woman's body. Closely related to this is the pivotal issue of trust. This system of Jewish law works only insofar as there is an assumption on the part of the rabbinic legislators and the husband of trust in the woman's word. Of course, there can be no question of "proof" that she is in fact menstruating, of her authenticating dates in some way. But before we leave the phrase "of course" unquestioned, could we not imagine a law, in a religion as rigorous as ours, whereby a woman would have her condition verified by another (perhaps as an extension of the function of the *shomeret*) to ensure that there was no manipulation of the system, that women could never exploit their authority? I have raised this theoretical possibility to demonstrate how utterly foreign and untenable such a mentality of suspicion is to any thinking about the arena of Family Purity laws.

No less surprising than the extent of the power the woman wields because of the function of her body — and because of the absolute trust of the halachic system on the reliability of the woman's word — is the area of the marriage that the woman controls. Women, Jewish and non-Jewish, have historically monopolized the domestic and child-rearing sections of family life, but sexual control has resided, or could always potentially reside, with men because of their superior physical strength. Rape, physical abuse, and sexual exploitation, where they exist, are almost universally acts of violence directed by men against women, not the other way around. The laws of Family Purity radically alter this paradigm for observant couples by taking the entitlement to and the possibility of sexual dominance out of the hands of men.

Quite simply, for non-Jews, marriage means that the other is always sexually available to them, subject to an unspecific, largely unenforceable notion of consent. The Jewish laws of Family Purity and those that mandate the woman's explicit consent to sexual relations make it clear to Jewish men from the outset that even marriage does not enable perpetual access to a woman's body and that sexual relations are not an inalienable and constant right purchased through the transaction of marriage. Therefore, in addition to inextricably binding sexual relations to self-discipline, the laws strongly encode the notions of the integrity of the woman and the woman's body and of her right to protection (I would even say, by extension, the right of every human to protect their body from another). Judaism also designs an extensive dimension of marital life to lie entirely outside of any sexual conduct.

Because of the rules of modesty governing the arena of the *mikvah,* there is a point where male involvement in the institution of the *mikvah* ceases and women take over. The *mikvah* is a major religious institution maintained to a significant degree by women. Women not only use the *mikvah,* they also supervise the use of it by other women. In this capacity, women often acquire considerable expertise in the laws of immersion. In addition, the position of the *shomeret* gives women the opportunity to extend their involvement with the *mikvah* beyond their own personal use of it—into the postmenopausal phase of their lives, for example. If the intimate exposure that is mandated by the role of the *shomeret* may be uncomfortable at times, it can also foster an unanticipated conduit of sisterhood in a religion so usually modest.

This is a surprising turn away from the manner in which patriarchal religions work to disenfranchise the woman from her body. Acts of sexual degradation such as prostitution, pornography, and exhibitionism are often accompanied by attempts to disguise the woman and to intervene between her and her body. Jewish women, however, need to attend closely to their bodies. The repeated internal examinations, the thorough cleansing of all body parts, the immersion without clothes, the examination in the role of *shomeret* of another woman's body, compel women to confront and come to terms with their bodies and the bodies of other women. The recitation of the blessing for immersion in the *mikvah* waters without clothing seems to me to point incontrovertibly to the sanctity of the woman's body and the propriety of blessing this ritual she is engaged in, in precisely this way.

Summation

It is a fundamental human need to justify one's choices, but the multiplicity of comment on the issue of Family Purity indicates it is impossible to produce a comprehensive set of interpretations that would definitively explain the rightness of these laws and unequivocally justify observance. One could validly argue for the laws' source in a notion of impurity or the laws' concern with the integrity of the woman's body or the necessity of discipline to circumscribe and impart a sense of sanctity to sexual relations. But the status of the laws of *Niddah* in the Torah as *chokk* (statute), that is, as that which must be observed independent of any reasoning or understanding, points precisely to our inability to ever exhaust our thinking about the rightness and wisdom of these laws. It seems to me, however, that this circumstance of making a decision one can never empirically justify to firmly observe a Jewish law one is never certain one entirely understands, points to the largely invisible prior decision by the individual Jew (it may be gradual, epiphanic, equivocal, permanent, etc.) to submit to Jewish law. The decision by Jewish women to unconditionally practice a vital law rendered to them, however oblique and problematic, powerfully repeats the "we will do and we will listen" (we will unconditionally observe as an act of faith; we will then try to understand) response of every Israelite upon the Torah's first reception at Sinai. We should not forget that the very enterprise we are engaged in here of locating rationales, persuading the other, describing our experiences, and so on, is a supplement only to that necessary earlier step. Even the readiness to listen to the words of this volume already constitutes, to my mind, a crucial act of faith.

5
God Is in the Details

Chana Silberstein

I

Many of us, when first encountering the *mitzvah* of *Mikvah,* find the concept deeply enriching. *Mikvah* represents the sanctification of the private and the personal. It tells us that what goes on behind closed doors is also sacred and holy. Teaching us never to take our partners for granted, it encourages us to value each other in multiple ways and makes our encounters constantly new and fresh. *Mikvah* adds meaning to our lives.

Despite this, for many Jewish women, a deep abyss separates the appreciation of *Mikvah* from its observance. There seem to be so many good reasons not to actually follow through on the teachings. Why can't the guidelines simply be used as an inspiration? One might assume that just reading and reflecting on *Mikvah* would be enough to inspire a deeper focus in our relationships.

Actually performing the *mitzvah,* on the other hand, can create a whole host of complications—*tevilah* (immersion) the night before a major business presentation due, finding a baby-sitter in a snow storm, driving to a *mikvah* across town to find the heater is malfunctioning. . . . Somehow, all the romance of the *mitzvah* fades in the face of the nitty-gritty details.

The more one considers the details, the stronger the hesitations become. Why a two-week separation? Five days seems more livable. Why drag out to a *mikvah* when there is a perfectly serviceable bathtub at home? If what matters is the cycles of separation and reunion, why not choose the times at our own convenience? Why lose the spontaneity that could ensure that the ritual is truly meaningful? Why not let our own feelings dictate the timing of the *mitzvah,* rather than some rigid, arbitrary timetable that is inexplicably tied to biology? Does God really care? Do these particulars make a significant difference?

The arguments crystallize as we mull them over. The little irritations, the personal discomforts, the tensions, the schedule juggling. . . . Shouldn't it be the *spirit* of the law that matters? Why does one actually have to *do* these things, and why in this particular way?

Letter and spirit. So often they seem to be at odds. How do we make peace between the limited and the free, the finite and the transcendent, the circumscribed and the imaginative in our lives?

II

Judaism compares the spirit of a *mitzvah* to a soul and its legal definition to a body. A body without a soul is dead—inert and unfeeling. But a soul without a body is ephemeral—fleeting and ineffectual. Only when body and soul are combined is real life possible. Just as the body needs the soul to come alive, the soul needs the body to act and to affect the world. The two, diametrically opposed, unite within us. Likewise, the spirit and the letter of the law interact, the spirit giving meaning to the act, the letter defining it.

But the connection between the two runs deeper still. Letter and spirit do more than complement and supplement each other. In Judaism, the letter of the law *is* the spirit of the law, setting the parameters of meaning for the *mitzvah.* The concept of *Mikvah* cannot exist in isolation of its practice.

The notions of purity and impurity around which the *mitzvah* of *Mikvah* revolves are not rational notions. There is no objective reason for why a particular time of month should necessitate a woman's separation from her husband. Neither is there an absolute, objective reason for why immersion must be in a pool built to particular specifications, filled with forty *se'ah* of natural rain or spring water. These are arbitrary legal definitions, defined by God; from our human perspective, they could just as easily have been otherwise.

Why, then, are we not free to redefine these parameters? Precisely because their only value lies in their God-given nature. Chasidism teaches that the word *mitzvah,* in addition to meaning "commandment" can also be defined as "connection." God is infinite and unknowable, and there would appear to be no common ground on which to connect with God. But by observing the command in its God-given form, we forge a link with the divine.

Although every *mitzvah* is characterized by the connective bond forged by total submission, this is most true of the *chukkim,* the *mitzvot* that defy logic. Whereas an atheist is capable of observing various moral precepts by understanding how they enrich the quality of human life, no such argument can be made about the observance of *mitzvot* such as *Mikvah*. While we may find meaning in the concept of separation and renewal, and symbolism in the use of water, the power of the immersion to actually transform a spiritual status is not something that fits within the framework of reason. By observing the *mitzvah,* we reveal that we behave not only in accord with our own sensibilities but first and foremost out of a sense of devotion to God. Thus, the very observance of the *mitzvah* serves to connect and bind us to God.

This notion of connection contains an additional layer of meaning when we discuss the *mitzvah* of *Mikvah*. The relationship between God and the Jewish people is often compared to the relationship between husband and wife.

Mikvah is paramount as a *mitzvah* that at once clarifies what is expected of our relationship with God and what is possible in our personal intimacies.

The *mishnah* in *Pirkei Avot* (Ethics of Our Fathers 5:19) says, "A love that is dependent on an ulterior motive ultimately fades away when the reason for the love fades. But a love that supersedes reason is eternal." Because it is not dependent on any rational reason, no circumstances can arise that can destroy that love.

In speaking of a relationship, we frequently speak as well of the factors that drew us to that relationship—our spouse's kindness, wit, compassion, humor. But ultimately, if the love is to be real, it must go beyond the parts, beyond the piecemeal definitions. True love means binding ourselves to the uncompromised whole. We must love our mates for who they are, not for what they have or what they do.

We live in a society that values self-actualization and individuality. These notions sometimes conflict with religious mores that find value in submission and in self-abnegation. These same notions are also at odds with the absolute devotion that a deep relationship entails.

The Hebrew word *ahavah* has its root in the Aramaic *hav,* meaning "give," for the measure of love is not the pleasure we take for ourselves in the relationship, but how willing we are to give to each other. The mark of a deep bond lies in the trust we are able to place in the wishes of the other and in our willingness to respond. To love means that it is enough to do something because we have been asked. It means we are prepared to give on the other's terms, because to do otherwise is not truly to give. To love means to totally accept. And to be loved means never having to explain.

Nowhere is this exemplified more than in the *mitzvah* of *tevilah* itself. In Hebrew, the root letters of the word *tevilah, t-v-l,* "immersion," are the same as the root letters of the world *bittul,* "nullification." Indeed, the notion of *tevilah* is nullifying ourselves before our Beloved God, immersing oneself totally beneath the purifying waters. Not even a hair may remain above the surface of the water. When we immerse in the *mikvah,* we lose all sense of ourselves. Beneath the waters, our lives are momentarily suspended. We exist and we do not exist at the same time. We are like a fetus within the mother, totally dependent, without even a breath of air to sustain us. When we are beneath those waters, we relinquish our very being to its essence. We are connected to God by an invisible strand—the bond of our absolute devotion—and that bond sustains us.

We emerge from the *mikvah* with a deeper understanding of the basis of lasting love. It is not enough for one's heart to be in the right place. Rather, it is acts of devotion that have the power to transform us. The measure of where we stand with God lies in our ability to translate a *mitzvah* into action, to accept it as a command, to let that command dictate to us, alter us, change us. Similarly, where we stand in our marriages lies in our ability to conform to each other's needs. In performing the *mitzvah* of *Mikvah* meticulously, these two devotions meet. We are able to contain our personal desires and sublimate them to God, and later, by extension, to each other.

III

In abstract terms, we may be able to recognize the vastness of God's wisdom and the value of submission to something higher than ourselves. We can extend the meaning by contemplating our gratitude to God for what is precious in our lives and recognize that doing a *mitzvah* is a way of giving something back. Thus we may be willing to submit to a *mitzvah* to forge a connection with the divine.

But all of this only touches the surface of the *mitzvah.* It makes the particulars irrelevant, spurious. And that makes it hard to be careful of the details. So long as we use the *mikvah,* does it matter when? Can't we personalize the experience by adapting the details to suit our needs?

The Baal Shem Tov describes the performance of *mitzvot* with a very moving parable about a poor country peasant who, after saving money for a long time, travels to the big city to observe the king's court. He has heard so much about the glories of the castle and is finally fulfilling a lifelong dream by observing it in person. As he enters the courtroom, he notices that all eyes are on a blind man who is pulling a bow of cat gut over some strings tied to a strangely shaped wooden box with a hole in it. He hears screeching and squalling, mewing and mauling, and the king and his courtiers are sobbing uncontrollably. The man puts down his hand. Then the pages read a request out to the king, but, saddened and depressed, the king responds in a perfunctory manner.

Soon the blind man raises his bow again, and this time the sounds are lighter and quicker. The king and his courtiers are smiling and vibrant, their heads nodding, their feet gently tapping. When the bow is finally put down and the page again reads out the people's requests, the king deals with the business of the court with enthusiasm and generosity.

The peasant is confused. He does not understand what has transpired here, for he has never seen a musician before nor heard the sounds of the violin. When he returns to his village, and people ask him what he saw in the king's palace, how can he explain?

Concludes the Baal Shem Tov: We are the blind musician, and we are the country peasant. When we fulfill the commandments, when we use the *mikvah* according to the *Halachah,* when we play the notes that we have been taught, a beautiful entity emerges that affects the heavenly court in ways that we cannot fathom. Like the blind musician who sees neither the tears streaming down the king's face nor the joyous nods as the king keeps time to a lively tune, we are unaware of the connections our actions forge with God. And like the country peasant, we do not even recognize the music when we hear it. We wonder at the power of a string of cat's gut to effect these powerful changes. Why not a string of silk, a block of solid gold? It is easy to observe and think of ways to improve upon a *mitzvah* and make it more meaningful. Like the peasant, we may be incapable of comprehending that the effect is dependent on the act being performed in a particular manner.

IV

While we may cherish the devotion that underscores our trusting obedience of the laws, while we may appreciate that there is much more there than meets the eye, there is still a fundamental disappointment that comes of not being able to rationally understand the import of our deeds. Why did God not reveal to us the meaning of the particulars, the divine correspondences? Why are we unable to see the spiritual counterparts of our actions?

We can achieve insight into this question by considering a passage in the Book of Hosea. The prophet describes God's disappointment with the Jewish people for abandoning their trust in divine providence. Hosea tells how the people will be cast out of the land of Israel into the desert, as an unfaithful wife is cast out of her home. And then, in a dramatic change of voice, the prophet describes how the Jewish people, with no alternative but to turn to God, begin to reinstate a new relationship. God says: "And I will betroth you unto me for ever; yea, I will betroth you unto me in righteousness, and in judgment, and in loving-kindness, and in mercy. I will betroth you unto me in faithfulness and you will know the Lord" (Hosea 2:21–22). The midrash describes this passage as the negotiation of a dowry. The Jewish people promise to behave rightly and justly; God, in return, promises divine kindness and mercy. The Jewish people promise faith and trust in God, and in return, God promises that ultimately they will know and understand God. The reward of faith is knowledge.

Why is trust of God a prerequisite to knowledge of God? Surely it would be easier to trust, to act with faith, if we understood what we were doing.

Imagine a king who has been lost in a forest for a number of days. His clothes are torn, his crown is lost—he looks like a ragged beggar. In hunger and exhaustion, he falls to the ground in a faint. A hunter finds the king and, unaware of his identity, carries him back to the hut. The hunter feeds the king and nurses him back to health. Then he offers to escort the king out of the forest. At this point, the king reveals his identity and promises to lavish rewards on the hunter for his kindness. The treasures the hunter will receive are valuable, but what is most dear to the hunter is the knowledge that he was able to help the king. And there is no doubt in our mind that the hunter is richly deserving of reward because of his selfless kindness to a stranger lying in the woods.

But imagine for a moment that when the hunter finds the crumpled figure on the ground, he notices at once the signet ring on the king's finger. He proceeds to feed and help the king as before. But it is impossible for him not to be affected by the realization that he is saving the king. The kindness is no longer pure, and there is always a lingering doubt that under different circumstances, he would have done nothing at all for the king.

Fundamental to Jewish faith is the belief in a Messiah, a time when the world will fulfill the ultimate potential placed in it from its inception. Maimonides describes the Messianic Era as a time when the whole world will be filled with the knowledge of God, just as the waters fill the seas. The secrets of creation will be revealed, and we will be able to apprehend that indeed God created a very good and just world. The joy of that culmination will be immense.

Through our belief in the Messiah, we illustrate our faith in the perfection of God and all that He has wrought. We demonstrate that our lives and all of creation have purpose and meaning. We affirm our trust that our efforts to do good will one day be amply rewarded. Thus, as Jews, all our efforts are directed to awaiting that time and bringing that day nearer. Through our actions, we attempt to elevate our lives and the world around us so that we can achieve that perfect state.

But if we could truly comprehend the secrets of the universe, could we serve God selflessly? Would not the knowledge of the rich rewards taint our devotions?

Chasidic philosophy teaches that in this way, our generation has a unique advantage over previous generations. The Jews in the desert experienced the Exodus from Egypt, the revelation of God on Sinai. Likewise, while the Temple existed, there was a very clear perception of God and a tangible relationship with Him. In other periods of our history, too, there were strong, central communities where Jews were surrounded by the knowledge and appreciation of God in ways that are uncommon today.

We live in an age when we are rushed, chasing after many phantoms, and it is hard to take the time to reflect on the spirituality within us. We live in an age that exalts the rational and emphasizes the material. Technology has brought the outside world into our homes, and it is difficult to maintain an unassimilated Jewish perspective in the face of these onslaughts. In the present environment, it can be hard to see why *mitzvot* matter, why we should bother, what difference our actions can possibly make. Yet these very difficulties afford unique possibilities in the service of God. For we more than any other generation, have the opportunity to show our unqualified commitment to God. In the words of Jeremiah, we follow God into a barren and desolate desert (Jeremiah 2:2).

Ultimately, we know, letter and spirit will unite for us, and we will come to appreciate the meaning of the *mitzvot* we do. We, who now curse our blindness, will become sighted musicians who understand the music and see the impact of the song we play. In the words of the prophet, on that day, we will all see that the mouth of God has spoken (Isaiah 40:5). But until that time, we can take comfort in the fact that our blindness only enhances the value of our devotion, that it makes our sacrifice all the greater. In our infirmity, our song plays ever sweeter to God's ears.

V

Perhaps when we first heard about *Mikvah,* it excited us, inspired us. But now our heart has gone out of it, and the wonder of it is gone. How can we recapture the moment lost? How can we recapture the spirit that held us once?

A story is told of Rabbi Shalom Dov Ber of Lubavitch who had an only child, a son. One evening, as he observed his infant son asleep in the cradle, he was overcome by an overwhelming feeling of love for the child. He immediately sat down and composed a philosophical discourse explaining some deep concepts in Chasidism (Jewish mystical thought). When his son grew older, he presented him with the essay, and said, "This is a kiss of Chasidism."

In some ways, his actions appear to be totally incongruous: His response to a poignantly emotional moment is a coolly reasoned intellectual work! Yet, in fact, his intention was to preserve that precious love. For he knew that emotions are fleeting. They come and go, and all that is left of them is an impoverished memory ill able to capture the intensity of the moment. But the discourse embodied the love and tenderness that overcame him then, and whenever that discourse would be subsequently read and studied, those heartfelt feelings would be reawakened and felt anew.

In the same way, each time we perform a *mitzvah,* we ground the spirit in reality. We give it permanence, we give it form, we make it tangible and graspable. Each time we immerse in the *mikvah,* we are able draw upon our earlier enthusiasm, and we keep our deepest inspirations from fading before our eyes.

VI

The preceding assumes a desire for the spiritual, a desire to find meaning in life and to connect with God. While the particulars of performance are perhaps difficult, the underlying spirit is present. But sometimes we lose even the essential desire to connect. In the absence of spirit, can the letter of the law still have meaning?

Chasidut explains that the soul has three garments, or outer manifestations. We express ourselves through thought, speech, and action. Though we are not defined by these garments, they are the only way for us to know ourselves. Which of these three comes closest to expressing our essential nature? It would seem that thought is most private and therefore most intimate. Speech, being more external, would seem somewhat more distanced from our true selves— yet, it has a constant connection to us by virtue of the fact that the flow of speech cannot exist without our presence. Action seems to be the furthest from our true nature. We can do something and walk away from it forever. The act, then, exists in total isolation from us.

While this is true of the garments of the soul in a revealed way, at its essence the opposite is true. While actions seem to be the most removed from our inner cores, they continue to exist without us because they emanate from the deepest parts of ourselves—parts so deep, so essential, that they have the power to grow apart from us and continue to feed on our essence even when we are gone.

Thus, we are told, for example, that the righteous do not die, for the good that they have done lives on after them. Their thoughts are lost to us. Their words will never again be heard, but their actions continue to exist through the ages, and through them they are immortalized.

In this volume, there are many essays capturing the beauty of the *mitzvah* of *mikvah* from many different perspectives. But ultimately, the *mitzvah* must go beyond the feelings of the moment, the transient vicissitudes of our lives. By performing the *mitzvah* faithfully, in spite of the way we feel at the particular moment, we build something bigger and more important than ourselves.

When we look down into the pool of waters and see our own faces, what do we see reflected back? Is it joy? Is it tension? Is it numbness? As we slowly descend the stairs of the *mikvah*, are we enveloped by wisdom? By ignorance? In the ebb of the gentle ripples, what voices will whisper? In the waters of that pool, we flow back in time and forward in time. Because of ourselves, in spite of ourselves, we join with our mothers and sisters. There is more here than we can ever know; we could not do this any other way. God is in the details.

6

Your Honeymoon Should Never End

Manis Friedman

There are two kinds of human love: the intrinsic, calm love that we feel for people to whom we're related by birth; and the more intimate, fiery love that exists in marriage. This is why the husband–wife relationship is very different from the parent–child relationship.

The love within a family, between relatives who are born of the same flesh, is innate. The love between a mother and child, a brother and sister, two brothers, two sisters, comes easily. Since they're related by nature, they feel comfortable with each other. There's an innate closeness between them, so their love is strong, solid, steady, predictable, and calm. There's no distance that has to be bridged; no difference that has to be overcome.

The love between a husband and wife isn't like that. Their love wasn't always there; they didn't always know each other; they weren't always related. No matter how well they get to know one another, they aren't alike. They are different from each other physically, emotionally, and mentally. They love each other in spite of the differences and because of them, but there isn't enough of a commonality between them to create a casual, calm love. The differences remain even after they are married, and the love between them will have to overcome these differences.

After all, husband and wife were once strangers. Male is different from female, so in essence they must remain strangers. Because of this, the love between them can never be casual, consistent, or calm.

This acquired love is naturally more intense than the love between brother and sister. When love has to overcome a difference, a distance, an obstacle, it needs energy to leap across and bridge the gap. This is the energy of fiery love.

Because the gap between husband and wife will never really close, their love for one another will continually have to reach across it. There will be distance, separation, then a bridging of distance, and a coming back together, again and again. This sense of distance intensifies the desire to merge.

To come together, man and woman have to overcome certain resistances. A man has to overcome his resistance to commitment, and a woman has to overcome her resistance to invasion. So, in coming together, husband and wife are reaching across great emotional distances, which intensifies their love. The absence of innate love actually makes the heart grow fonder.

If a brother and sister were to have a fiery love, their relationship would suffer. It's not the appropriate emotion for a brother and sister to have. Their love thrives when it's unbroken, unchallenged, constant, and calm. Not that they can't have disagreements, but those disagreements disrupt their love.

On the other hand, if a husband and wife develop a calm love for each other, their relationship will not thrive. If they are too familiar with each other, too comfortable with each other, like brother and sister, their love will not flourish. True intimacy in marriage—fiery love—is created by constant withdrawal and reunion.

If a husband and wife are never separate, their love begins to sour, because they are not creating an environment appropriate to that love. The environment of constant togetherness is not conducive to man–woman love; it's the environment for brother–sister love or parent–child love.

That's why the ideal blessing for a married couple is, "Your honeymoon should never end." A honeymoon—when two people who were once separate come together for the first time—should never end, because that's what a marriage thrives on.

The love between a man and a woman thrives on withdrawal and reunion, separation and coming together. The only way to have an environment conducive to that kind of relationship is to provide a separation.

There are many kinds of separations. A couple can live in different places, have differences of opinion, or get into arguments and be angry at each other. Often the arguing isn't for the sake of arguing, but for the sake of creating a distance so that husband and wife can feel like they're coming together.

That's not a very happy solution. Making up after an argument may be good for a marriage on occasion, but not on a regular basis. It isn't a good idea to go looking for arguments, especially since separations can take a more positive form.

The physical separation given to us by God for that purpose is a much happier solution. That separation is created by observing a collection of laws described in Leviticus as "the laws of family purity," but more frequently referred to as the "laws of *mikvah*" (Lev. 15:19–33). The word *mikvah* refers to the ritual bath in which traditional Jewish women, since the days of the Bible, have immersed themselves following their monthly period and before renewing sexual relations with their husbands.

According to these laws of *mikvah*, during the time that a Jewish woman is menstruating, and for one week afterward, she is physically off-limits to her husband. For those days, the physical separation is total: no touching, no sitting on a swing together, and even sleeping in separate beds.

Through the ages, all sorts of explanations have been given for the laws described in Leviticus, but all of them have one thing in common: Separation protects and nurtures the intimate aspect of marriage, which thrives on withdrawal and reunion.

This understanding is not unique to Jews. In most cultures throughout the world, the ancients practiced varying degrees of separation between husband and wife during the woman's menstrual period. Some, such as certain tribes of American Indians, actually had separate living quarters, menstruant tents, where a woman would stay during her period. Later these customs deteriorated into myths, taboos, fears, superstitions, hygienic arguments, and other rationalizations, in an attempt to make sense of a delicate and sensitive subject.

But separation was such a universal practice that I wonder if human beings know instinctively that male–female love thrives on withdrawal and reunion, on coming together following a separation. The body is actually reflecting an emotional state. Just as the love between man and woman cannot be maintained at full intensity all the time, but needs a certain creative tension without which it will not flourish, the body has a similar need.

As far as Jews are concerned, we know these cyclical changes were created for that very purpose. This is much more than a coincidence: It is how the body reflects the soul, how the body is created in the image of the soul.

Like everything else that exists in our lives, the cycle of withdrawal and reunion that exists in marriage is meant to be a reflection of our relationship with God. The two kinds of love, calm love and fiery love, exist not only among human beings, but between ourselves and God.

When we refer to God as our Father, it's an innate and intrinsic relationship. We don't have to work for it; it's just there. It's a steady, constant love, an indestructible love, a love compared to water—calm love.

But we also talk about how God is infinite and we are finite; God is true and we are not; God is everything and we are barely something. Because of these differences, we feel a great distance from God, and the need to create a relationship with Him. Establishing a relationship in spite of the differences, in spite of the distance, is more like a marriage. That's a stormy relationship—fiery love.

More precisely, our soul loves God like a child loves a parent, because our soul is of God. That love is innate and calm. When God tells this soul to go down into a body, that's a separation. Then our soul loves God with a fiery love, which, like the love between a husband and wife, does not come automatically. Acquired love is by nature intense and fiery.

Eventually, the soul will be reunited with God more intimately than before, just as the intimacy between a husband and wife is deeper when they come together following a separation. Therefore, when God says that a husband and wife have to be modest with one another, that they may be together and then separate, come together and separate again, according to a monthly cycle, it's not an artificial imposition. It may produce discipline, which is nice. It may keep the marriage fresh, which is important. But there's more to it than that.

It is, in fact, the natural reflection of the type of love that must exist between husband and wife. In order to nurture that stormy, fiery love, our way of living has to correspond to the emotions we are trying to nurture and retain.

If there's going to be a separation—and there needs to be one—consider the following: Rather than wait for a separation to develop, where a husband and wife get into a fight or lose interest in each other, let's take the cue from the body and create a physical, rather than emotional, separation.

Everyone is saying, "I need my space." It's true. Keeping the laws of *mikvah*, when they apply, is one way of creating that space.

7

Thinking Like a Jew

Chanoch Shuster

We live in a world that constantly impinges on us, whose atmosphere is so permeated with its particular values and attitudes and presumptions, that we absorb them without effort, unknowingly, unaware that we are being influenced. The American Jew is a tiny 2 percent or 3 percent of America numerically. Identifiably Jewish values, distinct and different from those of the other 98 percent, are so submerged, and unfamiliar to the "average" American Jew, that he doesn't realize any exist and certainly cannot share in them. Culturally, the Jew is thoroughly—shall we say—Western, for that is a neutral-sounding term. Actually, the culture, the values, the premises of Western culture are not an entity. They are to a tremendous degree Christian, and even if only in origin, nonetheless those roots are hardly obscure.

In the unquestioned, subterranean presuppositions of religion, in those basic statements that precede any discussion of religion, Christianity's views are a part of the West. The Jew should realize that these views are not universal, that they are specifically doctrinal, and that they are not in consonance with his own doctrines. In other words, the American Jew conceives of religion and discusses it in Christian terms.

He grapples with religious difficulties, because a Jew must examine Judaism, but he does so with alien categories. His conflict is not necessarily a Jewish one, but one of reconciling divergent viewpoints, the Jewish and the Christian, that were never intended to be reconciled, for they represent thoroughly different values. The "signs" of the Jew have been neglected, the demarcation between Jewish and non-Jewish faiths has been blurred, and the unaware Jew rejects or scorns his own religion because he does not have the tools for handling it appropriately.

Conventional thinking illustrates our adoptions from Christian thought, and they are often adopted, not adapted. The rabbi is regarded as the Jewish equivalent of the minister or priest, the synagogue parallels the church, *Shabbat* is the Jewish version of Sunday, both define faith in the same way though the content of the faith differs, and so on.

Many challenges of Judaism, many of the questions about Torah and *mitzvot* can be answered, not by answering the question, not by accepting its initial assumptions, but by eliminating the questions, by giving a fresh perspective, a view that makes the question irrelevant.

The institution of *Mikvah* and Family Purity is challenged constantly, and it is interesting to note that the sophisticated professor and illiterate laborer challenge it in virtually the same words. "In the olden days in the hot countries the purpose of the *mikvah* was to make sure that women bathed once a month, but nowadays, with water at hand in every home in the private white luxury of a tub, the *mikvah* hygiene is obsolete."

The defender of Family Purity will struggle with all sorts of refutations with intricate rationales, all trying to convince the questioner that *Mikvah* is indeed necessary and relevant and is not obsolete—and the challenger walks off unmoved. He framed his question in particular terms and it was answered in those terms. But those terms are only the verbalization, the tip of the iceberg. He is bothered by something far deeper. Treating the symptoms of his religious malaise will not help him.

Man is a composite of body and soul, of a wide range of faculties and talents. His body is "lower" than his "spirit," the intellectual is superior to the manual. The body is scorned as an instrument of Godliness, as an avenue to heights of spirit. It is ballast, deadweight, the anvil around the neck, the burden. The blessed, the truly dedicated, will spurn the flesh. The celibate is an ideal, the monastery is the religious institution. It is realized that the liberal will not subscribe to these statements baldly, but they are normative in Christianity. Even in rejecting Puritanism, the libertine is simply a reverse of the Puritan coin, still chafing under that onerous yoke, despite his desperate efforts at hedonism.

However our liberal will protest this caricature, it is reflected in his religious life. The "good Christian" refers to one who attends church regularly, every Sunday. Note what happens when we observe the "good Christian," the representative of religion in the Western World.

He has a day for serving God, for affirming his bond and debt explicitly. He has consecrated a place for this worship. Of man's countless abilities, he has dedicated some for divine service-prayer, faith, understanding, song—the "higher" faculties of man. And then, he has selected one person to stand apart and above, in a sacerdotal position, who is totally dedicated to the Divine service, his clergyman. What a snug, symmetrical compartment for religion. In time—a day; in space—a building; in man—his mind and heart; in mankind—a cleric.

What, now, is the appropriate, meaningful way to pray, to serve God, to be "religious"? Through prayer, through faith, through worship and song. "What goes out of your mouth is important, not what goes in"—who made that statement? It was an initial step in breaking away from Judaism and founding a new faith. We should know that.

Here is the real question about *Mikvah,* the assumptions that lead to the challenge; I can understand Judaism insisting on prayers, on *Shema,* on faith and on charity, our questioner is really saying. You can serve God with your mind and your emotions, with your "higher" faculties, but not with such a base animal function as procreation. Since Family Purity laws "cannot" be religious, then they must have some other origin and significance, logically hygiene. If that justification was warranted thirty centuries ago, it is anachronistic today. This is the challenge to Family Purity. Until the American Jew stops thinking in these alien categories of what is legitimate and authentic religious experience and service, he will never be able to meaningfully accept *mitzvot,* or Judaism for that matter. He must learn to think like a Jew and stop thinking like a gentile. The next man's ideas may be perfectly valid for him, but they are not mine.

Well what does Judaism have to say about serving God and authentic religious experience? There may be a single word to sum up Judaism, and of course that word must be understood: totality. All the man, all the time, in every place, under all circumstances, in every activity, in every fiber of his being, can serve God, can apprehend Him, can communicate with Him. Nothing human is alien to Torah, to God, to Judaism. Whatever the Jew does can be a channel, a bridge, between himself and God, or it can be a barrier, a wall separating him from God, an act to smother his sensitivity, to coarsen him.

Certainly mind is part of man, spirit, song, faith—these are all human, so these are all legitimate experiences of God's closeness. But so is man's food, and his business and recreation, and his family life, and his disappointments and ambitions, and fears and envies and gladness, and his esthetics. The mind and heart are avenues to God, true; so are food and family life. This is the meaning of totality, nothing is excluded from the purview of Torah. There is nothing intrinsically "higher" and "lower."

On Yom Kippur eve, in a *shul* jammed with worshippers, covering your eyes and crying out *Shema Yisrael,* meaning and feeling every word in the depths of the heart—this is worship, this is religious feeling. Anyone will subscribe to that. Torah tells us that in our marital lives, we can serve God just as well, when we conduct ourselves as He tells us. When we are conscious of Him through Torah-prescribed self-regulated abstinence and practice of the *Mikvah* rite— this too is an altar, sacred, man addressing God in a language other than words alone—and God sees and hears.

This is what we mean by thinking like a Jew, shedding the categories and presumptions of the Christian environment. The distinctiveness may be diffi- cult to maintain, the integrity of Jewish ideas may become diluted under the constant battering by the environment, so we have "signs" to remind us what we are. Let others decide for themselves what religion is for them, what will ennoble them, make them aware of God. We have no quarrel with that. All we insist is that we have our own standards, our own ideals, our conceptions, our communication with God, our awareness of His concern for us. Because Christianity scorns the flesh is no reason for us to be upset about *Mikvah.* We pray in many languages, in the language of the mind and the heart and the hand and the family and whatever we do. Which is the "superior" service of God? Who cares? We're not keeping score. We are living. On Yom Kippur we serve God one way. At the office we serve him in another. With our family life we serve Him, and in our intellectual pursuits we serve Him—the total Jew serves Him.

Now, what was that question about *Mikvah?* Isn't it obsolete now with modern hygiene? What in the world does health and hygiene have to do with the total human experience being a religious opportunity? We need not answer the question of the obsolescence of *Mikvah* laws. All we need do is examine our preconceptions, and reaffirm our Jewish perspective. The question disappears.

8

The Sexual Component in Love and Marriage

Maurice Lamm

Sex is the most powerful, all-pervasive force in human experience. It may be intensely personal, meaningful, and creative at one moment, and depersonalized, meaningless, and careless the next. Much of its glory is that it can bring us as close as we may get in life to experiencing the mystery of our mortality, and because of this it is sanctified. Yet it can also be a blind, nearly irresistible force seeking wanton release on the biological level, and in this way its sanctity is perverted. Paradoxically, sex—the most chaotic, powerful, and untutored drive—can only be fully experienced when it includes an element of discipline and precision.

Judaism on Sexual Boundaries

There is no single term for "sex" in the Bible. The title for the list of the Bible's prohibited sexual offenses is *gilui arayot,* "uncovering the nakedness" (Leviticus 18:6ff), and Maimonides classifies these chapters of the law under the rubric of *Kedushah* (Sanctity). Although Jewish tradition does not treat sexual experience systematically, reference to it can be found in every one of the Five Books of Moses, in every book of the Prophets, and *Ketuvim,* the "Writings." Even the Talmud contains candid, sometimes explicit clinical analyses and

Excerpted from the chapter in *The Jewish Way in Love and Marriage.*

intimate details that would make a Victorian blush. What emerges is a moral discipline that is strict, yet highly sensitive to the human condition; one that affirms the joyfulness of the sexual experience, but insists that it express itself in controlled circumstances; and one that never deprecates marriage and at every opportunity deplores monastic asceticism. Judaism's philosophy of sexual experience, love, and marriage begins with the Bible's first recorded paragraphs describing Adam's relations with Eve. This philosophy has weathered every new fad and every radical style that boldly declared its doctrine to the world, from the celibacy of Augustine to the free love of Bertrand Russell. Judaism has focused its greatest minds on understanding God's law and nature's demands, and throughout its history has succeeded in elevating sex, sanctifying marriage, and firmly establishing the family as the primary unit of the community.

Traditional Judaism makes the following general propositions about sex and its place in human society:

1. Sexual relations may take place only between a man and a woman. This means that sex with an animal is considered a perversion, and intercourse with a member of one's own sex prohibited.
2. Sexual relations and marriage are not permitted with someone outside the circle of the Jewish people (mixed marriage) or inside the circle of close relatives established by the Bible and the Sages (incest).
3. Sexual relations are a *mitzvah,* a religious duty, within a properly covenanted marriage in accordance with Jewish law. Outside of that covenant, premarital sexual relations are not condoned and extramarital relations are considered crimes.
4. Sexual relations within marriage must accord with the laws of family purity with respect to the wife's menstrual cycle.

Seven Axioms for Sexual Conduct

These propositions are based largely on the following axioms that form the fundamental concepts of human sexuality in Judaism.

1. The Human Being Is Not an Animal

Simple observation teaches us that we have the genitalia of animals and participate in a similar sexual process. Why, then, can we not act like animals? It does seem to be nature's way. Indeed, Freudian psychology teaches us generally that we must see ourselves as we are, pleasure-seeking animals, and that we will not succeed in negating our essential animality except at the risk of neurosis.

There are no rules for beasts to follow other than blind obedience to instincts, satisfaction of needs, and "doing what comes naturally." The consequences of this irresponsible behavior can be disastrous, resulting in broken homes, broken hearts, loneliness, children born out of wedlock, loveless marriages, and infidelity. Ecclesiastes (3:19) declares only in bitterness, "Man has no preeminence above a beast, for all is vanity." But if that is all we are, then the world, humanity, the soul, and all of life becomes meaningless and empty. We were created in the image of God, and Judaism does not permit us to squander our humanity. *Haneshamah lakh ve'haguf Pa'alakh* ("the soul is Yours [God's] and the body is Yours, too") is a cornerstone phrase of the Yom Kippur liturgy. At the wedding service, a blessing is recited to remind the bride and groom that the human being is created in God's image.

Despite the similarity of sexual anatomy and parallel reproductive processes, the essential humanity of our sexuality can be discerned in the very fabric of the physical act. If it is to be successful, the sexual act must be based on a sense of concern for the partner. Helmut Thielicke notes that "there is a two-way communication in the structure of the libido, for the prerequisite for the fulfillment of pleasure is that the other person give himself to it, that he participate. . . . The other person should not be a passive object upon which one's own urge is simply 'abreacted.' " Without this communication, coitus is disguised autoeroticism. We cannot successfully follow the animal instinct and achieve release, but must be synchronized with our partner in order to satisfy ourselves.

This "synchrony" required of sexual partners reflects a unique factor that is fundamental to our understanding of the difference between animal sex and human sex: A man's curve of sexual excitement tends to rise sharply and fall precipitously, while a woman's may rise more slowly and taper off gradually. At first this may appear to be an imperfection, when compared to the easy harmony of animals. But perhaps this apparent incongruity is designed to prevent human beings from merely following the erotic impulse in blind animal fashion. To achieve genuine satisfaction, we are forced to express our humanity. Sex exposes us to failure and success, and in all this it confronts us with the theme of human communication instead of mere animal copulation. It is precisely this human need to correct the natural impulse that impels the thirteenth-century author of *Iggeret Hakodesh,* a document on the mystical significance of marriage, to give detailed advice to his son on preparing his wife for the sexual act and designing the proper erotic atmosphere.

This exception of the human being from the rule of instinct in the natural realm teaches us that we must exercise our essential humanity in the area of sexual relations as in all other critical areas of life. We must reasonably and intelligently choose a life partner, make proper human covenants, order our lives and our priorities, control our urges, and submit to a higher discipline: a *Halachah,* the law we were given by God. This is a law that we need in order to protect our love, both from other humans who act like animals, and from the internal animal that we sometimes allow to crouch at the door of our souls.

While some segments of society attempt to animalize our humanity, Judaism tries to humanize that which is called animal.

2. The Human Being Is Not an Angel

If we are not animals — and thus not permitted to abuse our sexual gift — we are also not angels who may abstain from sex altogether. We must live according to a higher ethical and moral law as beings created in the image of God, but reality dictates that we are not, and will never become, angels.

Judaism therefore frowns on celibacy. As recorded in the Talmud, Ben Azzai (one scholar among the thousands recorded) chose to remain celibate in order to study Torah and was chastised severely. This is in stark contrast to the celibacy of the two founders of Christianity, Jesus and Paul, and the pronouncements against the institution of marriage (1 Corinthians 6 and 7), which accept it only as a concession to human frailty. To wit, Paul: People should marry only ". . . if they cannot contain . . . ; for it is better to marry than to burn" (1 Corinthians 7:9); and Matthew: "Be a eunuch for the sake of Heaven" (19:12); and John Calvin, at the beginning of the Protestant Reformation: Marriage is "a necessary remedy to keep us from plunging into unbridled lust." Reinhold Niebuhr considers the Christian development of the family a triumph over the negative Christian attitude to sex and marriage.

Judaism posits that sex is a gift from God. How could such a gift be considered evil or sinful? Properly used in a legitimate framework, sex is to be viewed positively as joy and as *mitzvah.* The patriarchs marry, the kings marry, the *kohanim* marry, the prophets marry, the Sages marry. Nowhere is there the slightest indication that sex or family interfered with their mission. The term used for Isaac's sexual relationship with his wife is *metzachek,* "rejoicing" (Genesis 26:8). The author of *Iggeret Hakodesh* writes: "Let a man not consider sexual union as something ugly or repulsive, for thereby we blaspheme God. Hands which write a *sefer Torah* are exalted and praiseworthy; hands which steal are ugly."

Sex is not sin, and it does not need to be spiritualized. It must, however, be humanized, by affirming the reality of its power and attractiveness, rejoicing in its presence, using it as a blessing for the benefit and development of humankind, and abstaining from it when its Creator forbids it. A corollary of the two statements—that we are neither animals nor angels—may be that we have aspects of both. In this case, our humanity would consist of proper resolution of the tensions and contradictory demands made upon us by our dual nature.

3. Human Sexuality Is Clean and Neutral

Judaism believes that sex is morally neutral. Libidinal energy is an ambivalent power, the effect of which depends on what the human being does with it. Sex does not even have the status of an intrinsic value, but can function as a means to express love and build family, or as random personal gratification. Sex is neither bestial nor sinful, neither sacrament nor abomination, and so may not be abused or discarded. It is not to be denigrated as a necessary concession to human weakness, nor is it to be worshipped as an idol.

Genesis (1:31) tells us that at the end of the creation, God saw everything that He made and that it was *tov me'od* (very good). Interpreting the verse, Rabbi Samuel ben Nahman said: "*Tov,* good—that is the *yetzer tov,* the good inclination; *tov me'od,* very good—that is the *yetzer hara,* the evil inclination. But how can an admittedly evil inclination be considered good, let alone very good? Because without it, man would not care to build a home, he would neither marry nor beget children, nor would he pursue a livelihood."

Judaism does not believe that sex in itself is evil, it is the abuse of sex that is evil.

4. Sexuality Cannot Be Separated from Character

If we agree that the sexual force is neutral and that its good or evil qualities depend on how we use it, we can begin to appreciate that our sexuality can never be separated from our total personality. Thus the way we handle our own sexuality is not primarily a matter of facts, but of values. Indeed, sex can be a revealing indication of character: is our partner a giver or taker, sensitive or gross, caring or selfish, religious or irreligious?

If sex were merely a matter of physiological function, it could be treated like a mechanical problem: get the best engine, use the best technique, and achieve the best result. If it doesn't work, trade it in. If this were the case, then sexual partners would be interchangeable and society would function as a warehouse for suitable parts. This mechanical concept is analogous to prostitution, which is concerned solely with the biological function. It follows, therefore, that the more one's life is motivated by isolated instinct, the more one tends to polygamy and the less one seeks a single person with whom to share everlasting love.

The Jewish worldview makes it clear that sex cannot be mechanically abstracted from the totality of human activity. Thus, the problems of premarital sex, adultery, and casual sex are really questions of values.

5. Human Sexuality Has Meaning Only in the Context of Relationship

Perhaps our greatest fear is that our lives will be meaningless. If sex, the most powerful and sensitive area of our lives is to have meaning, it must be used as an expression of love or affection for another person. If we depersonalize the act by relating to another person only on a biological level, we dehumanize our partner and rob ourselves of our own integrity. To be successful, the act of sex requires the sensitive involvement of both partners. Noninvolvement results in a mechanical orgasm that is ultimately meaningless and demeaning.

If simply sleeping together would produce happiness, then the prostitute would be the happiest person in society. According to Helmut Thielicke, what is an ethical deficiency for the person who seeks the prostitute—the need for the physiological function rather than the person—is for the prostitute a positive element of moral self-defense. She saves her sense of self-worth by withholding her "self" during sex.

It is this distinction that determines whether the act is merely another sensation, or a true step toward relationship. It is becoming characteristic of our society that old as well as young people seek experiences rather than relationships, episodes rather than the continuous growth toward greater love. Ramban, in his commentary to the fundamental verse of love and marriage in Genesis (2:24), notes: "First one must cleave to his wife, then they will become one flesh. There can be no true oneness of the flesh without first experiencing a cleaving together of the heart."

6. Sexuality Has Value Only in a Permanent Relationship

In the Jewish view, it is insufficient to affirm that the act must have meaning: it must also have value. For Judaism, value in human sexuality comes only when the relationship involves two people who have committed themselves to one another and have made that commitment in a binding covenant recognized by God and by society. The act of sexual union, the deepest personal statement that any human being can make, must be reserved for the moment of total oneness.

The sexual act is the first and most significant event of married life and its force and beauty should not be compromised by sharing coitus in the expectation that someday a decision will be made to marry or not to marry. The act of sex is not only a declaration of present love, it is a covenantal statement of permanent commitment. It is only in this frame of reference that sexual congress is legitimate, because only then is it a religious act, a *devar mitzvah*.

Love by itself is not a sufficient motivation for sexual expression; love that is authentic will want to reserve the ultimate act for the ultimate commitment. The test of a good marriage is not compatibility in bed, but compatibility in life. Given love and respect, sexual technique can be learned. Engaging in sex to "test it out" desanctifies the act. It is not a rehearsal for marriage, it is a rehearsal for divorce.

The Torah speaks of the sexual act as carnal knowledge, as in "Adam knew his wife Eve" (Genesis 4:1). *Yediah* is the most sublime human knowledge because it knows the mystery, the soul of the beloved. In the sexual act, knowledge comes not only from physical intimacy and harmony and oneness, but also from experiencing the very depths of passion and extremes of emotion emanating from the loved one. It is a knowledge from the inside. All such knowledge has two aspects: We learn about the other person, and we also experience ourselves at the extreme of our potential. Perhaps that is why taboos surround both love and death. A taboo is designed to protect us where we are most vulnerable and most mysterious: as we generate life in the privacy of our room, and as we take leave of life.

The increasing freedom from sexual restraint in this post-Freudian era is testimony to the demystification of sex and the irretrievable loss of precious "knowledge." We can conjecture further that perhaps the use of the term *yada* (revealing knowledge) for the sex act is contingent upon the prior existence of hiddenness, mystery. This *he'alem* (concealment) exists both on the biological level—the internality of the female genitalia—and the societal—the idea of modesty, *tzeniut*, and its use of clothing to cover the body. As society sheds its clothing, there is progressively less to "know" by means of sexual exploitation. If the object of carnal knowledge is to know our self as well as our mate, then the demystification of sex adversely affects our self-knowledge as well.

7. Sexuality Needs to Be Sanctified

If sexuality is that deepest personal statement, filled with ecstasy and informed by knowledge, it follows that even within marriage sex is not considered simply a legitimated biological function. The Torah motivated the Jew to sanctify sex within marriage, for sex as a part of daily routine threatens to become wearisome and a dread bore, and sometimes more divisive than supportive. The laws of "family purity," which require abstinence during and shortly following the menstrual period, place the sexual act in a special category.

On a basic level, sanctity means separating oneself consciously from immorality and illicit thoughts. Maimonides incorporates the laws of sexual morality in a section of *Kedushah* (the Book of Holiness) and states that the deliberate separation from the illicit is an act of self-transcendence that constitutes sanctification.

Kiddushin—which signifies sanctity and betrothal—leads inevitably to *nissuin*—nuptials, elevation. Thus sanctification raises the physiological act of sex onto a higher, more spiritual level. This understanding of sanctity as leading to elevation is implied in the suggestion of the Talmud that it is preferable for a pious scholar to perform the conjugal act on the Sabbath. Rashi explains, "It is the night of joy, of rest, and of bodily pleasure." Such an affirmation is descriptive of how the Sabbath invested even bodily joys such as wearing special clothes and eating special foods with a special significance, elevating them to the realm of sanctified physical pleasures.

Sanctity also implies mystery. The Holy of Holies of the Temple, its inner sanctum, was visited only once every year, and then only by the High Priest. In the imagination of the people, it was a subject of awe and mystery.

Our society has lost the sense of the sacred, and there is little mystery attached to sex. Its physiology and technique have become commonplace to children, and teenagers are already tired and bored veterans.

Judaism teaches that the erotic act has wide significance, and that this physical act operates transcendentally. The creation of family and the consecration of marriage are events of which Jews sing at the wedding feast: *shehasimchah bime'ono*, "there is joy in His [God's] abode."

There are two terms for the sexual act. The better known is that which is used in the Bible and Talmud, *bi'ah*, which means "a coming" as in "he came unto her." The second is a kabbalistic term, *chibbur*, which means "joining." It is used in *Iggeret Hakodesh*, which is subtitled *Sefer Chibbur Adam Ve'ishto*, "The Book of Joining of Man and His Wife." The word and concept are based on the mystical vision of the cherubim facing and embracing one another in spiritual mutuality. It also connotes the ideal of *yediah*, "knowledge from the inside." The Kabbalah considers knowledge and joining synonymous—true "knowledge" derives only from an interpenetrating and joining of the two bodies, the knower and the to-be-known.

Where *bi'ah* is simply descriptive of the physical position of the male, *chibbur* implies a coming together of equals. While rape or seduction must be referred to as *bi'ah*, *chibbur* implies a need for consent.

Chibbur also recalls the fundamental Jewish mystical drive of uniting and mending into oneness the fragmented world of "broken vessels." Genesis records the separation of the rib from ancient Adam, and *chibbur* refers to the rejoining of that rib to the side of Adam. Judaism strives for an understanding and an affirmation of the concept of *chibbur* in the context of *yichud,* the mutual love of husband and wife. The contemporary writer I. Lewald says: "In the consciousness of belonging together, in the sense of constancy, resides the sanctity, the beauty of matrimony, which helps us to endure pain more easily, to enjoy happiness doubly, and to give rise to the fullest and finest development of our nature."

9

A Most Delicate *Mitzvah:* Marital Challenges Related to *Taharat Hamishpachah*

Reuven P. Bulka

I

There is much in the rich expanse of Judaic literature that projects the Jewish marriage ideal. This projection of the marriage ideal is not intended as merely a theoretical formulation. It is intended as a practical guide for how marriage is ideally to be approached and lived out to the full. What is that ideal?

Marriage is not simply living the same as before but with someone else. Nor is it simply a change of lifestyle with added benefits and duties. Marriage is, and should be lived, as a higher dimension of existence. All that goes on prior to marriage ideally prepares for marriage, but marriage itself is a fresh start in the way life was meant to be. The ritual immersion in a *mikvah,* the Yom Kippur–like atonement for iniquity, and different customs prior to and during the ceremony all converge on this point.

What is one to make of this fresh start? It is a fresh start, but toward what? In a word, toward connectedness-cum-completeness. In creation, everything came in pairs, from the human being down; and the pairs comprised male and female.

With the human, it was two forms in one corpus, originally fused, then parted, only to be brought together in a spiritual fusion that was to reinforce their primordial oneness. Unlike animals, whose togetherness is primarily for copulation, human togetherness, while incorporating copulation, is much more. It is a togetherness that has no time limitations, a togetherness that is to be a oneness and a completeness. The idea of man (*adam*) in Judaic terms is that of man and woman together.

Oneness is more than partnership; it is connectedness without barriers, unity of mind, body, and purpose. To be interconnected is to be friends, confidants, and intimates in the most noble sense. Alone, man and woman are each exposed and spiritually wanting. Together, man and woman complete themselves by completing the other. To be united in mind, body, and purpose is to forge life together in total devotion, with utmost awareness of the other, alertness to the other's needs, and commitment to common ideals and values, in thought, and in practice. It is to be able to say, "My wife's foot hurts us," and to mean it. In essence, it is to be as God wanted us to be.

Unlike most *mitzvah* fulfillments, which are individual, Jewish family law involves two people, husband and wife, working in concert and harmony. Think of some high-profile *mitzvah* fulfillments: *Mezuzah, Tallit, Tefillin, Shabbat,* Yom Kippur, *Sukkah, Matzah,* and so forth. All these are fulfilled by the individual acting alone. Not so *Taharat Hamishpachah,* the Laws of Conjugality.

One major component of the Laws of Conjugality is *Onah. Onah* literally means "her time," and refers to the time that the husband must dedicate to his wife. *Onah* may also be related to *eenuy,* or "affliction," and relates to the notion that if the *Onah* obligation is not properly fulfilled, it can cause affliction. Conjugal union lived out as prescribed by the Torah is a sacred, ennobling experience. But conjugal union devoid of mutuality, and lacking sensitivity and caring, can indeed be an affliction.

There is a fascinating story in the Talmud about a student who stealthily made his way to his rebbe's bedroom and hid under the bed. In the evening, he listened to how his rebbe engaged in conjugal union with his wife and muttered to himself about the passion with which the rebbe approached his wife. The rebbe heard, and in understandable amazement, asked the student what he was doing under the bed. The student answered, "It is Torah, and I need to learn!" (*Berachot* 62a) Indeed, the proper fulfillment of *Onah,* of all matters related to *Taharat Hamishpachah,* is Torah at its best, and we all need to learn.

II

Mutuality is the key not only to conjugal union. It is also the key to the husband–wife fulfillment of the *Taharat Hamishpachah* obligations. If both husband and wife share a common commitment to the *mitzvah* and its details, in a loving and warm atmosphere, their married life is immeasurably enhanced.

Problems arise when husband and wife do not share a common commitment to *Taharat Hamishpachah*. The most dramatic instance of such discord is when one of the marital partners desires to fulfill the *Taharat Hamishpachah* laws, and the other is absolutely against adhering to these laws. The most problematic situation in this scenario occurs when it is the husband who wants to adhere, but the wife does not.

Before analyzing this problem in greater detail, it should be noted that difficulties arise not only when the divide between husband and wife is between one affirming and the other rejecting. Problems can also occur even when both agree "in principle" with *Taharat Hamishpachah* dictates but disagree on the details, on "how much" they want to observe the components of the precept.

For example, the husband may agree to refrain from conjugal union prior to immersion in the *mikvah* but may refuse to refrain from other affectionate physical contact with his wife. The wife may agree to immersion in the *mikvah* but may refuse to abide by the precise protocols leading up to it.

Additionally, other disagreements may become absorbed into *Taharat Hamishpachah* issues and used as a weapon by one or both of the spouses. When the disagreement is stirred into the pot of an already conflicted relationship, the result can be explosive.

The difficulties arising from the lack of a common agenda relative to *Taharat Hamishpachah,* as indeed to general Judaic commitment, are not new to the Jewish scene. What is new is the frequency with which this type of situation arises. This is due mainly to the welcome phenomenon of Jews returning to their roots and desiring to more actively affirm Torah precepts. One of the marital partners may latch on to Jewish affirmation before the other. Indeed, it is unlikely that the marital couple will completely synchronize their movements toward greater *mitzvah* fulfillment.

The discussion of the issues arising from absence of common commitment are thus hopefully useful in addressing existent difficulties, and also in preempting those difficulties from causing serious marital disruption.

III

On occasion, the disparity between husband and wife may exist even before marriage. For instance, the wife may have attended a premarriage class that is offered in the community and via that class became aware of Jewish marriage discipline. The engaged husband-to-be never intended to abide by these practices, and even now that his wife-to-be has a serious interest, he refuses to budge. So quite suddenly and unexpectedly, a problem arises between the couple that threatens their impending marriage.

Whenever this issue arises, it creates a serious complication, for it impacts directly on the unique language of the marriage: the sexual communication. That part of the marriage is by definition fragile and potentially volatile. The area of sex, demanding as it does the full cooperation and understanding of both partners, is sensitive to even the slightest nuances. Doubts about the other's love and respect, when they interact with one's own insecurity, may adversely affect the equilibrium between husband and wife.

The objections of either marital partner to follow Jewish Marital Law may be linked to a number of factors. These generally fall into four major categories: (1) religious objections, (2) the issue of control, (3) impact on sexual fulfillment, and (4) conflicted marriage.

Most of these objections can arise relative to other *mitzvah* fulfillments that demand husband–wife cooperation, such as *Shabbat, Kashrut,* and so forth. The focus in this article is strictly on the particular matter of the *Taharat Hamishpachah* issue.

1. *Religious objections.* The husband or wife may loathe religion and religious practice and therefore reject *Taharat Hamishpachah* discipline. There are many reasons why one may feel this way. The feeling may be related to unhappy childhood experiences, perhaps being forced into religious practice by teachers or parents. The religious models with whom one has had contact may have been less than ideal. One may genuinely feel that Judaic belief and practice is outmoded, irrelevant, unnecessary.

Alternatively, the husband or wife may fear this is the beginning of a frontal assault on their perceived identity, that is, he or she will be forced to change many other practices, including those related to *Shabbat, Kashrut,* etc. Here the reluctant partner is not hostile to religion but is afraid of too much religion.

The rabbinic instinct may be to say, So what is so terrible about keeping *Shabbat* and eating kosher? But that is clearly an inappropriate thing to say to someone who actually fears doing just that. It may be more effective simply to spell out the benefits of marriage governed by *Taharat Hamishpachah* rules and to urge the couple to give this an honest and genuine try for a period of time, say a year.

As for the fears that other religious practices may come next, fear of other consequences should not deter one from trying a discipline that has such a good chance of enhancing a marriage.

Neither partner should allow past experiences to deprive them of present fulfillment. Even if the resentment is related to hostility toward parents, it is still possible to convince the reluctant spouse to look at Judaism on its own merits.

Finally, even if one has a general resentment of religious practice, one should not reject an idea which will be to the benefit of one's marriage. It is of benefit if for no other reason than that the other partner desires it.

Another variation of this concern is the possibility that the husband or wife may feel that the status quo is just fine. One resists change for fear that one's partner will change, and thereby be a different person from the person one married.

Here we deal with the fear of change and its potentially negative impact on the union. Insecurity may be at work, or it may be a fear related to an experience of an acquaintance, for example, that a friend's wife started to keep *Taharat Hamishpachah* laws, then became very religious, to the point that she lost common thinking with her husband, and they divorced.

To avoid this potential pitfall, husband and wife should be urged to work together on this and all other components of their marriage.

Insofar as the fear of change is concerned, it is useful to realize that a more serious threat to marriage is stagnation. Growth in marriage, which effectively is *change,* is necessary for the marriage itself to endure and grow. But husband and wife must appreciate that the growth of one partner alone usually leads to growing apart, which is to no one's advantage.

Some women have a greater problem with this *mitzvah* than with any other that the husband might desire they embrace. Their preconceived notions about *mikvah* and the negative associations it has for them may cause them to vehemently oppose adopting this *mitzvah*. These varied concerns are addressed in many of the other essays in this volume.

2. *The issue of control.* Husband or wife may feel that by being "forced" into *Taharat Hamishpachah* discipline, he or she thereby forfeits the dominant role in the marriage.

Most husbands, for example, will not admit to this concern about losing the dominant role. Males may talk about this to other males, or may quietly believe it, but are reluctant to say this openly to their wives and for good reason. They know that such feeling is wrong, that they have no business desiring dominance or demanding it, even though they may want it.

Any man knows, or should know, that his wife would be repulsed upon learning that her husband wanted to dominate her. No one, not a man or a woman—or even a child, for that matter—wants to be dominated.

Conversation here should focus on the reality that marriage is a union of equals, each of whom has coresponsibility for the partnership and neither of whom has a right to dominate or subjugate the other.

Jewish law on conjugal union emphasizes that such togetherness can be experienced only when the wife is physically and emotionally ready. The Jewish marital discipline is especially geared toward avoiding abuse, and such avoidance is achieved through the wife's biological rhythm being the prime factor in resumption of conjugal activity.

Neither husband nor wife is dominant, and because of this, fairness and mutual understanding is predominant. Neither is in control; instead both are subordinate to God, Whose word is their guide.

3. *Impact on sexual fulfillment.* The husband or wife may feel that *Taharat Hamishpachah* laws deprive the marriage of sensual opportunity and spontaneity, since one can experience conjugal union only when "the law" (Torah) says it is permitted.

This is true, at least to some extent. During the menstrual period, and for seven days following, there can be no spontaneous sex because sex is off limits. And the night of immersion in the *mikvah* is not a night of spontaneity, since both husband and wife expect to resume conjugal union.

There are a few points relative to this issue of spontaneity. First, what is lost in spontaneity on the night of immersion is more than compensated for by the heightened sense of anticipation, the fresh coming together and renewal of marital intimacy. Additionally, spontaneity, even on immersion night, need not focus exclusively on the physical reunion. Making the evening a night of celebration, with special affectionate gestures such as taking one's mate out for supper or going together to a play or movie, are nice surprises that have the same impact, if not a greater impact, than sexual spontaneity.

Second, the argument for spontaneity can sometimes be a facade masking a desire to indulge when one wants, without assuring the eagerness of the other— that other usually being the wife. More important than spontaneity is sensitivity to one's spouse.

Finally, there is still ample room for mutual spontaneity during the more than two weeks when conjugal union can take place.

4. *Conflicted marriage.* The husband or wife may feel that the other is using *Taharat Hamishpachah* laws to punish, to send a message about marital unhappiness and resultant lack of desire for sexual intimacy. This feeling may indeed be accurate, and even if not accurate it reflects a mindset about the marriage that demands further scrutiny.

Why does the spouse feel this way? Perhaps his wife has sent the husband such signals, because she is unhappy at the way he treats her, be it in the bedroom or in other aspects of their union.

Perhaps the wife feels a certain coldness or distancing from her husband, and his desire to observe *Taharat Hamishpachah* rules is the final straw.

If these feelings are based in reality—and these feelings sometimes are— then one should see this as a welcome opportunity to correct what has obviously gone wrong in the relationship.

Each must be honest about their real agenda in this. If it turns out that the husband or wife is correct in their hunch, the reason for the other wanting to send such a message should be further explored. There may be clear and legitimate complaints that should be shared with one's spouse.

If the relationship between the couple is already shaky, the husband or wife may reject *Taharat Hamishpachah* simply because they resent being dictated to by their spouse, being forced into something against their will. This concern is quite serious, not merely for *Taharat Hamishpachah* issues but for the very essence of the marriage. The spouse who feels this way may have had unpleasant exchanges with his or her mate and rebuffs attempts to once again be forced to abide by the partner's agenda.

There may be other factors in the presenting difficulty. Whatever the factors, the couple now has a serious problem. They threaten to be driven apart by the very laws designed to enhance marital togetherness.

In the process of clearing the air, in which the couple are hopefully committed enough to each other to give the marriage the serious attention it deserves, introducing *Taharat Hamishpachah* as a new ingredient in the relationship can even help set matters on course. The couple must be made aware that these laws are not to be wielded as weapons and should be apprised not to think of *Taharat Hamishpachah* as a punishment.

Rather, each should see this as a new opportunity to renew and reinvigorate their marriage.

IV

When the wife desires but the husband rejects, the situation is uncomfortable but not impossible. The wife can maintain adherence to the *Taharat Hamishpachah* protocols without her husband's involvement, up to and including her immersing in the *mikvah* without his knowledge.

However, the situation is still potentially explosive. The husband may want to kiss his wife during her menstrual period, and the wife refuses to allow this. The husband may show his disdain for his wife's religiosity by refusing to engage in marital relations following her immersion in the *mikvah*. In the worst case scenario, the husband may want to show his machismo, that he is the boss, by literally forcing himself upon his wife when she is in a menstrual state. This is marital rape.

When the husband desires to maintain the *Taharat Hamishpachah* protocols and the wife does not, the husband is forbidden to have any physical contact with her. As such, it is patently obvious that the wife's refusal, coupled with the husband's insistence, leads to an impossible situation. True, the husband and wife can live in the same home, but they are only acting as if they are husband and wife, for there would be no physical intimacy between them. But it is unlikely that such a situation could endure for more than a short period of time without adverse and potentially explosive consequences.

Because of the fact that the husband's desire and the wife's lack of desire create a situation wherein sexual fulfillment is impossible, the situation demands more immediate intervention and hopeful resolution by (1) the couple themselves, (2) a community rabbi, and/or (3) a competent therapist.

There are many ways the resolution can be attained. There is also a distinct possibility that no resolution will be forthcoming.

In a case of *conflicted marriage, Taharat Hamishpachah* is really a side issue. The real issue is the marriage itself, and appropriate intervention by a sensitive and astute professional is imperative.

Religious objections can and should be addressed to a rabbi the couple trusts, or some other knowledgeable person or persons in this area, assuming of course that the religious objections are essentially matters of theology rather than psychology.

It is usually best for husband and wife to dedicate quiet, reserved, inviolable time to discuss the issue between themselves before venturing outside. Sometimes, because the situation is so delicate, it is best that they communicate in writing. Writing is a good mode of communication, and unlike talking, is relatively free of high-pitched verbal abuse or temper tantrums. The wife should put down on paper why she is so interested in abiding by *Taharat Hamishpachah* laws, and the husband should write his objections, or vice versa.

Both must be absolutely honest, even though unconscious desires may be at work in the issue. If the couple are not honest to the best of their ability, the difficulty may be temporarily resolved, only to reappear at a later time.

The husband, who, in a calm atmosphere, reads of his wife's sincere desire and finds it is not a power play to exert control, may thereby feel somewhat reassured and less reluctant to be cooperative. The wife, who reads that her husband is concerned that their love life may suffer, may thus appreciate that the husband's reluctance is related to his strong desire to maintain a viable and fulfilling marriage.

That is the easy part, when the couple bridges the gap separating them with relative ease. What if the couple is not able to come together on their own? What if the gap between them remains unbridgeable? The next step is to approach a third party, someone they both trust and who understands the issues on a religious and psychological level. A community rabbi noted for his understanding and wisdom is a good choice. The situation may at times be beyond the rabbi's capacity, in which case a competent therapist, his or hers, working together with the rabbi is another possibility. This is especially the case in places where a competent therapist schooled in religious nuance may not be available.

V

The proper implementation of *Taharat Hamishpachah* regulations can involve problems even for the best-intentioned of couples. Two issues that are of crucial importance are self-control and intimacy during the menstrual (*niddah*) period.

Regarding self-control, it is nice to talk of it, of the need to be the master over one's drives. But actually achieving self-control is much more complicated than simply acknowledging that control is needed. The program for self-control is too much of a challenge to be left totally for the couple to devise.

The couple may have the best intentions, but they will be hard-pressed to prevent personal preference — be it toward overindulgence or overdenial — from interfering with a fair and balanced approach. An approach that in its general framework is the same for all but at the same time allows for individual differences and preferences is the norm for the Jewish community. That norm is incorporated into the *Taharat Hamishpachah* package.

A few more observations about the control issue are in order. People desire to be in control, and that is natural. It helps address fundamental insecurity. But one person's exercise of control means that another person is being controlled, and no one really wants that.

When both husband and wife submit to God's will, they both relinquish control and thereby allow the best in themselves to flow naturally. Each is pushed to a higher level of love rather than merely allowing internal desires to express themselves.

This higher level of love, this transcending love, is also a strong hedge against the husband falling into the allure of extramarital affairs. When the marriage is treated as sacred, that sanctity pervades one's life.

Several other benefits accrue from this sensitive complex of rules we refer to as *Taharat Hamishpachah*. The husband is programmed to adjust not to his need, but to his wife's availability.

The wife need not impose this discipline and thereby incur the husband's wrath. The Torah does it for her, and the husband, equally dedicated to the union, is obliged to respect his wife's timetable. More than making him respect his wife's schedule, the law serves to inculcate respect for the wife, for her dignity as a person, one entrusted with control of the rhythm of family life.

Another benefit concerns the possibility of the couple arguing because the one is not responsive enough to the sensual needs of the other. This possibility is significantly minimized, since responsiveness during certain times is impossible and at other times is obligatory. The obligation of responsiveness is clearly delineated.

Additionally, potential conflict arising from uncoordinated desires, in which one is in the mood but the partner is not, is likewise minimized. Almost two weeks apart is an effective way to establish correlated moods.

This is not to suggest that the *Taharat Hamishpachah* rules guarantee the couple will be blissfully happy. There is still plenty of room to create problems, since the *Halachah* only establishes a framework but refrains from legislating all the nuances within the framework. This would ruin the excitement and openness the *Halachah* itself endeavors to create.

Under normal circumstances, however, the couple who live by the letter and intent of the *Taharat Hamishpachah* regulations cannot help but be better off for it. The community, too, is much better off with happy couples, so much so that, in the scale of priorities, the building of a *mikvah* — the effector of closeness — takes precedence over the building of a *shul* or the writing of a Torah scroll. The foundation, happy and committed families, comes first. The rest follows.

VI

Another intrinsic challenge for the couple is how to relate to each other during the menstrual period, the so-called off time. Aside from the natural difficulty of being together with but apart from the one you love, the separation itself comes at a time when the wife needs her husband's support. The couple should realize that although the time for separating is ideally situated in the menstrual period, when conjugal relations are less desirable, this should in no way be an excuse for total withdrawal.

If physical intimacy is not possible, emotional intimacy is highly desirable. With conjugality out of the question, the couple can and should forge ahead in developing a caring relationship. This is an ideal time to comprehend what each is going through, how each feels, what aspects of the relationship can be improved.

The couple who effectively use the separation period to prepare for a greater, more meaningful togetherness will likely view the night of immersion as more than a mere reunion. For them, it is a festival of its own, an event to be celebrated.

The appropriate atmosphere for conjugality is created long before the actual conjugal experience. Without authentic love, physical intimacy loses its true meaning. Functionally, such relations may succeed once or twice, but over a longer duration, conjugality cannot effectively materialize from a sudden burst of affection.

Conjugality is an expression of love; love itself is an ever-evolving reality, not a machine to be turned on or off when it so suits the desirous partner.

Biologically, arousal is possible without love, but true human intimacy is more than a biological act. It is a spiritually infused emotion, an emotion that yearns for an unconditional loving and caring relationship.

It is absurd to focus on what is commonly and unfortunately called "foreplay" and not give proper attention to the prime elements of the marriage. Foreplay conjures the notion of a game plan, a technique. But conjugal relations is not a combination of foreplay, play, and afterplay; it is not play or a game. Conjugal relations is a periodic contextual peak, evolving from a growing love and itself intensifying that love.

The most important "foreplay" for conjugal relations is the daily infusion and effusion of love between husband and wife.

There are times when one or another of the partners is genuinely tired, though the other is in the mood. Sometimes the tiredness is a convenient shield hiding a disappointment at the way one is being treated.

Emotional closeness developed during the time when ulterior motives for niceness are nonexistent help the couple through this challenging time—and also enhance the conjugal period.

VII

Both husband and wife must realize that in addition to *Taharat Hamishpachah* concerns, there is another fundamental *mitzvah* that pervades the marital union, the famous *mitzvah* to love your *re'ah* (spouse) as yourself (*Vayikra* 19:18).[1] This *mitzvah* places *sensitivity to one's spouse in all respects* as the highest priority for each of the married couple.

It must be stressed that this *mitzvah* is an essential component of the *Taharat Hamishpachah* package. Especially in a situation wherein one of the couple has a stronger penchant to observe *Taharat Hamishpachah* regulations, it is imperative that sensitivity to the other spouse be prevailing.

To love one's spouse as oneself is a biblical obligation. Anyone who wishes to intensify the religiosity of the marital union must appreciate the difficulty that one's partner is experiencing in trying to commit to a discipline that heretofore was quite foreign, even alien. To love one's spouse as oneself is to put oneself in the shoes of the other and fully understand the difficulties that are at hand.

It is not the Torah way to step on other people on the way to *mitzvah* fulfillment. It is certainly not the Torah way to become harsh and insensitive to one's spouse in the desire to abide by Jewish Marital Law, if for no other reason than that an essential part of Jewish Marital Law is to genuinely and completely love one's spouse.

The way to *Taharat Hamishpachah* is via love. By showing that love in its full unconditionality, one paves the way for the reluctant partner to experience God's word as promoting and enhancing love.

VIII

In conclusion, it is clear that *Taharat Hamishpachah* is quite a challenging *mitzvah*. Aside from the fact that it takes two, it also takes two who act in concert and harmony. That is not easy, but it is fulfilling. A well-intentioned couple who fully understands and implements their respective responsibilities will raise their marriage into a transcending joy of togetherness.

Those who face the formidable challenge of trying to convince a reluctant spouse to embrace *Taharat Hamishpachah* protocol should do this in a loving and caring manner. And those who are reluctant are well served by giving it a genuine try. The results will speak for themselves.

Notes

1. See my book *Jewish Marriage: A Halakhic Ethic* (New York and Hoboken: KTAV Publishing House and Yeshiva University Press, 1986), pp. 90–92.

10

The Institution of the *Mikvah* in America

Joshua Hoffman

For most American Jews, the institution of the *mikvah* and the laws of Family Purity—*Taharat Hamishpachah*—are strange, remote areas of Jewish life. If they have heard of them at all, it is usually in connection with Jews in the European *shtetl*. Even among generally religious Jews, it is only in recent years that the *mikvah* has enjoyed an upsurge in popularity.[1] The casual observer may therefore conclude that this crucial area of Jewish law was simply abandoned by Jews upon their arrival in America. A closer study of American Jewish history, however, will reveal that the matter is more complicated than it initially appears.

In July 1902, several of the most prominent rabbis in the United States met in New York City for the purpose of founding an organization to strengthen the observance of Jewish law in this country. The organization they formed, the Agudat Harabbanim, or the Union of Orthodox Rabbis, issued, at that time, a constitution stating its goals and how it proposed to achieve them. One of the most important issues mentioned was that of the *mikvah*. The rabbis stressed that *mikvahs* must be supervised by competent rabbinic authorities rather than by laymen. Localities that did not have *mikvahs* should be urged to build them, under proper rabbinic supervision rather than by lay people.[2] In its jubilee volume, published in 1928, the organization noted that thirty years earlier, before the founding of the Agudat Harabbanim, many communities in the country did not have any *mikvahs* at all, and some communities that did have a *mikvah* were under such inferior leadership that the wives of the local rabbis did not observe the laws of *Taharat Hamishpachah*.[3] Rabbi Moshe Weinberger, a Hungarian–Jewish immigrant to New York, wrote in 1889, in his *Jews and Judaism in New York*, "In this great matter as well, we must rely on the evidence and trustworthiness of one person: the bath attendant. In New York the bath attendants are not all righteous people. . . . The few poor rabbis whom we have here make the *mikvah* kosher initially, and get paid. After they have certified it, they have nothing more to do with it. . . ."[4] Although Rabbi Weinberger went on to express his happiness over the fact that one congregation in the city had made improvements in its *mikvah,* the general situation did not improve much over the next fifteen years.

Despite the Agudat Harabbanim's declared goal of building *mikvahs* throughout America, by 1919 it reported at its annual convention that observance of the laws of *Taharat Hamishpachah* had become, in large part, a thing of the past.[5] The rabbis decided that they needed to educate Jewish women in these laws and, to that end, published in 1920 a small pamphlet written in Yiddish entitled "A Handbook for the Jewish Woman." The pamphlet presented a summary of the various duties of the Jewish woman, focusing especially on the laws of *Niddah,* explaining their importance for the perpetuation of the Jewish family. The author, Rabbi Elozor Meir Preil of Elizabeth, New Jersey, wrote in his introduction that the situation in America had deteriorated to the point that even Jews who were scrupulous in their observance of the laws of *Kashrut,* separating milk from meat and avoiding *chametz* on Pesach, neglected the laws of *Niddah.*

Rabbi Preil placed the blame for this development largely on the doorstep of the parents, who had failed to provide a proper Jewish education for their children. Although in Europe Jewish girls did not receive a formal Jewish education, the condition of Jewish life there was different from that in America. In the closed society of the shtetl, wrote Rabbi Preil, the very atmosphere was permeated with the spirit of Jewish tradition, and the Jewish home was conducive to the practice of religion. In such an environment, parents were assured that their daughters would, as a matter of course, adopt the laws of *Taharat Hamishpachah,* just as their mothers had. In the more open American society, however, where children were susceptible to all kinds of influences, and the Jewish home was often not permeated with Jewish values, the only hope for the children to adopt traditional Jewish practice was to educate them in Jewish schools. The Agudat Harabbanim published the pamphlet in the hope that by distributing it to prospective brides, they would in some way compensate for the failure to educate the younger generation in this crucial area of Jewish law.[6]

Basing himself mostly on the reports of the Agudat Harabbanim, Charles S. Liebman wrote, in a widely cited article, that *Mikvah* was one of the first areas of Jewish law to be abandoned by Eastern European Jews upon their arrival in America.[7] Although this notion has become the conventional wisdom in works on American Jewish history, there is ample evidence to the contrary.

J. D. Eisenstein, the famed author of many volumes of Jewish scholarship, wrote in 1895, in an article on the history of the Beth Midrash Hagadol synagogue on New York's Lower East Side, that one of the characteristic features of that area of the city was the occasional *mikvah* that could be seen heralded by its Hebrew sign.[8] Charles Seligman Bernheimer, a social worker from Philadelphia, wrote in 1905, in reference to the Russian Jews in New York, that "a Jewish woman must visit a bath at least once a month. . . . These religious rites and customs are carefully observed by the older generation who are generally pious; the younger people, though they do not observe these rites religiously, follow some of them."[9]

In a recent study, Andrew R. Heinze has demonstrated that Eastern European Jews in New York were very active in building *mikvahs* and apparently used them as well.[10] He cites, for example, an article in the *New York Tribune* on December 7, 1884, which mentioned that Russian Jews commonly used the free *mikvahs* in the local synagogues and that this practice would serve as a check on the potential outbreak of cholera in the city. The reporter wrote that there were at least fifteen *mikvahs* in the downtown synagogues. Heinze notes that in 1884 the population of Eastern European Jews in New York City was not greater than fifty thousand, so that each *mikvah* served, on the average, about three thousand people. Taking into consideration the fact that this figure included men and children and that many of the women were too young or too old to need a *mikvah,* the ratio was sufficient, not worse than the average community in Eastern Europe and, in fact, better than some. The existence of *mikvahs* in downtown synagogues was again noted in the Yiddish daily, the *Tageblatt,* in 1899. That newspaper criticized a plan to resettle Jewish immigrants in New York suburbs because their religious needs, including the availability of a *mikvah,* were better served in the downtown area. Again, in 1902, an article in *Century* magazine noted the existence of *mikvahs* in downtown synagogues. Insurance maps from 1903 and 1905 also indicated many *mikvahs* in the area, as did the journalist Ray Stannard Baker, who wrote about the neighborhood for *The American Magazine* in 1908 and 1909.[11]

Eastern European immigrants to American cities outside of New York also built and used *mikvahs.* In Atlanta, Georgia, the local German–Jewish community, which was mostly nonobservant, assisted the Russian immigrants in building a *mikvah* in 1896. Interestingly, they were motivated by the hope that the availability of the *mikvah* would assure that the immigrants would maintain an appropriate level of cleanliness.[12] In 1895, Rabbi Shalom Elchanan Jaffe, a Russian immigrant who later became the rabbi of the Beth Midrash Hagadol in New York, wrote a lengthy responsum about the *mikvah* in St. Louis, where he then served as rabbi.[13] He sent a copy of the responsum to Rabbi Shmuel Salant, chief rabbi of Jerusalem, asking for his opinion and noting the importance of the *mikvah* for the continuation of Jewish life.[14] In New Brunswick, New Jersey, Eastern European immigrants, more traditional than the members of the liberal congregation in the city, founded an Orthodox synagogue, Ahavas Achim, in 1889. Some of its members later recalled that in the early years of the synagogue, a *mikvah* stood behind the building. Others recalled a little *mikvah* at a different location at the turn of the century and, later, another *mikvah* in the Ladies Sheltering House.[15] In Minnesota, one woman recalled that traditional Eastern European women, who did not find a *mikvah* available, would go to Lake Geneva and break through the ice to immerse themselves.[16]

There is thus no doubt that the older generation of Eastern European immigrants to America made an effort to conform to the laws of *Taharat Hamishpachah*. However, as noted by Bernheimer, the younger generation did not continue to observe the laws scrupulously. Still, *mikvah* was not totally abandoned even by the younger generation. In New Brunswick, some women recalled that when they were married, a *mikvah* was no longer available in the city, and to conform with the practice of going to the *mikvah* before the wedding ceremony, they had to travel to Elizabeth.[17] Apparently, although they no longer followed the laws of *Niddah* during married life, they did go to the *mikvah* before marriage, probably at the urging of their parents. A woman who came to this country with her family as a small child shortly after the turn of the century recalled undergoing a ritual immersion before her wedding in the 1920s: "My mother called the *mikvah* to make the arrangements, to keep it open. My mother went with me. It was a nice experience. You take a bath and in spite of what people say, dirty smirty it is not. It is clean, it's sanitary, and they make you feel very comfortable, not to be nervous. Wash your hair, cut your nails. Each bathtub is in a separate room, private. They cut your toenails. Actually in the Jewish religion, when a bride gets married she is clean and that is what she is supposed to be. Really clean. I even planned the date of my wedding that I shouldn't have my period."[18]

The references to the cleanliness of the *mikvah* reflect a widespread notion that the *mikvah* was a dirty place. Although this particular woman's experience belied that notion, the cleanliness factor was, in fact, a long-standing problem in connection with the *mikvah* and played no small role in its abandonment by many younger Americans. Shortly before World War I, the New York City Board of Health declared many of the *mikvahs* in the city to be health menaces. Health officials estimated that an average of three hundred people used a *mikvah* before its water was changed, and this practice created a very high bacteria count. Working together with health officials, Jewish laity established a Mikveh Owners Association to eliminate the worst abuses.[19] Ads for new *mikvahs* during this period emphasized the cleanliness of the facility.[20] Rabbi Leo Jung, of New York's Jewish Center, who was a major campaigner for the *mikvah* beginning in the 1920s, wrote in his autobiography that he was shocked at the condition of the *mikvah* in Cleveland, where he held his first rabbinical position in this country. He started a fund in that city to build a new, aesthetically pleasing *mikvah,* which was opened in 1922, after he moved to New York.[21] He subsequently helped establish about fifteen *mikvahs* in various cities in America, always insisting that they be both halachically and aesthetically acceptable.[22] During the 1930s and 1940s in New York, a number of model *mikvahs* were established to attract the modernized American woman to the observance of *Taharat Hamishpachah.*[23] The perception of the *mikvah* as a filthy, unsanitary place, however, persisted and continued to discourage women from using it.[24]

Actually, the complaint that *mikvahs* were not being maintained in the clean condition that the dignity of the *mikvah* demanded had been voiced already in the mid-1800s. Rabbi Bernard Illowy, a Bohemian-born talmudic scholar, arrived in America in 1852 and held pulpits in several important American Jewish communities, including Baltimore, St. Louis, Philadelphia, Syracuse, New Orleans, and others, until his death in 1871. In 1914, his son, Dr. Henry Illowy, wrote a short biography of his father as an introduction to his book of responsa, *Milchamot Elokim.* Enumerating the various duties his father had to fulfill in his rabbinic positions, he included the maintenance of the *mikvah.* His father, he wrote, "saw to it that it was kept in a perfectly sanitary condition, and that absolute cleanliness which the character of the institution implied was maintained, so that none of the numerous charges that were (and still are) frequently made against the *mikvah* could be set forth against the institution pertaining to his congregation and his supervision."[25]

From Dr. Illowy's comments it is apparent that the many communities in which his father served as rabbi did in fact have *mikvahs.* Indeed, a survey of various Jewish communities in America in the nineteenth century reveals that the *mikvah* was a common feature in many of them. Jewish immigration to America, in the early- and mid-eighteenth century, was from Germany, Austria, and Central Europe. One of the first things these immigrants did in the communities they founded was to build *mikvahs.* For example, in Charleston, South Carolina, there was a *mikvah* as early as 1809.[26] Congregation Brith Shalom of Easton, Pennsylvania, established its synagogue in 1839. Among the duties of its *chazzan,* mentioned in a contract drawn up in 1848, were the supervision of the *mikvah* and the provision of the "necessary kettles of hot water."[27] Beth El synagogue in Buffalo, New York, was founded in 1847. Its *mikvah* is first mentioned in the synagogue's minute book in 1849. Apparently it was used quite frequently, because in 1853 and again in 1856 funds had to be allocated for its repair.[28] On April 10, 1857, San Francisco's *Weekly Gleaner* carried the following announcement: "The managers of the Hebra Shomre Shabbat hereby give notice to the scrupulous Israelites that a proper *Mikweh* is now constructed at the Bath Establishment of Dr. Brun, North Beach. Those whom such an arrangement interests may avail themselves of it. . . ."[29]

This pattern was followed in numerous cities throughout the country settled by Jews from Germany and Central Europe. Although the Reform movement had begun in Germany in the early 1800s, there has been in recent years a scholarly debate regarding the extent of its influence on Jews who immigrated to America.[30] Moreover, in its early years, the movement in Germany did not abandon the institution of *Mikvah*. At the 1841 Reform conference in Frankfurt, the community of Bingen asked whether it was permissible to use drawn water for its *mikvah* instead of the halachically required rainwater. Apparently, women in the community avoided using the *mikvah* because of its filthy condition. Therefore, permission for leniency was requested. Although permission was granted by the conference, constituting a direct violation of *Halachah,* it is significant that the rabbis there did affirm the need for the *mikvah.*[31] Statistics for southern Germany, in fact, show that 119 out of 165 communities in Hessen-Nassan and 75 out of 97 in Baden had *mikvahs* as late as 1906. It was from these communities that large numbers of German immigrants came to this country.[32]

While it is true that nineteenth-century immigrants to America built *mikvahs* soon after their arrival, it is uncertain how long they continued to use them. Although in Buffalo it appears that the *mikvah* was used for many years, Hyman Grinstein, in his study of the early years of the Jewish community in New York, has argued that *mikvah* use there was on the decline in the 1850s. Making a sample study of the use of the *mikvah* of Anshe Chesed over a seven month period in 1851, he found that, during that time, one hundred women used the *mikvah*. Based on that figure, he estimated that, in all, two hundred women used the three *mikvahs* in New York during that period, out of about 4,000 Jewish families. His conclusion was that the newer immigrants to the country used the *mikvah,* while the native Americans did not. The very fact that the Shearith Israel congregation, which by 1759 had built a *mikvah* in its synagogue on Mill Street, did not build one when it moved uptown to Crosby Street in 1833, he argues, indicates that women were not observing this ritual.[33] This pattern was also followed by Eastern European Jews who came to this country from the 1870s until the 1920s. While the arriving immigrants, as we have seen, built and used *mikvahs,* the younger generation began to neglect this institution.

When immigrants moved uptown or to the suburbs, that is, to second and third area settlements, they often failed to build *mikvahs*. When the previous Lubavitcher Rebbe, Rabbi Yosef Yitzchak Schneerson, moved to America in 1940, for example, he was surprised to find there was no *mikvah* in the neighborhood of Kahal Adath Yeshurun on the Upper East Side.[34] As the immigrants and their children acculturated, they apparently began to neglect observance of *Taharat Hamishpachah*. In the suburbs, moreover, the Conservative synagogue became the dominant Jewish institution. Until the late 1960s, the Conservative rabbinate, with a few exceptions, virtually ignored the Family Purity laws, thus furthering their abandonment by second- and third-generation American Jews.[35] Although there has been some improvement, on the whole, the Conservative rabbinate continues to treat the subject of Family Purity and *Mikvah* with benign neglect.

Another factor that contributed to the growing laxity in observance of *Taharat Hamishpachah* seems to have been the influence of the Reform movement in America. Between 1859 and 1860, a European Jewish traveler, Israel Joseph Benjamin, visited America and later recorded his findings on the condition of the various Jewish communities he encountered throughout the country. One of the things he noted was the existence of *mikvahs* and women's societies devoted to their maintenance in many of the communities. Invariably, congregations that had begun to adopt reform practices did not have *mikvahs*. In one congregation in Louisville, Kentucky, he recorded, a member objected to the proposed acceptance of a Christian candidate for conversion to Judaism because, she argued, conversion entails imposing new commandments, including use of the *mikvah*. Since the congregation itself had abandoned that practice, how could they expect a convert to observe it?[36] A history of Congregation Beth Israel of Hartford, Connecticut, notes that the congregation, founded by German Jews in 1843, was originally strictly Orthodox. When in 1852, funds were raised for the building of a synagogue, money was also given to build a *mikvah*. The plan was abandoned, however, and by the time the synagogue was built in 1856, the congregation had turned to Reform.[37] A popular writer of Jewish history described the pattern as follows: "One could almost state the phenomenon of the *mikvah* as a law. As the *mikvah* appears, Orthodoxy is in ascendance, as the *mikvah* vanishes, Orthodoxy is in the decline."[38]

As noted above, the early Reform movement in Germany did not totally reject the institution of the *mikvah*. In America, too, one can discern a change within Reform leadership in regard to the *mikvah*. The pioneer Reform leader, Rabbi Isaac Mayer Wise, recalled in his memoirs that one of the charges brought against him in 1850 by his congregation in Albany—which wanted to dismiss him because of his Reform tendencies—was that he had publicly ridiculed the women's ritual bath. Wise wrote in his defense that he "never mocked women and always treated them with dignity and courtesy" and that he "certainly never made sport of religious customs."[39] In contrast, Wise's student, the more radical Rabbi David Phillipson of Cincinnati, upon learning that the Orthodox Jews in that city were trying to raise funds to build a *mikvah*, was appalled that they would deem it necessary "in this age of bathrooms public and private."[40] Later, in the 1930s, when Rabbi Eliezer Silver began a campaign in Cincinnati to replace its rundown *mikvah*, which was located in the old Jewish neighborhood, with a new, remodeled one, to be located on a street near a major Reform temple, Phillipson, the rabbi of that temple, joined many people in the neighborhood in vigorously opposing the move. In a letter published on May 6, 1932, in the *Cincinnati Enquirer*, he wrote "The institution of the *mikvah* or ritual bath . . . is entirely foreign to our modern interpretation of Jewish faith and practice."[41] These remarks of Phillipson were echoed by Sally Priesand, the first woman to be ordained by the Hebrew Union College, who wrote in 1975 that the laws of Family Purity are "senseless and irrelevant to modern society."[42]

The rapid growth of the Reform movement in America in the latter half of the nineteenth century, then, was an important factor in the gradual decrease in observance of *Taharat Hamishpachah* and helps account for the fact that when Eastern European immigrants began to arrive in this country, they found that in many cities there were no *mikvahs* in operation. Another factor was the lack of Orthodox rabbinic leadership in this country. The first ordained rabbi to come to the United States was Rabbi Abraham Rice, in 1840. Soon after his arrival he accepted a pulpit in Baltimore, and later he served as rabbi in a number of other cities. Over the next several decades, a few more Orthodox rabbinical scholars—most notably Rabbi Illowy—came to America, but, by and large, there was virtually no Orthodox rabbinic leadership in this country until the influx of Eastern European immigration in the 1880s. It was, in fact, this influx that saved American Jewry from being totally dominated by Reform.

Because of the scarcity of rabbinic scholars until the latter part of the century, most communities lacked any guidance in the intricate laws of *Mikvah* and *Niddah*, and, as a result, *mikvahs* in many communities fell into disrepair. Moreover, women, lacking proper instruction, may well have concluded that a bathtub could serve the same function as a *mikvah*. This was a common mistake made by women in the early decades of the twentieth century in this country, as pointed out in books and pamphlets on *Taharat Hamishpachah* written at the time,[43] and it is very likely that the same mistake was made in the nineteenth century.

While it can be demonstrated that the initial waves of immigrants to the United States in both the earlier and the latter parts of the nineteenth century were active in building *mikvahs* and observed *Taharat Hamishpachah*, it is not certain that the same can be said about the first immigrants to this country, the Sephardim. In 1654, the first group of Sephardim to arrive in this country came to New Amsterdam, later renamed New York. Congregation Shearith Israel of New York drew up its constitution in 1728 and completed its first synagogue building, on Mill Street in 1730. At that time the building did not have a *mikvah*. By 1759, after many German Jews had joined the congregation, a *mikvah* was built.[44] In Philadelphia, a substantial Sephardic community existed by the 1730s, but not until the Mikve Israel Synagogue was built in 1786 did the city have a *mikvah*.[45] The *mikvah* in that synagogue was built, to a large extent, upon the urging of Manuel Josephson, a German Jew who lived in the city. In 1784, Josephson wrote a letter to the board of Mikve Israel, lamenting the fact that there was no proper *mikvah* in the city. He added that "should it be noted in the congregation abroad that we had been thus neglectful of so important a matter, they would not only pronounce heavy anathemas against us but interdict and avoid intermarriages with us, equal as with [a] different nation or sect, to our great shame and mortification."[46]

The failure of the New York Sephardic community to provide a *mikvah* for its women has led one writer to the conclusion that the "worldly Sephardim" had simply rejected the entire institution.[47] This conclusion, however, can be challenged. There was, in fact, a tradition in New York that next to the location of the Mill Street synagogue was a brook of free-flowing water, over which a bathing house was erected to be used by the women as a *mikvah*. In 1836, while digging in that area, a laborer found a ring with the inscription Isaac Lopez 1728. That ring may very possibly have been lost by one of these women.[48] In Philadelphia, too, tradition had it that the women immersed themselves in the Delaware River.[49] Moreover, the synagogue in Newport, Rhode Island, completed in 1763, did by tradition have a *mikvah,* and the congregation that built it consisted mostly of Sephardim.[50] The failure of the communities of New York and Philadelphia to build *mikvahs* earlier than they did may have been due to their reluctance, as newcomers in the country, to incorporate in a public building an institution that related to so private a matter, especially in light of the puritanical moral stance of the populace.[51] By the mid-eighteenth century, when the communities were already firmly established, these misgivings diminished. In South America, by contrast, where such misgivings were not a factor, we find that the Sephardic communities built *mikvahs* at a very early stage. In Curaçao, for example, where Sephardic Jews had begun to arrive in the 1650s, excavations in 1970 uncovered remains of a *mikvah* that was three centuries old.[52]

The general trend of immigrants to the United States, then, was to build *mikvahs* and observe *Taharat Hamishpachah,* with observance slacking off in the next generation. By 1920, as we have seen, observance had fallen to an alarmingly low level. Some of the reasons for this development have already been pointed out: the influence of Reform, the lack of proper rabbinic leadership, the acculturation of the younger generation along with the move to new neighborhoods in which Conservative synagogues were dominant, and the unclean state in which the *mikvahs* were maintained. The core problem, however, seems to have been the one emphasized by Rabbi Preil in his 1920 pamphlet, namely, the lack of Jewish education and consequent ignorance of the laws of *Niddah* and their importance. In an effort to correct this situation, a number of dedicated people began to publish works on the topic to educate Jewish women. In 1924, Rabbi David Miller of Oakland, California, a European-born rabbi who made a fortune in oil wells after moving to America, published a book in Yiddish entitled *Mikveh Yisroel.* In 1930, he published a much-expanded, English-language version of the work, under the title *The Secret of the Jew.* The book explained the laws of *Niddah,* their philosophical underpinnings, and their beneficial effect on married life. Rabbi Miller noted in the book the growing neglect of those laws and listed eight reasons that he thought were responsible for that situation.[53] These eight reasons can actually be reduced to three or four. The most important was the failure to recognize the significance of the institution of *Mikvah* in Jewish life.and the ignorance of the laws of *Taharat Hamishpachah* common among Jewish women. Another was the reluctance of women to immerse themselves in the public *mikvahs* because of the unattractive manner in which they were maintained. In addition, they did not wish to use the same water already used by many others, nor did they wish to participate, in public, in matters that pertained to intimate personal relations. Finally, many Jewish communities did not have *mikvahs* because there was a popular notion that building a *mikvah* involved great expenses that were beyond the means of the community.

Rabbi Miller, in his book, proceeded to offer a solution to the problems he had enumerated. He devised a method of building a small but halachically acceptable *mikvah* in one's own home, disguised as a piece of furniture.[54] The problems of cleanliness, public usage, and availability were, thus, all eliminated. To help combat the prevailing ignorance about *Mikvah,* he distributed the book free of charge, and traveled around the country to promote his plan for *mikvah* construction. Rabbi Miller felt his campaign was so important that in his will he left ten percent of his considerable estate for the purpose of publication and distribution of material on *Mikvah* as well as on Sabbath observance, about which he also had written. The fund was to continue for twenty-five years after his death, which occurred in 1939. In his will, he named a five-man committee to manage this fund.[55] One of these men, Moses Hoenig, was the brother of Rabbi Sidney Hoenig, who wrote a pamphlet on the laws of *Niddah* entitled *Jewish Family Life: The Duty of the Jewish Woman.* The first edition of the pamphlet, published in 1942, was sponsored by the committee. It was subsequently reprinted many times and is still widely distributed to newlyweds. One of the interesting features of the pamphlet is its *mikvah* directory. Listed in the directory are *mikvahs* in Jewish communities as remote as Cheyenne, Wyoming, and Tucson, Arizona, an indication that Jewish settlers in these areas did, in fact, observe *Taharat Hamishpachah*. In a private meeting held in 1968, the Lubavitcher Rebbe, Rabbi Menachem Mendel Schneerson, told Rabbi Gedaliah Finkelstein, who is Rabbi Hoenig's son-in-law, that the pamphlet was responsible for countless Jewish women in remote communities observing *Taharat Hamishpachah*. It was, in fact, Rabbi Hoenig who coined the term "ritualarium" to refer to the *mikvah,* instead of the less appealing "ritual bath," as part of his effort to attract women to the *mikvah.*[56]

Another important campaigner for observance of *Taharat Hamishpachah* was Dr. Jacob Smithline of Brooklyn, New York. In 1930, he published an essay entitled "Scientific Aspects of Sexual Hygiene," in which he demonstrated that complete compliance with the laws of *Niddah* promotes the physical health of the woman and also helps prevent cancer of the uterus. In his essay, he cited the findings of Dr. David Macht, an Orthodox Jewish scientist from Baltimore, who wrote a lengthy essay in 1924, "A Pharmacological Study of Menstrual Toxin," explaining scientifically why sexual abstinence should be observed during the menstrual period.[57] Dr. Smithline received letters of approval for his pamphlet from several prominent rabbis, including the Chofetz Chaim and Rabbi Abraham Isaac Kook, and was encouraged in his efforts by the Lubavitcher Rebbe, Rabbi Y.Y. Schneerson, during his visit to America in 1929–1930 and also after he moved to America in 1940. Dr. Smithline continued to publish works of this nature and traveled widely, delivering lectures on the importance of *Taharat Hamishpachah,* until his death in 1963. In 1937, at the annual convention of the Orthodox Union, a resolution was passed to form a committee to work together with Rabbis Miller and Jung and Doctors Smithline and Macht, in promoting the observance of *Taharat Hamishpachah.*[58] Mrs. Yetta Rothman, who had been Dr. Smithline's nurse, promised him before his death that she would carry on his work to increase observance of these laws, and so she created an organization, United Jewish Women For Torah Traditions, to teach Jewish women about their religious duties. The organization reprinted Dr. Smithline's pamphlet on sexual hygiene in 1962 and again in 1968 and, in addition, endeavored to organize women throughout the United States to promote observance of *Taharat Hamishpachah* and to build *mikvahs* in areas where none existed. The organization, however, was basically a one-woman operation and ceased to exist after Mrs. Rothman's death.[59]

A more enduring organization, dedicated, among other things, to teaching women about *Taharat Hamishpachah,* is the Lubavitch Women's Organization, created by the Lubavitcher Rebbe, Rabbi M. M. Schneerson, in the early 1950s. The organization increases awareness of these laws through various publications and the sponsorship of educational programming on the topic.[60] The previous rebbe himself was very active in establishing *mikvahs* in various communities throughout the United States, both during his 1929–1930 visit and after settling in this country in 1940.[61] His work in this area, too, was continued by his successor, who directed his emissaries to build *mikvahs* in Jewish communities in the United States and throughout the world. In 1975, Rabbi Schneerson launched a concentrated campaign to build *mikvahs* and increase the observance of *Taharat Hamishpachah,* making a commitment to provide a *mikvah* for any community that requests it.

With all the work being done to increase observance of *Taharat Hamishpachah,* writers on the topic, as we noted, continued to complain of its neglect. A dramatic improvement in the situation began to take place after World War II, with the arrival in this country of refugees from the Nazi Holocaust. A large percentage of these refugees were observant Jews, for whom *Taharat Hamishpachah* was an important part of their lives.[62] Availability of *mikvah* was essential for them, and so interest in the institution increased. This change is reflected in the remarks of Rabbi Nisson Telushkin of Brooklyn, New York, who in 1947 published a detailed and comprehensive book on laws of *Mikvah, Taharat Mayim.* In his introduction to the third edition of the book, published in 1964, he wrote that when the book first appeared, his colleagues expressed surprise at his choice of topic and told him that very few people in America would be interested in such work. However, the book quickly sold out, and went into a second printing in 1950. By 1964, he wrote, it had sold 1,600 copies and needed to be printed again. The book continues to be popular and was most recently reprinted in 1990. The relatively wide popularity of a book on such a specialized topic in the 1940s and 1950s indicates a reawakening of interest in the construction of *mikvahs* in this country.[63] This interest, it seems, can be seen as a response to the needs of the newly arrived European immigrants. Emblematic, perhaps, of this development is the fact that the Fountainbleau Hotel in Miami Beach, a popular vacation spot for religious Jews, had a *mikvah* installed in 1958.[64]

In the 1960s, a further increase in the observance of *Taharat Hamishpachah* occurred, coinciding with the rise of the *baal teshuvah* movement.[65] Pamphlets on the topic, especially that by Rabbi Hoenig, were reprinted, and new ones were written. Two of the most popular of these newer works are *A Hedge of Roses,* by Rabbi Norman Lamm, which presents a modern, psychological exploration of these laws, and *Pardes Rimonim,* by Rabbi Moshe D. Tendler, which touches on the biological aspects of the topic. A more recent book, *Waters of Eden,* by Rabbi Aryeh Kaplan, which explores the kabbalistic significance of the *mikvah,* has also gained popularity. Mrs. Tehilla Abramov has authored a work on the laws of *Niddah, The Secret of Jewish Femininity,* which has been well received. She is very active in this area, traveling to Jewish communities throughout the world to teach seminars on the subject. Lubavitch continues to build modern, elegant *mikvahs* in communities throughout the country, and other organizations have recently been established to aid in the construction of *mikvahs.* One of these organizations, based in Denver, Colorado, is the Mikvah Team of Torah Community Project.[66] Rabbis Zeev Rothschild of Lakewood, New Jersey, and Gershon Grossbaum of St. Paul, Minnesota, constitute one-man *mikvah* committees. Their expertise in all areas of *mikvah* construction, both halachic and technical, have aided in constructing many new *mikvahs* in communities both in America and abroad. Rabbi Rothschild served as a consultant for the recently completed, state-of-the-art *mikvah* in Boca Raton, Florida, which has generated a new interest in *Taharat Hamishpachah* in that community. Women there have organized committees to reeducate patrons of the *mikvah* in these laws and to reach out to members of the wider Jewish community.[67]

The increasing observance of the laws of *Taharat Hamishpachah* in this country constitutes a reversal in the trend that we have observed in previous periods of American Jewish history. As we have seen, while immigrant Jews built *mikvahs* upon arriving in this country and observed the laws of *Taharat Hamishpachah,* their children generally neglected these practices. The Jews who came to America after World War II also frequented the *mikvah,* following the well-established trend. However, the next generation, rather than abandoning the practice, continued and, in fact, increased it.

We have suggested a number of reasons for this development, but the central reason, it seems, can be found in the argument presented by Rabbi Preil in 1920 that the root cause for the abandonment of the *mikvah* was the failure of Jewish parents to provide their children with a Jewish education. Addressing the annual convention of the Agudat Harabbanim in 1952, Rabbi Preil's son-in-law and successor to the rabbinate in Elizabeth, New Jersey, Rabbi Pinchos Mordechai Teitz, assessed the state of traditional Jewish observance in this country at the time. He pointed out that a new generation had arisen in America, sixty percent of which had parents who were not observant. While the children of Eastern European immigrants could recall Jewish observance in their parents' homes, much of the new generation could not. This state of affairs, he said, presented the American rabbinate with a new challenge. However, he expressed optimism for the future because of the increase in day schools and *yeshivot,* launched largely by the militant Orthodox rabbinic leaders who had recently come to America from Europe. If this trend continued, he told his audience, a reinvigorated observant Orthodoxy would emerge in the coming years.[68] His prediction has proven to be accurate, perhaps to a greater extent than he envisioned. Day schools and *yeshivot* have been, and continue to be, built in communities throughout the country. Out of them has emerged a generation of committed Jews, for whom *Taharat Hamishpachah* is as much a part of their lives as is *Kashrut*.[69] This new generation, in tandem with the growing number of *baalei teshuvah,* has helped bring about a rebirth of American Orthodoxy. Traditional observance has now become a matter of pride rather than of embarrassment, as it once was. In this environment, and with the continued construction of modern *mikvahs,* outreach efforts have great potential to attract increasingly larger numbers of women to the observance of *Taharat Hamishpachah*. Thus, within the Orthodox community, observance of the Family Purity laws is on the increase. Outreach programs, as we have seen, have begun in some quarters to educate the wider Jewish community in this neglected area of *Halachah*. Hopefully, these efforts will succeed in influencing growing numbers of Jews to use the *mikvah* and thereby reclaim this important institution, which as we have shown, has deep roots in American Jewry's past.

Notes

1. Samuel C. Heilman and Steven M. Cohen, *Cosmopolitans and Parochials* (Chicago: University of Chicago Press, 1989), p. 60, report that in a survey of 1,000 Orthodox Jews in New York City, 99 percent of those who identified themselves as "traditionally observant" and 79 percent of those who identified themselves as "centrist Orthodox," used the *mikvah* regularly.

2. *Sefer Hayovel shel Agudat Harabbanim: 1902–1927,* (New York: Arias Press, 1928), p. 27.

3. Ibid., p. 125–127.

4. Jonathan S. Sarna, trans., *People Walk on Their Heads: Moses Weinberger's Jews and Judaism in New York* (New York: Holmes and Meier Publishing, 1986), pp. 117–118.

5. Elozor Meir Preil, *A Hantbukh Far Die Yiddishe Froy* (New York: Agudat Harabbanim, 1920), p. 5.

6. Ibid.

7. Charles S. Liebman, "Religion, Class, and Culture in American Jewish History," *The Jewish Journal of Sociology* (December 1967): pp. 231–232, and, by the same author, "Orthodoxy in American Jewish Life," *American Jewish Year Book* (1965): p. 28.

8. J. D. Eisenstein, *Ozar Zichronothai* (New York, 1929), p. 246, reprinted from *Ner Ha-Ma'aravi,* 1895.

9. Charles Seligman Bernheimer, ed., *The Russian Jew in America* (Philadelphia: John C. Winston, 1905), pp. 287–288.

10. Andrew R. Heinze, *Adapting to Abundance* (New York: Columbia University Press, 1990), pp. 56–58.

11. Ibid., 57–58.

12. Steven Hertzberg, *Strangers Within the Gate City* (Philadelphia: Jewish Publication Society, 1978), p. 88.

13. Shalom Elchanan Jaffe, *Shoel Ke'inyan* (Jerusalem, 1895), pp. 24–36.

14. Ibid., 37–45

15. Ruth Marcus Patt, *The Jewish Scene in New Jersey's Raritan Valley, 1698–1948* (New Brunswick, NJ: Jewish Historical Society of Raritan Valley, 1978), p. 52.

16. W. Gunther Plaut, *The Jews in Minnesota—The First Seventy-Five Years* (New York: American Jewish Historical Society, 1959), pp. 90–91.

17. Patt, op.cit., p. 52.

18. Neil M. Cowan and Ruth Schwartz Cowan, *Our Parents' Lives* (New York: Basic Books, 1989), pp. 151–152.

19. Jenna Weismann Joselit, *New York's Jewish Jews* (Bloomington, IN: Indiana University Press, 1990), pp. 119–120.

20. Ibid., 170–171, n. 121.

21. Leo Jung, *The Path of a Pioneer: The Autobiography of Leo Jung* (London: Soncino, 1980), pp. 48–49.

22. Ibid., 49–50.

23. Joselit, op. cit., p. 120. The architectural drawing of one of these *mikvahs,* circa 1941 and located on 311 East Broadway in lower Manhattan, can be found in the Benjamin and Pearl Koenigsberg papers, 33/1, housed in the Yeshiva University Archives.

24. Rabbi Norman Lamm, in a conversation in August 1994, related that this perception was common among congregants in New York's Jewish Center in the early 1960s.

25. Bernard Illowy, *Milchamot Elokim* (Berlin: M. Poppelauer, 1914), p. 18.

26. James William Hagy, *This Happy Land* (Tuscaloosa: University of Alabama Press, 1993), p. 74.

27. Leon A. Jick, *The Americanization of the Synagogue, 1820–1870* (Hanover, NH: Brandeis University Press, 1976), pp. 51–52.

28. Selig Adler, *From Ararat to Suburbia, The History of the Jewish Community of Buffalo* (Philadelphia: Jewish Publication Society, 1960), p. 63.

29. Hasia R. Diner, *The Jewish People in America,* vol. 2, *A Time for Gathering—The Second Migration, 1820–1880* (Baltimore: Johns Hopkins University Press, 1992), p. 136.

30. This is the main topic of Jick's work, cited in n. 27.

31. Michael A. Meyer, *Response to Modernity* (New York: Oxford University Press, 1988), p. 138.

32. Steven M. Lowenstein, *Frankfurt on the Hudson* (Detroit: Wayne State University Press, 1989), p. 282, n. 14.

33. Hyman B. Grinstein, *The Rise of the Jewish Community of New York, 1645–1860* (Philadelphia: Jewish Publication Society, 1947), pp. 197–198.

34. Shalom Duber Levin, *Toldot Chabad Be'Artzot HaBrit* (New York: Kehot, Ottzar Ha-Chassidim, 1988), p. 396.

35. Telephone conversation with Dr. Dov Zlotnick, a faculty member of the Jewish Theological Seminary, on October 14, 1994. Dr. Zlotnick delivered a sermon on *Taharat Hamishpachah* at the seminary synagogue in 1966 and has, subsequently, taught classes in *Mishnayot Niddah* and *Mikvaot* at the seminary. At the urging of the Lubavitcher Rebbe, Dr. Zlotnick had the sermon published. It is reprinted on pp. 107–111 of this volume. See Marshall Sklare's *Conservative Judaism: An American Religious Movement* (Glencoe, IL: Free Press, 1955) for a discussion of the appeal of Conservative synagogues in suburbia. For a reevaluation of this work, see *American Jewish History*, no. 2 (1984): 102–168.

36. I. J. Benjamin, *Three Years in America*, vol. 1, trans. Charles Reznikoff (Philadelphia: Jewish Publication Society, 1956), pp. 334–335.

37. Abraham J. Feldman, *Remember the Days of Old* (Hartford, 1943), pp. 25–26.

38. Max I. Dimont, *The Jews in America* (New York: Simon & Schuster, 1978), p. 91.

39. Isaac M. Wise, *Reminiscences* (New York: Central Synagogue of New York, 1945), pp. 161 ff.

40. Michael A. Meyer, op.cit., p. 292.

41. Aarón Rakeffet-Rothkoff, *The Silver Era* (New York and Jerusalem: Yeshiva University Press and Philipp Feldheim, 1981), pp. 82–86.

42. Sally Priesand, *Judaism and the New Woman* (New York: Behrman House, 1975), p. 25.

43. Preil, op. cit., pp. 13–19; Jacob Smithline, "Scientific Aspects of Sexual Hygiene" (New York, 1930), reprinted in *Torah Laws for the Modern Woman* (New York: United Jewish Women for Torah Traditions, 1968), pp. 31–32; Elyahu Mordechai Ha-Cohen Maza, *Sefer Niddah, Challah Vehadlakat Haner* (New York: M. Zitver, 1940), pp. 3–7; Sidney B. Hoenig, *Jewish Family Life: The Duty of the Woman* (New York: Spero Foundation, 1949), p. 22.

44. Grinstein, op. cit., p. 297, and Dimont, op. cit., p. 91.

45. Edwin Wolf and Maxwell Whiteman, *The History of the Jews of Philadelphia from Colonial Times to the Age of Jackson* (Philadelphia: Jewish Publication Society, 1975), p. 142.

46. Jacob Rader Marcus, ed., *American Jewry—Documents—Eighteenth Century* (Cincinnati: Hebrew University Press, 1959), pp. 134–136.

47. Dimont, op. cit., p. 91.

48. "Historical Sketch by Naphtaly Phillips," in *Publications of the American Jewish Historical Society,* no. 21 (Baltimore, 1913), p. 194. See also Eli Faber, *The Jewish People in America,* vol. 1, *A Time for Planting—The First Migration 1654–1820* (Baltimore: Johns Hopkins University Press, 1992), p. 34, who writes that the congregation constructed a *mikvah* around 1731.

49. I. Harold Sharfman, *The First Rabbi* (Malibu, CA: Pangloss Press, 1988), p. 144.

50. Morris A. Gutstein, *The Story of the Jews of Newport* (New York: Block Publishing, 1936), p. 103.

51. Diner, op. cit., p. 136.

52. Bernard Postal and Michael H. Stern, *A Jewish Tourist's Guide to the Caribbean*, n.p., n.d., p. 25. See also Isaac S. Immanuel, *Precious Stones of the Jews of Curaçao, 1656–1957* (New York, 1957), p. 72.

53. David Miller, *The Secret of the Jew* (Oakland, CA, 1930), pp. 277–280.

54. Ibid., 334 ff.

55. Koenigsberg Papers, Yeshiva University Archives, 20/1.

56. Conversation with Rabbi Finkelstein, August 1994, and telephone conversations with Bernard Hoenig, son of Moses Hoenig, in November 1994.

57. Smithline, op. cit., pp. 26–27.

58. *The Orthodox Union*, July–August 1937, p. 2.

59. Telephone conversation with Rabbi Sherman Siff, spiritual leader of the Young Israel of Manhattan, July 1994. A letter from Rabbi Siff to Mrs. Rothman, praising Dr. Smithline's work, was included in the 1968 reprint.

60. *Aura: A Reader on Jewish Womanhood* (New York: Lubavitch Women's Organization, 1984), p. 108.

61. S. D. Levin, op. cit., pp. 51–53, 355–359.

62. William B. Helmreich, *Against All Odds* (New York: Simon & Schuster, 1992), pp. 78–79.

63. Nisson Telushkin, *Taharat Mayim* (New York, 1964), p. 1.

64. Deborah Dash Moore, *To the Golden Cities* (New York: Free Press, 1994), p. 32.

65. Liebman, 1965, op. cit., p. 90, wrote: "Observance of the laws of 'family purity' and *mikveh*, which once seemed to be on the verge of total desuetude, are rising. There are 177 public *mikvaot* in the United States—36 in Greater New York area alone—and a number of private ones. There is even a Spero Foundation which assists communities planning to build *mikvaot* with architectural plans, specifications, and suggestions."

66. Hillel Goldberg, "Retrieving a Critical Mitzvah: Mikveh," *Jewish Action* (Summer 5752/1992): 34.

67. Telephone conversation with Rabbi Kenneth Brander, spiritual leader of the Boca Raton synagogue, November 1, 1994.

68. *Hapardes*, January 1953, pp. 33–37.

69. See also Liebman, 1965, op. cit., p. 90.

II

Voices

11

Tkhines and *Techinot:* Ancient Prayers

Chava Weissler

Introduction

Tkhines are prayers in Yiddish written for and sometimes by women. They are closely related to Hebrew *techinot* written primarily for men but occasionally for women. In fact, it seems that the genre of *tkhines* arose because women knew of private prayers in Hebrew and wanted similar prayers they could recite in Yiddish. Books of *tkhines* in early modern Yiddish were published in Germany and the Netherlands from the middle of the seventeenth until the end of the eighteenth century. These books were anthologies of prayers to be said on many occasions of a woman's life, such as lighting Sabbath candles, visiting the cemetery, confession of sins, blessing the New Moon, and *niddah,* pregnancy, and childbirth. The early collections of *tkhines* were almost all published anonymously, and we don't know for certain if they were written by women or men.

In the course of the nineteenth century, collections of private devotions for women continued to be published in Germany, but increasingly in German rather than in Yiddish. In Eastern Europe, the older Yiddish anthologies were reprinted, and new *tkhines,* often written by women, began to appear in the mid-eighteenth century. These texts confined themselves to a smaller range of subjects, preeminently the Days of Awe, the Sabbath, and the blessing of the New Moon.

With the decline of Yiddish, in America because of immigration and acculturation, in Europe because of the Holocaust, and in Israel because of the rise of modern Hebrew, the *tkhines* (Yiddish, German, and the Hebrew *techinot*) were largely forgotten.

These prayers are firmly rooted in the realities and consciousness of the seventeenth and eighteenth centuries, in many ways foreign to our way of thinking. Nonetheless, we may find that they yet have the power to surprise and move us.

The following is translated from the Yiddish *Seder Tkhines Uvakoshos* ("The Order of Supplications and Entreaties") published anonymously in Furth in 1762. (Translation by Chava Weissler.)

> Send me the good angel to wait in the womb to bring the seed before you, Almighty God, that you may pronounce, from this seed will come forth a righteous man and a pious man, a fearer of your Holy Name, who will keep all your commandments and find favor in your eyes and in the eyes of all people, and who will study Torah day and night. . . .

The following is translated from the Yiddish *Seder Mitzvas Hanashim* ("The Order of Women's Commandments") compiled by Rabbi Benjamin Aaron Solnik (c. 1550–c. 1619), first published in Cracow in 1577. Translation made from the Basle 1602 edition by Chava Weissler. This is the only *tkhine* in the book. It is just about the earliest datable *tkhine* in existence.

Say this tkhine *just before you go into the water (of the mikvah).*

> I pray you, God, Lord of all the world, God of Abraham, God of Isaac, God of Jacob, that you have mercy on me that I may conceive tonight by my husband. May the child whom I conceive after this immersion be a sage and a fearer of the Name of your holiness, and a keeper of the commandments of your holy Torah. God, Lord of all the worlds, hear my prayer and permit your angel who is in charge of the souls to take a pure soul and put it into my body, and protect me from a soul which is impure, that I do not burden myself with children who do not become pious and are not blessed. Destroy all my evil thoughts and protect me from a soul which is not pure, and protect me from the evil inclination, so that it does not incite me, and does not bring me to evil impure thoughts. Strengthen my heart and my thoughts for good and to keep the commandments of your holiness, in expectation that I will be worthy that you, God, Lord of all the world, will hear my prayer and will fulfill my bidding which I bid, for you are God, the One who hears the prayers of all creatures. **So may it be your will, Amen, Selah.**

The following series of *techinot* is taken from the Hebrew *Tefillot Lenashim* (Prayers for Women), an anonymous, undated, manuscript found in the collection of the Hebrew Theological Seminary. (Translation by Shaindy Jacobson.)

When the course of her menstruation is finished, she should (close up and) count exactly seven clean days. Every day, in the day of the cleaning, she should say:

I am hereby prepared and ready to fulfill the command of my Creator, as it is written "And she shall count for herself seven clean days and afterwards she shall undergo purification."
    Today is the first day in the counting of my purification.
    Today is the second day . . .
    Today is the third day . . .
    Today is the fourth day . . .
    Today is the fifth day . . .
    Today is the sixth day . . .
    Today is the seventh day . . .

On the seventh and last day she should add:

Master of the universe, You have listened to Channah the righteous one and You have graciously bestowed upon her a righteous and holy offspring, Godly and awe-inspiring. So too, in Your abounding mercy and great kindness, be aroused to hear the prayer of Your maidservant and tear asunder all the barriers that stand between me and holiness, because I have done all that You have commanded me and I have cleansed myself and changed my garments these seven days; and in these days I have not done less (than what is incumbent upon me), and examined myself each day at the times designated by our Sages of blessed memory. And here I am on this seventh day, prepared and ready to observe Your commandments, my Father in Heaven, to wash my entire body and to cleanse it of any impurity and to be purified as the sun sets, in a ritual bath so that I be able, this approaching night, to unite with my husband with clean body and pure soul, as You, my God, have bid me.

In the house before going to the bath or in the bath (house or room) before undressing:

Master of the universe, You have consecrated Your nation Israel from amongst all other nations, commanded them to purify themselves from their impurities, and to wash their bodies in pure waters. God, my God, may this purification and washing and immersion be favorable and acceptable to You as the purification of all the pious and righteous Jewish daughters cleanse themselves and immerse in the proper time. O, God, hear my voice for You hear the prayers of Your nation Israel. May the words of my mouth and the thoughts of my heart be acceptable before You, Lord, my strength and my redeemer.

May it be Your will, Lord my God and God of my fathers, God of Abraham, God of Isaac and God of Jacob, that You be gracious with me so that I conceive from my husband on this night approaching in peace, and may the child created as a result of this immersion be a Torah scholar and God-fearing person in the innermost recesses of his heart, and fulfill Your commandments, Your statutes and Your laws for their sake. Master of the universe, accept my prayer and endow within me an untainted and pure soul, so that I not be dishonored, God forbid, with children who are unworthy; dispel from me any alien thoughts, and save me from the evil inclination that it not entice me with evil thoughts. And grant to my husband good thoughts in his heart, that when he will want to unite with me he will be joyous and glad of heart, and be gracious and kind to me, so that I and my husband will merit to bear a child untainted and pure and with a good heart. And may it be that all my reflections and thoughts be for good so that I merit that my prayers be accepted before You and my requests be fulfilled, for You are the One and only mighty King, just and faithful, who accepts the prayers of Your creations. May it so be Your will, Amen.

Do it for the sake of Your name, do it for the sake of Your right hand, do it for the sake of Your Torah, do it for the sake of Your holiness. May the words of my mouth and meditations of my heart be acceptable before you, Lord, my strength and my redeemer.

When going out of the house (to the mikvah) she kisses the mezuzah [and says]:

Guard me like the apple of the eye; and shelter me in the shadow of your wings. Shelter me from ruination by the wicked, and from the tumult of those who perpetrate evil. Save me from powerful enemies and those who hate me and are stronger than I.

While going to the bathhouse she should say many times in the street, until she will arrive, Esah Einay *(Psalm 121):*

A Song of Ascents. I lift my eyes to the mountains—from where will my help come? My help will come from the Lord, Maker of heaven and earth. He will not let your foot falter; your guardian does not slumber. Indeed, the Guardian of Israel neither slumbers nor sleeps. The Lord is your guardian; the Lord is your protective shade at your right hand. The sun will not harm you by day, nor the moon by night. The Lord will guard you from all evil; He will guard your soul. The Lord will guard your going and your coming from now and for all time.

And while she is getting undressed she should say Vehi Noam:

May the pleasantness of the Lord our God be upon us; establish for us the work of our hands; establish the work of our hands.

When she goes down to the water she should say the blessing:

Blessed are you, Lord our God, King of the universe, who has sanctified us with His commandments and commanded us concerning the precept of immersion.

12

We Must Act

Sara Hyamson

It is in keeping with the spirit which permeates the Women's Branch, that on this festive day we should be taking counsel on so important a subject as Jewish family life.

It is a well-known fact that the Jewish people owes its vigor and its strength, its sobriety and its modesty to the system of laws which, Biblical in its origin, teaches its followers purity and holiness. These laws have the approval of scientific experts, and the whole-hearted support of eminent medical men. Only a month ago, at a festival dinner of the Jewish Hospital in London, England, Sir Berkeley Moynihan, Bart., President of the Royal College of Surgeons, England, made the significant statement "that the Jew is very interesting as a patient, because of the personal purity of his life." In Sir Moynihan's judgment, the Jew stands supreme in this respect. He hoped that he was not giving offence when he said that he felt that if the Jew failed in personal purity, it was only when he relaxed or relinquished something of the faith of his fathers. This surely is a commendable recommendation, coming from so high an authority.

It might have been expected that I would discuss the spiritual values of these laws. But to the women who represent the bulwark of Orthodoxy in America,

Address before the Women's Branch of the Union of Orthodox Jewish Congregations of America, delivered at a Chanukah Gathering, December 7, 1926.

there surely is no need to explain or stress their spiritual significance. However, we cannot shut our eyes to the disquieting condition which prevails among a large section of our people, and we must take counsel as to what can be done to alter it.

Our religion has assigned to woman the highest position in the economy of Life, and has formulated many regulations for the protection of her health and for her safety. Throughout the ages, we find that Jewish women have been treated with tenderness and with care. While ancient nations regarded women as slaves or playthings, our ancestors held their women in high respect. When in the Middle Ages women were placed on a fantastic and unreal pedestal by the knights of chivalry, and also in our days when there has emerged a new principle of sex equality which may result in a lowering of moral standards, we can justifiably claim that our Jewish law has given women their proper position, neither too high nor too low. The Jewish woman is queen in her home, the helpmeet, friend, and companion of her husband, the guide and guardian of her children, watching over their conduct and teaching them by precept and by example. This status naturally brings with it great responsibilities. It is our duty to impress upon the rising generation the beauty and necessity of our holy laws. We must imbue them with a sense of their sacredness, convince them of their worth, and help them to realize their vast importance in the preservation of the peace, purity, and blessedness of Jewish home Life.

In these days of irreverence and materialism, when restlessness and pleasure-hunting are the keynotes of life; when youth, impatient of restraint, irresponsive to old traditions, will take nothing on trust, will only believe what is apparent to the senses; when the beautiful ceremonials which protected the Jewish home are flagrantly neglected; and when even marriage is no longer recognized by many as a permanent bond—it behooves us to erect the necessary barriers to check the lowering of the influences of religion. Our paramount duty it must surely be to strengthen our children's faith, instruct them in our holy laws, and the observance of them. It is no light task which we shall be undertaking.

Chanukah teaches us courage in times of difficulty. We can never forget the great part which women played in the achievements of which Chanukah so forcibly reminds us. Who is not thrilled at the recollection of the heroic Judith, a worthy sister of Judas Maccabees? Who can keep back tears of sympathy, mingled with admiration, when recalling the bravery of Hannah, who could see her seven sons suffer tortures and death rather than see them forswear allegiance to their God? Throughout that desperate struggle the women stood loyally at the side of their fathers, brothers, husbands and sons, and they, like their male relatives, endured martyrdom. When the time came for active resistance it was the Jewish women who nerved the hearts and arms of the

Jewish warriors. The divine spirit which animated them we hope will give us courage in our own Herculean endeavor.

In the Victorian days ending the nineteenth century, it was the fashion to be very reticent on human sex life. Mothers and fathers did not consider it their duty to enlighten their sons and daughters on the mysteries of their bodies and inclinations.

Today, however, every phase of life, including its aberrations and perversions, is depicted on the stage, transcribed in novels, and discussed in parlors. Our young people have knowledge of things which wise and hoary-headed grandfathers and grandmothers have never heard about. It is stated that all knowledge is good, and that our young people benefit by it, and that, far from being a detriment, it makes for a finer, more honest, more reliant, and more self-controlled young manhood and womanhood. But we cannot, dare not hide from ourselves the fact that there is unfortunately another side to the story.

I would therefore suggest that we openly face our problem and frankly examine the situation. First, let us ask, have we taken the necessary steps against the general neglect of the last of the three duties incumbent upon the Jewish wife. Are we to blame for this dereliction? Secondly, have we inspired our children with belief and faith in God's Law? Have we zealously instilled in our daughters supreme trust in and obedience to His Will? Thirdly, have we taken practical steps to build *Mikvaoth,* which will enable our daughters to fulfill this duty without reluctance? Whilst sex hygiene is now taught even in schools, and our special sex laws are being more and more observed by many enlightened and intelligent women of other faiths, the coping-stone of a sacred married life, the use of the *Mikvah* (Leviticus 11:36.) at the prescribed periods, is more honored in the breach than in the observance. Various excuses have been given for this laxity. It is contended by our non-observant sisters that these places are not sanitary, that they are unnecessary relics of ancient times, and that the swimming pools and baths at home fulfill the same purpose. I regret to state that our sisters who offer such excuses entirely overlook, or are unaware of, the spiritual and sacramental value of this duty. They do not realize that a law which is Biblical in its origin and has been observed throughout the ages, is binding on our conscience even in these days. Surely it should be apparent that a law which shows so much understanding of human nature and so much kindliness in all relationships, may be taken on faith, even if some of its requirements are difficult and seem obscure and inexplicable.

The time has certainly come when the *Mikvaoth* in our cities should be more attractive buildings. The Jewish women of past generations were so devout and so pious that no difficulties prevented them from carrying out their duties. The spirit of this age is not quite as ready to accept the hardships our grandmothers and mothers endured. Youth of today longs for greater ease and comfort, for more beauty in its surroundings. In this regard our leaders have not been sufficiently alert and foresighted. They have done their duty to the rising generations in religious education. Agreeing that Talmud Torahs are the foundation on which rests the future of Judaism, nevertheless we must grant that the provision of proper, sanitary, attractive *Mikvaoth* is equally important, and should come even before the establishments for religious instruction. It is certain that the women whose faith makes them obedient to the injunction contained in Leviticus will see to it that their children are properly instructed in the tenets of their faith. When synagogues, centers, Talmud Torahs, and Yeshivahs are vying with one another in beauty and efficiency, let us also raise to its proper level the *Mikvah*, that Cinderella among religious institutions. Let us build up-to-date *Mikvaoth*, both in accordance with the requirements of Jewish law, and such as will satisfy the most fastidious and exacting, so that the objections now raised by those out of sympathy with their use will be overcome. There is great need for the formation of local committees everywhere for this purpose. These could enlist the moral and material support of all Jewish residents and build *Mikvaoth* which would have the sanction and supervision of the synagogues in the neighborhood. The establishment of such model *Mikvaoth* will demonstrate our earnestness, and prove to our children that we believe that these laws of Family Purity are a preservative of chastity, a talisman against evil influences, a protection to our well-being and the guardian of our happiness.

If we do our duty conscientiously, we can hope that the Almighty will give us victory as He gave to the Maccabeans of old; that He will help us to imbue our young with such understanding of the value of our holy laws, that they, too, will realize their spirituality and become convinced that they are indispensable factors for the continuance of a sturdy, strong, loyal and law-abiding Jewish people.

Just as during Chanukah week we light more candles each night, we hope that the observance of these laws will gain the appreciation and adherence of larger and larger numbers, till the Light of our religion will illuminate the world and help to make it perfect.

13
In the Merit of Righteous Women

Aidel Dubin

Today all of humanity is experiencing a terrible crisis; materially, politically and morally. Specifically, the Jewish nation suffers.

A stormy wind of anti-Semitism is blowing across the entire world. Not only in one country; it is both in the Diaspora and [even] in Israel that Jews are tortured. With our intellect and understanding we cannot see any way out of this situation. . . .

Both believing and nonbelieving Jews recognize that through natural means there is no source of hope. Something supranatural must occur to help us out of our current situation.

Just as in Egypt, when extraordinary salvation came to the Jews in the merit of the righteous women, must we today who seek salvation become righteous women.

The beautiful Jewish way of family life is the secret of our existence as a nation. Healthy family life is the secret of a healthy national life, and only as a nation which adheres to the Jewish family laws can we hope for Godly redemption from our *tzoris*. It is for this reason that I will address the issue of Jewish family life today. . . .

Excerpted from a speech delivered in Yiddish at a conference for Jewish women in Riga in May of 1938. Translation by Rivkah Slonim.

. . . *Taharas Hamishpachah*—there are many laws under that category which for specific reasons I cannot explicitly enumerate. But I will in a few words describe that which I speak of: according to Jewish law . . . there are certain times during which husband and wife must keep at a distance. It is upon the woman's loyalty to these laws that her fortune, the fortune of her husband, her children, and in fact the fortune of the entire Jewish nation, hinges.

How many sacrifices does each mother bring during the course of raising her child! And the one which is not so difficult and is most important for her child—that of *Taharas Hamishpachah*—she will not bring?

We must keep all of God's laws—those that we comprehend and those that we do not—because our human understanding is finite.

Very aptly does the prophet Jeremiah state: "The grass dries out, the blossom fades, man's youth passes swiftly and life even more so, but the word of God remains eternal. . . ."

Many do not understand why a bathtub in one's home is not as good or even better [for immersion] than the *mikvah*. The essential reason for this matter is shrouded in deep mystery and according to my opinion is totally incomprehensible. God gave the *mikvah* waters the wondrous powers to cleanse and purify. This may be better understood by contemplating the following analogy: If a doctor sent an ailing patient to drink the waters of a specific well, the patient will not go drink waters of another well. He understands that the remedy for his sickness is found specifically in the well the doctor ordered him to drink of. How much more so is this true of God who heals all sick. He has ordered us to immerse in specific waters which will purify us and cleanse us of all ailments. . . .

In answer to women who asked, What is the difference between bath water and the waters of the *mikvah?* the Kasnover Rav said: "And the spirit of God hovered upon the face of the waters." Godliness hovers upon the *mikvah* waters. . . .

I have recently returned from Western Europe where I was quite shattered and depressed to learn of the neglect in those countries in regard to this all important observance of Family Purity, which is a corollary of our faith and the foundation of our existence. The ritual is observed only by a select few, the poor and simple. The intelligentsia completely deride the notion. When I applied further scrutiny to this matter—in my search for an explanation for this abandonment of *Taharas Hamishpachah*—I found numerous reasons.

The primary reason is simply an overwhelming lack of understanding of the importance of this rite. Secondly, there is a sense of embarrassment. This rite is a source of embarrassment before the greater society in which they find themselves. They are afraid of being mocked and scorned for their adherence to such an outmoded belief system. But we must not be embarrassed before others who do not share our understanding of, or commitment to, religion.

A third reason for its decline is the perception of the masses of *mikvah* as an unhygienic place, but there do exist first class, modern, well-ordered *mikvahs*. As a result of their laxity—after not attending the *mikvah* once—they are hesitant to go back. . . . They (erroneously) feel that if they sinned once, how can they go back?

The Talmud states: There are three partners in (the formation of) a person: God, mother, and father. The master of the universe gives the person their spirit and soul, and the father and mother give the body. Only through adherence to the laws of Family Purity can parents be the proper partners with God in this process.

We know what kind of preparations are made when one greets a human king (of flesh and blood); how much more so should this be when we greet the King of all Kings with whom we enter into communion, a partnership. The Divine gardener shows the parents how to plant the Godly seedling and later how to cultivate it and care for it. And father and mother want to be irresponsible in a moment of such importance, holiness, and great responsibility?

You may not understand why I am according such import to a subject which is not generally thought of as being so pivotal. But the Creator alone placed such unparalleled emphasis on this ritual. . . . We must visualize our connection with God as if we are a branch of a tree. As long as the branch is connected to the tree and derives thereof its vitality, it can live, grow, and produce leaves and fruit. But it is very different when the branch is cut off. One cannot discern the difference immediately, but over time, gradually, it becomes completely dried out. So it is with those who do not keep this holy *mitzvah;* they and their children and grandchildren become as a dried out tree—bereft of the vital juices of *Yiddishkeit.*

Esteemed ladies, we women were always ready to offer everything for our children. A mother does so much for her children—the pains of childbirth, sleepless nights, and yet we are not eager to do for our children this easy thing?

. . . As I mentioned earlier, the redemption from Egypt came about only because of the righteous women. Additionally, at the beginning of my speech I underscored the fact that it was always the Jewish women who helped the Jewish nation during its terrible and difficult times.

We are currently experiencing the most difficult times and we are in need of a complete salvation. We await for the Holy One Blessed Be He to show us the miraculous. But the Jews are in need of a *zechut* (great merit) to be deserving of such a crucial moment. Let us hasten to become righteous women, and just as in Egypt, will the Jews now also prove themselves worthy of being redeemed. Let us be proud and devoted Jewish women and help our persecuted and downtrodden nation experience redemption.

14
Today's *Met Mitzvah*

Dov Zlotnick

I wonder whether we feel a small part of that terrible insignificance that our grandparents felt as they gathered in *shul* on Rosh Hashanah in the large cities of Lithuania, in the villages of the Ukraine, in Vienna, Budapest and Prague, and in so many other places where no Jew lives today. They were not all saints, nor were they all scholars, but they did feel that they were part of an *"am kadosh"* a holy people, and they knew what was required of them. And although their lives were bleak and unadorned from so many points of view, they were not devoid of warmth and purpose. I don't mean to imply that they fulfilled every *mitzvah;* I am merely saying that they knew what they were. They knew that there are things that a Jew should do, and things that he must not do: A Jew should study Torah; he should honor his parents; he gives *tzedakah,* and he does *chesed;* he doesn't work on the Sabbath; he tries to *daven* with a *minyan.* And along with all the other commandments, they knew that *taharah,* ritual cleanness, had something to do with *kedushah,* holiness.

The ordinary Jew, the one referred to as *amcha,* may or may not have known that more than one-sixth of Tannaitic literature was devoted to the laws of ritual cleanness—and that most of these laws became *inoperative* with the destruction of the Temple. They may or may not have known this—but they did know in a very real way that this too was part of being Jewish.

"Today's *Met Mitzvah*" was originally delivered by Rabbi Zlotnick as a sermon on Rosh Hashana 5727 (1966) at the Jewish Theological Seminary in New York.

As Rosh Hashanah drew near, a sense of inadequacy would grip the Jewish community in Eastern Europe. I am told that people used to say: "Even the fish in water tremble." At this time of the year the people were worried; they were worried about the magnitude of their sins. Their sins, they felt, were many and *Yom ha-Din,* the Day of Judgment, was approaching. The more righteous they were, the more unworthy they felt; the greater their *kavanah,* their concentration in prayer, the more convinced they became that they were not as good as they should be. They were clearly not historians, but in their own unsophisticated way they had a sense of history, a glorious sense of Jewish destiny. They were not theologians—but who can deny their experience of "fear and trembling?" This was no time for sham. Time was slipping by, and they had not as yet done *teshuvah.*

When they did something wrong, they had a sense of sin, and this sin increased the distance between them and God. They were able to do *teshuvah,* to return, because they were able to admit that they had wandered. But what about their grandchildren and greatgrandchildren—the vast majority of American Jews? It is much more difficult for the *am kadosh* to do *teshuvah* today—not only because so many of our people no longer feel that *Halakha* has a mandate upon them, but because there are areas of Jewish life that most of our people do not even know exist.

How is the *"tinok shenishbah"* to do *teshuvah?* As you know *"tinok shenishbah"* is a term that is employed in legal contexts to describe the Jew who is taken captive as an infant and raised without any knowledge of Torah. He is not culpable for what he does or does not do. And this is what so many of our people are today: captive infants in a free and affluent society.

Let us take the area of *taharat ha-mishpahah,* the laws that govern the intimate relationship between a man and his wife, which is part of the Torah reading on Yom Kippur. How can our people do *teshuvah* in this area, if they don't even know it exists? I am not so naive as to believe that knowledge of a *mitzvah* will assure its observance, but I know you will agree that there is no possibility of observance if one simply doesn't know it exists.

At this point you may well ask: In an atomic era, when man is on the threshold of space; at a time when a social revolution is going on in America; when tens of thousands of American soldiers are at war in Viet Nam—is this what one should talk about? And if, indeed, you are going to discuss a ritual— why this one? What about *Shabbat?* Clearly most of our people do not observe the *Shabbat.* What about *kashrut?* Most of our people do not observe *kashrut.* Does one say to a person who doesn't fast on Yom Kippur, "You really ought to fast on *shivah asar betammuz."* Does one say to a person eating a bacon sandwich, "You know you really ought to wash before you eat and say Grace after you eat." Is there no hierarchy of Jewish values? Aren't there *mitzvot* more important than this?

As in the case of so many questions of this kind, the question is often better than the answer. But let me try to answer it.

First I want to say that from the point of view of Jewish law *taharat ha-mishpahah* is very important. From the Torah and the first Mishnah in *Keritut,* we see that it is as important as circumcising a child. It is as important as not eating bread on Pesach. It is as important as fasting on Yom Kippur.

In calling your attention to this *mitzvah,* I am also trying to follow the council of Rabbi Judah of Regensburg who lived during the twelfth century. He wrote: "Favor that *mitzvah* which is similar to the *met mitzvah.*" What is a *"met mitzvah?"* It is the obligation to bury an abandoned corpse, and everyone—even a High Priest, who may not defile himself at the death of his own father and mother—must attend to the burial of a *met mitzvah.* So, continues Rabbi Judah, when a person sees a *mitzvah* fallen into disuse, let him be drawn to it and favor it, and his reward will be as great as the number of people neglecting it are many.

The abandoned *mitzvah* of yesterday is not necessarily the same one today. A hundred years ago in Lithuania when the study of Torah flourished and there was no lack of scholars, Rabbi Israel Salanter felt it necessary to point out to his contemporaries that it is easier to go through all of the Talmud than to correct one character flaw, for the abandoned *mitzvah* of his generation was the correction of the perennial vices of envy, lust and the desire for public acclaim.

To their own contemporaries, the early Chassidim were notorious innovators, yet they did not advocate major halakhic deviation, but rather championed a change of emphasis. The *met mitzvah,* as they saw it, was the vast number of Jews who felt rejected by the learned aristocracy of Eastern Europe. And so they tried to instill in their followers a sense of their own importance as they stressed prayer and the joy of observing a *mitzvah.*

I feel it is up to us here—without going to extremes—to communicate to our generation of Jews the *met mitzvah* of our day. For, I feel, the whole question of *taharat ha-mishpahah* has been overlooked by all rabbis in our generation—whatever their school.

I also believe that this *mitzvah* is of supreme importance to the survival of our people. In the steps to perfection of Rabbi Pinhas ben Yair (Sotah 9:15) we find: "Purity leads to separateness, and this separateness leads to holiness." In the past it was *perishut*—separateness, that assured our survival. By choice our forefathers lived within the four cubits of the law. Of necessity, they also lived within the four cubits of the ghetto. Not that they needed it—but this too served to remind them of their Jewishness.

We have seen the four cubits of the law give way to the broad horizons of the *Haskalah.* And although we were delighted with many aspects of "Enlightenment," many of us were alarmed when it led to a weakening of Torah; and, I believe, all of us were grieved whenever it led to assimilation. Now we have also seen the four cubits of the ghetto, the persecution of millennia, give way to a modicum of understanding and we have watched this understanding grow into ecumenicism—and this we welcome. But what of its side effect—will it also be assimilation?

This summer I spent a month visiting in Oklahoma. I met a number of students attending the local universities and I learned from several girls that the Jewish boys on campus follow a principle of behavior all their own. They simply don't date Jewish girls.

We have a talmudic principle which states that we must examine rules very carefully before coming to any conclusions. So I did some research. I found myself reading many unsettling statistics on religious affiliation on campus and on intermarriage. I found that at one large urban state university, where students were asked: "What is your greatest loyalty?," seventy-four percent of the Catholic students said it was loyalty to God, and so did fifty percent of the Protestant students. But only eleven percent of the Jewish students claimed God as the object of their greatest loyalty. When these same students were asked a question of *ma'aseh,* about attendance at weekly religious services, seventy-eight percent of the Catholic students said they attended once a week; thirty-six percent of the Protestant students replied similarly; and, I quote, "not a single Jew attended synagogue once a week."

If a student wants to assimilate, it has never been easier. Fraternities and sororities that were once "exclusive" are now open to Jewish students. Unless a student has strong intellectual commitments and emotional ties to his Judaism, there is a very good chance that he will intermarry. For intermarriage is increasing today at a tragic rate—from almost twenty percent in the city of Washington to more than forty percent in the state of Iowa. And the most disturbing statistic of all is that seventy percent of the children of these intermarriages are lost to Judaism.

My friends, we cannot afford this loss. At a time when six million of our people have been killed and more than two million in the Soviet Union are being systematically alienated from us—we cannot afford this loss.

We will not stem this tide by watering down our Judaism, by giving our people less and less in an effort to meet them halfway. To stem this tide, we, of course, need intensive education—more day schools and more Ramah camps with renewed emphasis on study. And it seems to me that at a time when morals have broken down, when restraint is out of fashion, we should try in some way to make *taharat ha-mishpahah* relevant. Our people have a right to know what Judaism has to say on the subject. I think that what it has to say is very important for our day. The laws are clear, and the reasons for observing them can be made intelligible to college students. Since the college years have been called the "marrying years," this is the group we must reach. They may or may not choose to follow these laws. They may or may not be persuaded by what we have to say—but they should at least be given the opportunity to make that choice. At a time when sex is being openly discussed on every level, we should not be hesitant about suggesting to our people, and especially to a young couple about to be married, that they add this measure of sanctity to their lives.

> Happy are you Israel!
> Before whom are you cleansed?
> Who cleanses you?
> Your Father in Heaven.

For it is written: "the Lord is the hope *(mikveh)* of Israel."

Mikveh, which means hope, is here understood midrashically (Yoma 8:9) to refer to the pool for ritual immersion. Just as the *mikveh* cleanses the defiled, so the Holy One blessed be He cleanses Israel. (Yoma 8:9)

We have said that purity leads to separateness. In the past it was separateness which permitted our survival: both that separateness which we chose on our own and that which was forced upon us. Today we are fully part of a non-Jewish world and so are wholly dependent on the separateness we ourselves choose to follow to insure our continuance as a people.

When, asks the Talmud, is a corpse considered a *met mitzvah?* Whenever he calls out and the people do not hear his cry. According to the Tosafot in *Nazir,* "Whenever he calls out" refers to the deceased; if he were alive and cries out but no one responds, then this is a *met mitzvah* (Nazir 43b).

In a little while we will hear the voice of the *shofar.* It is a call to *teshuvah.* May we hear in it the call of the neglected *mitzvah* of our day—and may we all respond.

15

The Sexual and the Sacred: Newly Observant Women Speak

Debra Renee Kaufman

Rachel's Daughters (Rutgers University Press, 1991), from which the following excerpt is taken, began as a personal journey for me. Not toward Orthodox Judaism, but rather toward a better understanding of what was happening for some young women just a generation or two younger than me, as they came into young adulthood. Most particularly, my interest was peaked by those young women who in their young adult years "returned" to Jewish Orthodoxy. Most of these women were the inheritors of the women's movement, many came from liberal households and many had experienced the social movements of the sixties and seventies. My interest in young adult women comes from both personal and professional sources. I am a mother of a young adult daughter and I am a women's studies professor. My connection to young women of that age is critical to me, not only as a scholar, but as a Jewish woman, as a mother, as a feminist and as a supporter of all areas of women's liberation.

It is with this personal information that I often began the interviews I held with 150 women from five major urban areas, with large Orthodox populations, within the United States (New York, Cleveland, Boston, San Francisco, Los Angeles), who had become Orthodox in their young adult or adult years *(baalot teshuvah)*. I shared with my respondents as much information about myself as they wished to know. It only seemed fair, since I was asking them to share their personal lives with me.

Leading Jewish activists in each community, Rabbis and personal friends helped me locate *baalot teshuvah* in their respective cities. Once within a community, interviewees then provided more names.

Indeed, they provided more than names, they involved me in a round of activities: stories, meals, holidays, cooking, diapering, strolling in the park, learning, praying, and even *Mikvah*.

The following describes some of their attitudes toward and their experiences with *Mikvah:*

. . . When asked about the Family Purity laws, these newly Orthodox women almost unanimously used the "graceful" rather than the "demonic" to characterize their experiences and feelings about *Niddah* and *Mikvah*. Most eschewed the understanding of themselves as "unclean" and referred to the counting of the postmenstrual days as the "white," not "clean" days. "During *Niddah*," explained one particularly articulate woman, who, although a *baalat teshuvah*, had come so far in her own studies that she taught seminars on the laws of *Niddah*, "the woman falls between categories of life and death." She noted that she often calls upon nonlegal but traditional sources of explanation to frame discussions of *Niddah* and *Mikvah*. "For instance, when it is questioned why women and not men are still subject to impurity rituals, I look to traditional explanations. . . . You can find one that suggests that women are closer to God because of their ability to create life and that they are therefore subject to purity rituals. Still another views the woman's body as a "holy" temple. I like to think of a woman's cycle as part of all the sacred time rhythms in Judaism—the *Shabbat*, holidays. . . ."

The following quotations underscore how important and meaningful the laws of *Niddah* are to these women: "Even before I became religious and was living with my boyfriend (now my husband), we began to practice the laws of *Niddah*. I thought it the most wonderful thing, it made good sense."

A Ph.D. in psychology who lived with her then lover, now husband, in Jerusalem noted that the laws of *Niddah* most fully interested her when she was introduced to Orthodox Jewish law, while occasionally attending a *baal teshuvah* institute in Israel:

I had counseled many young people about sexual practices when I lived in the United States. When I first read about *Taharat Hamishpachah* they made absolutely good sense to me, psychologically speaking, that is. I leaned over in bed and shared with Daniel [a fictitious name] what I was reading. We made a commitment to try this practice for at least one month. We got separate beds. I went to the *mikvah* and when next we made love it was wonderful. I smile now, really not because I am embarrassed, but because of how much I have grown since then. You see, then it seemed like a lark; it made good psychological sense to me. Now it has so much more meaning. . . . I practice *Niddah* with other women and we share in a sacred ritual that connects us to our past and with our children and their children.

But not all introductions to sexual orthodoxy are so sanguine. Another woman recalls her first introduction to the laws of *Niddah:*

I was terrified of water and immersion. I knew I could not be an Orthodox mother and wife if I was not able to use the *mikvah*. I went for counseling and it did not help. My boyfriend [now husband] said that we should marry anyway and that this would somehow be resolved. We loved each other and would live like sister and brother if necessary until I could overcome my fear. I tried going to the *mikvah* several times before we were married. The first time I went to the *mikvah*, the attendant talked with me for several hours; I could not immerse myself. After several tries over the first few months, I finally decided to try it slowly, very slowly. As I went under for the first time I concentrated on how this one act linked me to generations of other women. . . . I lost my fear completely. I truly felt renewed, like a new woman capable of anything I really set my mind to. I'll also say that my friends were especially supportive in this. . . . We all had a big party at my house afterward.

Almost all women noted the positive functions of the Family Purity laws. Most frequently cited were claims of increased sexual interest and pleasure within the marriage. Although newly married women were more likely to complain about sexual separation, those married over longer periods of time and with more children found the laws quite positive over the adult life cycle. One woman notes:

When we were first married I found it hard to consider sexual separation as a positive thing. In fact, during my menstrual cycle I felt I wanted to be held and loved more than at other times of the month. But I must admit over the years it truly serves as a renewal . . . it is really like being a bride again . . . well, almost.

Even among the newly married, many claimed that forced separation heightened desire.

Others referred to the autonomy and control they experienced when practicing the laws of *Niddah*. Invoking Virginia Woolf, one woman noted, "It allows me a bed of my own." Others referred to the increased time for themselves: "I can curl up with a good book during *Niddah* and not feel in the least bit guilty." Other women emphasized the increased time for themselves, and still others spoke of a kind of control over their sexuality. "I can say no with no pretense of a headache if I wish," claimed one newly married woman. Other women suggested that the Family Purity laws provide a sexual rhythm to marriage for both partners.

Because these women have to attend intimately to their bodies to engage in sexual activity according to religious law, many speak of an increased awareness of their bodies they had never known before, evident in the following response:

> At this time of the month I am acutely aware of myself, everything is heightened because I am paying attention to what is happening inside of me. Over the years it is building a cycle for me; it's a rhythm that is related to me and my body alone.

While most of the women seem to enjoy the rejuvenation and spiritual uplifting of going to the *mikvah,* not all were uniformly happy about the length of time they were separated from their husbands during the month. Indeed, if anything, it was length of time, not the practice of the laws, about which women complained. However, even their complaints were expressed in positive terms. A good number of women suggested that the practices surrounding the period of *Niddah* force them and their husbands to learn new forms of communication and, perhaps more important, to use those newly found skills. "Most men don't know how to talk things out," claims one woman, "but since approximately one-half of my year is spent in *Niddah,* I have found that we are forced to talk about things more and that he has learned to show his love in ways more important than just physical contact."

. . . While they do believe that the laws encourage men to respect them as sexual beings, increase their own self-respect (particularly toward their bodies), and heighten sexual desire, there seems to be more than that. The symbolic framework emerging from their language, imagery, and experiences moves beyond the self and the dyad to the community at large. Indeed the pride with which one leader of her community took in taking me on a tour of the newly completed *mikvah* was unmistakable. The women had raised the money in their own sisterhood and helped the architect with the design. The more affluent the community, the more commodious and luxurious the *mikvah.* One *mikvah* I visited was constructed all in redwood with a sauna and an elaborate dressing room. Blow dryers and vanity tables were also available. One community boasts the only solar-heated *mikvah* in the country.

Without the *mikvah* the community of believers that calls itself Orthodox could not be reproduced. Therefore, the immersion in the *mikvah* is more than personal sanctity. It also represents the sanctity of the community. The *mikvah,* although legally required for women only, has deep symbolic and communal meaning. It is used as the final step in conversion to Judaism. A groom sometimes uses the *mikvah* before his wedding, some Jews purify themselves before the Sabbath or holy days, and it may be used by men and women whenever they want to renew or establish a deeper commitment to Judaism. No woman doubted the importance of the *mikvah* to the community. As one woman put it: "There is no doubt about it. If a choice has to be made, a community has to build a *mikvah* before it can build a *shul* or even acquire a *sefer Torah.*"

But it is to yet another larger community that *mikvah* unites these women. "I feel connected to history and to other women," says one *baalat teshuvah* who has practiced the laws of *Niddah* since her marriage twelve years before. Feeling a sense of history, one woman mused: "The Jews at Masada used the *mikvah.*" "Each time I use the *mikvah* I feel I come back to the center of Judaism and to my own core," a woman married fifteen years proclaimed. What became clear after several years of interviewing was that for these women the core of Judaism emanates from activities and obligations shared with other women even, and perhaps most ·ironically, when speaking of the religious ritual surrounding their heterosexuality.

A heightened air of sensuousness and intimacy surrounds the practices of *Niddah* and *Mikvah.* These rituals create a world in which women, not men, are the central actors despite the heterosexual goals. "I have been to the *mikvah* all over the world," stated one *baalat teshuvah,* "and there is a sense of togetherness. There are unspoken codes among women. No one ever counts or questions another woman's use of the *mikvah.*" Indeed there is something private, almost secretive, and emphatically intimate about the ways in which the women describe their experiences. "I feel closer to all women who share in the practice of *mikvah,*" claimed one woman. "We share all kinds of unspoken secrets with one another. After all we celebrate our bodies, our sexuality, our regenerative powers in the same way. . . ."

After immersion in the *mikvah,* women and men are allowed to resume sexual intercourse. Forgetting that completion of the *Mikvah* ritual is often a prelude to sexual activity, I once almost overstayed my welcome at one respondent's home. I had accompanied one woman to the *mikvah,* where we met others from the same community, including the woman with whom I had the next interview. My next interviewee and I spoke for a while at the *mikvah* and then I accompanied her to her home to continue the interview. As we concluded the interview, she smiled at me and said that although she was enjoying the conversation she really did not want to make it a long night. She then hesitated, and I, belatedly picking up her cue, left soon thereafter.

Nothing attests to the social construction of sexuality and the true meaning of the erotic better than how these women describe the religious rituals which heighten their sexuality. Many find erotic fantasies in the social act of "cleansing the body" for purity purposes. A woman married three years states:

> All the connotations of being a bride again are brought back. It is even more than
> the anticipation of making love but the whole secret sharing of it with other

women, a friend I may meet at the *mikvah* or the friend who might take care of the baby when I go, that makes it all more, I don't know, sort of sexy.

By maintaining and preserving appearances of chastity and not talking directly about their sexuality, the *baalot teshuvah* seem to stimulate and deepen their sense of sexuality. Although headcoverings and hemlines may vary from community to community and from woman to woman, all women abide in some way by the code of modesty in dress, conversation, personal habits, and in public displays of affection with men. Prior to their entrance into the Orthodox community, most would have found *tzniut* an alien concept; or as one woman put it, " 'Victorian'—you know, 'prudish.' " Eschewing prudish and Victorian reasons for abiding by these modesty customs, one woman compared them to the values of a sexually liberated society. The same *baalat teshuvah* who taught seminars on the Family Purity laws notes: "I find that those things we consider so intimate—like a kiss or a hug—are meaningless if you give them to everyone. It's easy to 'turn on' in this community, hard to do so out there."

The practices of *Niddah* and *Mikvah* celebrate the woman, body and soul. The ritual both constrains and extends. For the *baalot teshuvah,* the Family Purity laws represent the purity rites surrounding the entrance to the Second Temple. Renewal and regeneration of life forces are themes that run throughout these women's commentaries. The themes of sexual and sacred are concomitant for them. Immersion in the *mikvah* nullifies their state of impurity and gives rise for them to another cycle of sexuality and generativity.

16
Men and *Mikvah*

Daniel Lapin

I

I had grown up and spent all my life in the conventional *yeshivah* world. Suddenly becoming rabbi of the hip, beachfront community of Venice, California, in the late '70s came as a shock. It wasn't the derelict who strolled the boardwalk outside the *shul* with a python wrapped around his neck. Neither was it the crowds of gawkers drawn to Venice by its reputation as Southern California's number two tourist destination. No, the shock was the earnest band of upscale and well-educated young people who constituted my new community. Instead of being content with information on *how* to perform the *mitzvot* of the Torah, they actually wanted to know *why* perform them in the first place. I was dumbfounded. I had never before met anyone who not only wanted to wash with a cup before meals but also wanted to know why we should do so. For the first time in my life I was confronted by people who sought a religious lifestyle but for whom the answer "Because God says so" was part of the answer but not the entire answer.

My father, Rabbi A. H. Lapin, of blessed memory, had served congregations in South Africa since his arrival there from Lithuania during World War II. During the years I had assisted him, he trained me well. In spite of that broad experience, I was unprepared for my encounter with young Jewish Californians who came from homes with almost no Jewish content and yet who inexplicably wanted to know more about Torah Judaism. There was a challenge here. These young people had not been conditioned to "Jewish normality" by years of Jewish upbringing; in fact, most of them grew up in homes with no candle lighting on Friday night, not even a commitment to Israel. Naturally, every statement I made needed to be backed up by an explanation that "made sense." I was forced to learn far more creatively during my first year in Venice than I had during many years in a *yeshivah*.

Most Jews fall into one of two categories. They either entirely ignore the dozens of daily details of Jewish life or they observe them because they are prescribed in the Torah. It dawned upon me that there was a third category. Consider for a moment how you might explain why we shake a *lulav,* why we wear *tefillin,* or why we eat kosher to a sincere and sophisticated individual who doesn't yet believe in God but wished he did. As difficult as these examples are, they fade in comparison to the consternation I felt while preparing the first few Venice couples for marriage. "We have to do *what?!*" the wild-eyed bridegroom-to-be usually exclaimed.

My wife, Susan, explained the mysteries of the *mikvah* and the halachic structure of its rules to prospective brides. She focused on the benefits rather than the costs. Almost invariably they responded to her with genuine appreciation for the wisdom of the Torah. That their fiancés responded far less enthusiastically to me and my information, I prefer to attribute chiefly to the differences between men and women. Not surprisingly, I quickly found that I had to delve deeply into our holy sources to develop an approach that made sense to modern Californian males. I am fortunate to have had well over one hundred opportunities to hone this approach during the past fifteen years.

Human physiology allows us to become accustomed to almost anything eventually. Provided the stimulus is constantly and consistently applied, we will continually become less aware of it. This century provides tragic but compelling proof that even unthinkable horrors become accepted as almost normal existence once they have gone on long enough. The opposite is also true. We can become jaded by pleasure and enjoyment constantly and consistently applied. This problem is, of course, well known in the dark world of drug usage. The addict's response is to increase the dosage each time, in an effort to regain the original euphoric sensation. Similarly, in the Western world, eating is no longer a matter of survival. It has become a sensual pleasure requiring newer and more exotic restaurants to overcome bland familiarity. The best advice for the gourmand would be to impose a fast upon himself at regular intervals. This would enable him to reset his "sensual odometer" back to zero, as it were.

Society suffers because it has no means to set the sensual odometer back to zero. The solution is to the relationship between husband and wife what the regular fast day is to the gourmand: a means of recovering the original euphoria and banishing the tedium of familiarity. It is so brilliant a technique that it is hard to fathom why it hasn't spread throughout any society in which observant Jews have lived.

I had found the first key to presenting this *mitzvah* in a way that made sense. It was not necessarily an approach for everybody but it helped privileged young Californian men of the baby-boomer generation to grasp the idea of the *mikvah*.

> Howard was a serious young lawyer with a large West Los Angeles firm that specializes in show business transactions. Unlike his friends, he had not been promiscuous as a young bachelor and was now engaged to an accomplished young woman trained as a CPA. Karen had been involved in my Jewish community for far longer than Howard and was eager to incorporate what she referred to as "THM" into her marriage. After a number of sessions with me, Howard began to see "THM" as something he should be embracing, not merely allowing Karen to impose on the marriage. Said Howard during one unforgettable conversation: "This is as much for me as it is for her."

I suspect that *Taharat Hamishpachah* has not become more popular for the same reason that *Shabbat* observance has not become more widespread than it is. Despite its lifesaving qualities, observing *Shabbat* is irrational in the face of compelling business demands. "Start your Sabbath day off a little later," urges an important customer awaiting your attention late on Friday afternoon. In the final analysis, there will always be a logical reason to defer or cancel *Shabbat,* just this week. Declaring it a religious issue won't make the Friday afternoon customer any happier, but it will help to reconcile him to the inevitability of your business closing. Making *Shabbat* a central pillar of religious observance confers upon me the energy and conviction to make it work. If working on *Shabbat* violates the essence of my relationship with God, very few demands can make it worthwhile.

In a similar way, for a couple to agree to impose upon themselves a regular restraint on the ordinary intimacy of married life makes a lot of sense. However, the call to sexuality is too compelling, the summons too urgent for it to work reliably. It would prove hard not to rationalize from time to time that right now, in spite of an earlier commitment to the contrary, physical intimacy is precisely what the marriage needs. For this reason there is no alternative to adopting these family rules as central to our relationship with the Almighty.

II

Marriage itself is enormously ennobling for men. From adolescence onward, most men are self-centered and even selfish. Marriage is the first time that most men realize how much more of a thrill it is to give than to take. For the first time in his life, trudging off to work on Monday morning has real meaning. No longer is he working to satisfy his needs, like any animal that spends its days gathering nuts or hunting prey. As a married man, he is working also to satisfy the needs of another person.

The Torah assists the husband in becoming more giving by stating that a primary obligation of the man in marriage is to give his wife sexual satisfaction according to her wishes. Nonetheless, since it is often the husband that initiates intimacy, he thereby reveals his own desire for gratification, and this once again casts him as the taker. This contradicts his primary role in the marriage but can fortunately be avoided. Once the rhythm of intimacy is to be established not chiefly by desire from within, but by an objective and holy external source, the husband can reclaim his proper role as giver.

> Charles was a Harvard-trained dermatologist who was raised in New York in an Orthodox home whose traditions he had rejected. He was gradually reclaiming his religious heritage but regularly assured me that the one thing he would never accept was Torah's jurisdiction over his bedroom. Then he became enamored of a young woman with little Jewish background and considerable hostility to religious practice. He told me that he had decided to marry her if she accepted the centrality to their marriage of *Kashrut, Shabbat,* and *Mikvah.* When I asked why the last, he explained that *Mikvah* completely contradicted feminism's angry denunciation of the husband as a sexual predator.

There exists yet another way in which *Mikvah* ennobles men. It is reflected by the metaphor constantly used by the Torah for a man—a tree. Like a tree, we are rooted in the ground of materialism, but our leaves grope upward, reaching for the sky. The Torah's commandments are all intended to give us an opportunity to raise our material side from the ground toward the sky. We are most concerned by those activities we have in common with animals. Thus the *mitzvah* structure surrounding those areas is detailed and complex, whereas activities that are unique to humans require limited elevation; they are already halfway to heaven. There is little complex ritual surrounding activities like prayer, the wearing of clothes, reading a book, or listening to music. This is because these activities in themselves already distance us from the animal and materialistic world. But activities like eating, using a bathroom, and even dying are so similar to what animals do that we are grateful to our Creator for providing us with a complex web of spiritual threads that helps us maintain our perspective of who we really are. Nowhere is the similarity between animal and man more threatening to us than in the area of male/female intimacy. Perhaps this accounts for the awkwardness and embarrassment surrounding this subject. It also helps explain why people often attempt to dispel their discomfort with false bravado and by ostentatiously stripping away the natural cover of modesty with which most people clothe the subject.

The Torah offers a splendid solution to this dilemma. Animals eat and we eat. But animals eat whenever and whatever their instincts demand; we eat only after preparations and blessings and only what has been prescribed. Animals relieve themselves publicly and instinctively; we use a special and private room constructed for the purpose, and we follow it with a blessing. Animals witness death dispassionately; we surround it with specific mourning observances. Finally, animals simply mate; we announce our intentions to our communities. We demonstrate an ability to wait through a preparation period and we formalize the bond between us with a ceremony. Above all, we ensure that the most physical aspect of the union is sanctified in a way that no animal could ever comprehend.

According to Torah, women need fewer acts of self-elevation because their natural life-giving abilities already contains a touch of the divine. Not surprisingly, men are commanded to perform many more *mitzvot* than women. The gift of *Mikvah,* for instance, is far more valuable to the husband than the wife. To her, a physical relationship with her husband is already imbued with a conscious awareness of its life-giving potential. This thought is not at the forefront of most men's minds. The husband's entire spiritual self-esteem therefore depends upon some affirmation that he is not merely engaging in a ridiculously animalistic act. The awareness that his wife has come to him from the *mikvah* provides that precious assurance.

> David was a director of an investment bank when he became involved in the Venice community and serious Judaism. He was good-looking, talented, and successful but at forty-two years old had never married. During the daily Talmud *shiur* one morning, it was necessary to discuss how *mitzvot* elevate the physical, particularly with reference to marriage, and David's eyes lit up. I had never seen him so bright-eyed. He seemed totally transformed, and I could hardly wait for our next private conversation. Later that week he talked to me about his "hang-ups," the problems that a succession of therapists had identified as the root causes of his reluctance to commit to marriage. He now felt that it was not a reluctance to commit that had restrained him, but something else, something far deeper. It was answered by the Jewish approach to marriage that he had just understood. He was jubilant that marriage did not mean renouncing dignity and discipline. He married Annette shortly thereafter.

III

Had the Torah been written by a mortal, surely the first person on earth would have been a woman. Eve would have fallen into a deep sleep, and Adam would have emerged. Readers would recognize it as the model for all future child-birth; after all, it is simply more plausible for a woman's body to yield a man than the reverse. We consider Adam and Eve to have been the most perfect couple and the paradigm for all marriage; after all, look at who the Match-maker was. God chose not to create two humans simultaneously, a man and a woman, who would then bring forth future generations. Instead He selected a subtle parent–child schematic for marriage. He created one, whose body would then yield the other. The choice was a mother–son paradigm or a father–daugh-ter paradigm. By selecting Adam as that first person, God implies that a man is obliged to conduct himself in the marriage more like a father than a son. In other words, a man is obliged to be giving, selfless, disciplined, restrained, and responsible. According to the marriage contract, women have the right to be taken care of—not that they will always choose this. In fact, women are natural givers; men need God's assistance. It would be hard to find an area in which a husband ought to display more self-restraint and discipline than that of physical intimacy. The delicate rhythm of the *mikvah* provides an opportunity for the husband to demonstrate his acceptance of God's rules.

Those selfsame rules also offer a refuge from the most haunting and destructive aspect of life, which is a subconscious but overwhelming awareness of death. So powerful a factor is this in most human lives that we Jews even have a term for it—*Tumah*. It is indescribably difficult to coerce our minds into ignoring our inevitable mortality and this can affect everything creative we attempt. The genius of the Torah is in recognizing that it is far simpler to avoid the circumstances of *Tumah* than to rid ourselves of its effects. For this reason we attempt to keep the life and death motifs of our existence quite separate. For instance, everyone recognizes that meat, while permissible, is a food for which a living creature had to die. Milk, on the other hand, is not only made available with no death, it is the very substance of life. *Kashrut* therefore decrees the separation of dairy foods and meat foods. Not surprisingly, it is less stringent in the naturally occurring sequence of life followed by death than the reverse. Which is to say meat may closely follow dairy but not the reverse. We observe the same concern in the Torah's prohibition of spiritualism. The living should have no communication with the dead. Indeed the Torah conspicuously lacks any after-death information because the Torah is called "a tree of life" and we wish to keep the zones of life and death quite separate.

For this reason, the most life-affirming act that two human beings can engage in must be insulated from the slightest hint of mortality. One such hint is the monthly loss of an egg that human females undergo. This is different from men whose production of seed is seemingly infinite and for whom the loss of any quantity of seed does not represent a diminishing balance. For women however, each loss of an egg represents one less chance at life; in other words, a minideath. Even this tiny taste of death should be kept far from the life-affirming act. The question is how? With the substance that every human associates with life — water, of course. And not just any water, but water that constitutes an almost mathematical model of the original water, the cradle of all life, the primeval amniotic fluid described in the opening verses of the Torah, the *mikvah*.

> Philip was a psychologist and an atheist. He began dating Judi, who had been observant and committed for a number of years. She was feeling increasingly pessimistic about the relationship ever leading to marriage, so I began a series of lunch meetings with Philip in the hope of helping things along. Eventually Philip became religious and married Judi. Years later I asked him what did it for him. He told me two things. First, there was no way that any human founder of a religion could have figured out how to create a role for a father in a family as does Judaism. Second, no human could have figured out how to handle the exquisite life/death tensions of marriage that we find in *Halachah*.

It is hard to think of any area of Torah observance that can claim greater credit than the *mikvah* for the durability of the Jewish people. Other nations rise and fall over a period of several hundred years, sometimes more. The end usually comes not with a bang but a whimper, the whimper of decadent excess and spiritual weakness. It is not only the Jewish people but each Jewish community and each Jewish family that benefits from the rigorous discipline of these rules with which God has blessed us. I am certain that the widespread observance of these laws in the Venice community of Pacific Jewish Center conferred not only enormous communal vitality but also extraordinary families and remarkable children. It was my privilege to serve those spiritual heroes as rabbi for fifteen years and it is to them that I dedicate this discussion.

17
The *Mikvah*

Lis Harris

It is probably safe to say that no aspect of Orthodox Jewish life has so piqued the curiosity of interested outsiders as the so-called Laws of Family Purity, the rules that govern sexual relations between all Orthodox men and women. Men and women in this context means husbands and wives. There are no Jewish sexual laws that apply to unmarried men and women, except those that forbid sexual congress between them and those that help ensure that transgressions will not take place. Like most people, I knew that Orthodox married women did not cohabit with their husbands while they menstruated and for a week afterward. I also knew that they immersed themselves in a ritual bath—a *mikvah*—at the end of this time and that the immersion officially ended what I had heard described as their period of "uncleanness." To the extent that I'd thought about it, which wasn't much, it all sounded like some unwholesome misogynist ritual from the pages of *The Golden Bough.*

   . . . I was interested in knowing what Sheina thought about the *mikvah,* but reluctant to discuss what seemed like such a private matter with her. As it happened, the subject came up naturally one day. Sheina and a friend had for years talked about trying to replace the crumbling old women's *mikvah* on Albany Avenue and Union Street with a better equipped, more modern one, she

---

Excerpted from the chapter in *Holy Days.*

told me. Eventually, they had interested the women of the neighborhood in making a new *mikvah* a community project, and, after months of discussions, planning, fund-raising (and of course the obligatory go-ahead from the Rebbe), the *mikvah* was finally on its way. Sheina wanted to show me how it was coming along. The new *mikvah* was being built in a gutted brownstone next door to the old one. There were actually going to be three baths in the new building, all built to extremely rigorous religious specifications. They looked like small swimming pools, something like the indoor pools that are built next to saunas in Scandinavia. Like all *mikvahs,* they were fed by two sources of water; in each of the baths, two hundred gallons of rainwater commingled with ordinary city water. It is this rainwater that gives a bath its legitimacy as a *mikvah.* Gleaming tiles covered the walls, dressing rooms and showers were being installed, and rolls of carpeting leaned against the walls. The Lubavitcher laborers, wielding trowels and hammers, looked like displaced M.I.T. philology professors. They greeted Sheina cheerfully and spoke to her about the progress of their work. Sheina had been more or less in charge of seeing that things went along smoothly from the beginning of the project and it was apparent that she was immensely proud of the new *mikvah.* As we left, she glanced up at the old building (the plans called for its being gutted and incorporated in the new complex, but its baths were still in use until the new ones were completed) with its somber Ritualarium lettering etched above the doorway and said, "We want people to like coming here. It's a beautiful ritual, and we think it deserves a welcoming setting."

"I'd like to know a bit more about how it affects you," I said.

Sheina said that she had a doctor's appointment in Queens (for months she had been waging a valiant battle, with the help of a nutrition expert, to shed some pounds, but as soon as she lost a few, a particularly lavish Sabbath meal would render the previous week's efforts meaningless) and another one later on at the neighborhood *sheitl macher* (wig maker) but that she would be happy to continue the discussion if I could come along for the ride. I agreed, and as we drove along Eastern Parkway past miles of decrepit, once-elegant buildings and boarded-up brownstones, Sheina talked about the Laws of Family Purity.

"You know, I suppose, that according to Jewish law women may not have sexual relations or any physical contact whatever with their husbands while they menstruate and for a week afterward. This may seem unnatural and a strain on a marriage to outsiders, but I think it is fair to say that no Orthodox couple I've ever known thinks of it that way. In the first place, it's a time when couples stress all the other ways that they have of communicating with one another, and secondly, most people find that abstinence whets their sexual appetite so that the boredom that many marriages suffer from has no chance to develop."

Contrary to popular belief, *chasidim* are not discouraged from enjoying sex and have as part of their inheritance a wide variety of quite specific talmudic and posttalmudic exhortations to enjoy the act of love, complete with Masters-and-Johnson-like suggestions as to how to go about it. One can only assume that they respond to these tracts as scrupulously as they respond to all the other advice of their sages. Much of the literature on the subject has as its theme the obligation of husbands to give their wives pleasure. This excerpt from the Epistle of Holiness, by Rabbi Moses ben Nahman, a thirteenth-century mystic, is illustrative: "Therefore, engage her first in conversation that puts her heart and mind at ease and gladdens her. Speak words which arouse her to passion, union, love, desire and eros. Never may you force her, for in such union the Divine Presence cannot abide. Win her over with words of graciousness and seductiveness. Hurry not to arouse passion until her mood is ready."

"I don't know if it's the separation or the beauty of the ritual, maybe it's both, but I feel like a new bride every month," said Sheina. "How many married women can say that?"

"Why are the rules so strict about all physical contact between husband and wife in this period? Why, for example, are you not even allowed to pass a table utensil to Moshe?"

"The prohibition against men and women cohabiting while a woman menstruates comes from the book of Leviticus. But our rabbis spelled out the ways such a prohibition could best be carried out in the Talmud tractate *Niddah* [the word *niddah* means removed or separated] and in the Code of Jewish Law. Most of the customs are there for the same purpose, to keep the flames of passion [Sheina used this expression without the slightest note of irony in her voice] banked for a while. Nowadays, the casual touch of a woman's hand or the gesture of sitting on a woman's bed [another prohibition] would probably be considered ridiculously unstimulating to a lot of people. But to men and women who don't take casual physical contact for granted, the most ordinary acts can be erotic. We have an extremely low divorce rate in this community; no one's really counted but I would say it is less than five percent. I know that people think that it's low because of the social stigma attached to divorce, but that isn't it at all. I really believe that marriages are stronger here, certainly sturdier than most that I've seen in the outside world."

. . . Sometime after my visit to the unfinished *mikvah* with Sheina, and after the birth of my second child, I returned to pay a visit myself. It is about a forty-five minute subway ride from Lower Manhattan, where I live, to the Kingston Avenue IRT stop. After Brooklyn Heights, mine is the only white face on the subway car. It is sundown (the prescribed time for taking a *mikvah*) when I surface and, as usual, there is a large group of bearded, black-hatted, somberly dressed men milling in front of 770, which is just across the street from the subway exit. The neighborhood still seems dreamlike, but the faces above the beards have begun to look more individualized to me; the perceptual trick seems to be to read them from the nose up. Union Street, where the *mikvah* is, cuts into Kingston Avenue, and as I walk down it toward the *mikvah* I find myself trailing behind a black teenage boy bopping down the street with an enormous radio that is blasting out reggae music. Formalizing the occasion, I imagine that the music is a kind of fanfare for the ritual I am going to experience, and that the boy and I form a kind of procession. The farther away we get from Kingston Avenue the more deserted and rundown the street gets. Across the street from the tan brick-face *mikvah* building, which glows faintly in the fading light, is a large deserted apartment building with broken windows. There are no windows at all in the new *mikvah,* and the old ones have been cemented over. A fancy brown canvas canopy arches over the front door, giving the entranceway the appearance of an elegant salon. I am buzzed into the building, ascend a flight of stairs and give eight dollars to a Slavic-looking attendant who tells me that she can't remember ever having seen me before. At the *mikvah,* many women shower and bathe in preparation for the ritual immersion itself. I explain to the attendant that I have already bathed at home so she leads me to a dressing room with only a shower in it. The shower has a sliding frosted-glass door; there is burgundy, white, and gold deco paper on the walls; and a beveled diamond-shaped mirror over a Formica dressing table. There is also a wig stand, a bright red Clairol Son of a Gun 1400 hundred watt hairdryer, a long cream-colored terry cloth bathrobe, and a pair of brightly colored rubber slippers. The attendant shows me a tan intercom and tells me to pick it up when my preparations are completed and tell the *mikvah* lady that I'm ready. As I close the door, I notice several other women flitting down the corridor. The *mikvah* is considered an extremely private ritual, and there is no socializing here, none of the affectionate banter that is so prevalent in feminine chasidic society. Women generally go to the *mikvah* alone, and even Sheina, who was always eager to act as my cicerone to landmarks of Jewish Orthodoxy, had not offered to accompany me to this one. The lower half of the dressing room is covered with gleaming off-white tile. I had always imagined *mikvahs* to be rather oriental: vaporous dim places, chaste seraglios. Nothing could be further from my preconception than this sleek Swiss spa.

The toilette one makes in preparation for the *mikvah* is elaborate. Having read about (and followed) the complicated preparations before I came, I was not surprised to see a small tray filled with cotton swabs, cotton balls, tissues, shampoo, baby oil, toothpicks, bleach, alcohol, soap and Adwe New Fluoride Formula Kosher toothpaste. It is considered extremely important that the waters of the *mikvah* touch every part of a woman's body; even minute particles of matter that prevent this from happening make the immersion invalid. The kinds of matter that might (literally) gum things up have been spelled out in excruciating detail by rabbinic authority. "A splinter," for example, "which protrudes from the skin, or even if it does not protrude the skin but nevertheless is on the same level with the outer skin must be removed." Even particles of food that get caught in one's teeth are considered impurities, so a little box of dental floss is provided. But then again, the floss might get stuck, so, taped to the little plastic box is the typed message "Don't floss if your teeth are tight together." Most of the people who come to the *mikvah* already know everything there is to know about preparing for it. As a precaution, however, a lengthy checklist has been taped to the wall. Among other things, it suggests that "Rabbinic advice should be sought for temporary fillings, root-canal work or capping in progress, nits in the hair, stitches, casts, unremovable scabs, unusual skin eruptions." It is further suggested that one ask oneself, "Have I cut finger and toe nails and removed dirt in crevices (bleach helps)? Removed all foreign bodies: false teeth, contact lenses, paint and makeup, nail polish, artificial nails, Band-Aids, bobby pins?" The list goes on, and suffice it to say that no crevice or orifice of the body is neglected.

Scrubbing myself in the shower, I remember the woman who commented on the "dirtiness" of the *chasidim* and laugh out loud. The last words on the checklist are "Now you are ready for the great *mitzvah* of *Tevilah* [immersion]." A French version of the list has been taped below the English one (many French-speaking Jews have been visiting the community recently). With characteristic Gallic grace, the French version adds a little coda to the English one: Now, it says, you are ready to perform the great *mitzvah* of *Tevilah* "*avec joie et assurance.*" I ring for the *mikvah* matron. I do not feel "*joie et assurance.*" I feel nervous. I find myself wishing my mother were here. Then, one of the kindest most benign faces I have ever seen appears smiling at the door, and my worries evaporate. The woman, who is middle-aged and wears a dark wig, tells me as she leads me through the climate-controlled corridor that her name is Brachah. Brachah, of course, means blessing. These Lubavitchers really know how to do things. I tell Brachah that I've never taken a *mikvah* before. She folds her hands over her stomach and beams. "Well, then, we'll treat you like a *kallah* [a bride]" and proceeds to explain some of the basics of the ritual to me. Then she asks, enumerating the various items on the checklist one by one, if I have remembered to do all of them. I have not. I have forgotten to comb my wet hair and I have forgotten my nose, which I proceed to blow, rather showily. Then, after blotting my eyes with a linen cloth to make sure no mascara lingers on my lashes, Brachah leads me over to the *mikvah*. I take off the robe and stand expectantly in the chest-deep warm green water. Brachah tells me to keep my eyes and lips closed but not too tightly and to keep my feet and arms apart, so that the water will touch my whole body. When I go underwater I instantly curl into the fetal position because of the position of my body. When I come up, Brachah places a linen cloth over my head and I repeat the *mikvah* blessing after her. Then, the cloth removed, I go down two more times. The second time down, I see a little speeded-up movie of all the religious people I know, performing this ritual. I think of all the generations of people I have not known who have considered the impurities of the world dissolvable. My grandmother floats by, curled up, like me, like a little pink shrimp. I see her as she was in her very old age, senile and mute, curled up in the same position on her bed. The third time down, I think of my boys suspended inside me, waiting to join the world. I look up and see Brachah's smiling face through the water. I feel good. As I am climbing out, Brachah tells me that some people prefer to immerse themselves with their bodies in a horizontal position and asks me if I'd like to try it that way. I try it, but find it less satisfactory. It's too much like going for a swim.

When I finish dressing, I find Brachah and the other attendant huddled together at the reception desk. I've told Brachah that I live in Manhattan and that I came by subway. "We don't think you should go home by subway," Brachah says. "It's really not safe to walk alone out there now." It's only a little after eight, but I take their word for it and call one of the local car services, Black Pearl. (No city radio cabs will come to Crown Heights. No yellow cabs cruise the neighborhood streets.) Five minutes later, a blue Chevrolet station wagon pulls up. I thank the women for their help, say good-bye, and climb into the car. The driver is a garrulous, handsome Haitian. Loud, monotonous music blasts out of the radio. Hanging over his rearview mirror is an air deodorizer, which fills the car with an overpowering sickly sweet smell. Competing with the air deodorizer is the sharp scent of his after-shave, which he keeps in a kit on the front seat. At a long red light, he splashes a little extra on. My ablutions have made me feel tender, almost porous, and the harsh smells are overwhelming. Is this how Moshe and Sheina feel when they traffic with the outside world? The driver tells me that his company is often called upon to pick up women at that spot, which he seems to believe is a kind of shrine.

"You're Jewish, right?" he says, shouting to be heard over the music. "You have a lot of rules you have to follow?"

I hesitate. I am not up to any discussion.

"Yes, I'm Jewish," I say, as I roll the window down and point my nose toward the fresh air.

18

A Different Time

Roni Loeb Richter

I am writing these words from a different time. The year is the same, the days are the same, but the months are different.

The time in which I exist today is neither solar nor truly lunar. It is a time quite individual—created by God, especially for me. Today is one cyclical month since my first immersion in the *mikvah*. This day, this time, is shared among only three: God, my husband, and me. Today I am brought back to the very moment of recreation of self that took place for the first time on the day of my wedding.

In the excitement and anticipation that preceded the wedding, I had counted the days, checking them against God's calendar and my own body's. The rebirth for which I was preparing would take place in a home of sorts, under the *chuppah* (marriage canopy). My fiancé and I, often swamped with the details of wedding plans, finally began to focus more on the spiritual preparations we needed to make in order to escort the *Shechinah* (God's presence) to our wedding and into our lives. The most important part of this self-preparation was gaining the ability to slip ourselves into *Mikvah* time. This step would prove monumental, for within the entire planning process, there was nothing so full of potential and meaning for me as *Mikvah*. Somehow I felt that only after I had experienced this immersion would I be able to understand the oneness that defines the relationship between husband and wife.

I walked to the *mikvah* on a beautiful Thursday morning, on a sunny *Rosh Chodesh,* on a sparkling *Mikvah* day. I had spent the early part of the day preparing my body for immersion. Filing, trimming, scrubbing, soaking, combing, and inspecting, I realized that this was the first time I had ever spent such concentrated time focused on my body. Yet, inherent in this moment of complete physical absorption was a palpably electric surge I felt run through me as I connected, for the first time, the spiritual and physical aspects of myself.

As I walked up the hill to the *mikvah,* a song came into my head and I stopped short. The song was *Shir Hamaalot,* a song of ascents, originally sung by the Levites as they stood on the stairs that led to the holy Temple. The words of the psalm speak of the Jews returning to Jerusalem as if in a dream, filled with laughter and singing. And here I was, a modern Jewish woman, feeling that the boundaries of time had blurred. I walked on smiling, simultaneously there at that moment and a part of all time.

I approached the *mikvah* alone, and as I reached it, I saw the smiling face of a friend who said, "You shouldn't have to go to the *mikvah* alone the first time." My joy and nervousness blended with the comfort I took in the familiarity of her presence and with a sense that I would never really be alone at the *mikvah.* I felt as we entered, that there exists a collective *neshama* (soul) shared by all Jews throughout history. The *mikvah* is the link of all those years, the container of that soul. The waters of the *mikvah* today are the same waters that have filled *mikva'ot* since the beginning of time. I imagined that by immersing myself in those waters, I could in that silence under water hear the voices of my ancestors.

Later, as the *shomeret* held my shaking hands in hers, the power of this process filled me with tears. For when I was completely enveloped by those waters, I had realized that this birth was not of a new me alone. The still voice of the *mikvah* told me that this was the birth of "we." From now on, *mikvah* time would be counted by two. From now on, this merging with the collective Jewish soul would enable me to merge with the other half of my own soul, this man I love.

19

The Groom's Wedding Plans

Andrew Klafter

Submerged underwater at the southern Long Island shore on the morning before my wedding, I prayed to the Master of the Universe: *May the words of my mouth and the meditations of my heart be acceptable to you. Allow me to feel Your holiness and not be distracted by selfishness. When You consecrate my bride to me, grant me perception of Your presence.*

For months prior to our wedding, I prepared for a spiritual metamorphosis. I needed to make the transition from independence to a state of mind where I would act as part of a greater whole. Up to that point in my life, all decisions and plans in my life had revolved around myself, exclusively. My most consuming responsibilities had been to do well in school and take care of my own personal needs. I knew that husband and wife, unlike business partners, have goals that are greater than merely establishing an arrangement where self-interests can be better served. Marriage presented an opportunity to extend the limits of my role in this world beyond my own physical limitations — not only through the creation of more Jews, God willing, who will devote their lives to serving the Master of the Universe, but more directly by internalizing the dreams and aspirations of my wife and working with her to accomplish them. There were two aspects of my preparation for this role. There is a standard course of study in the Jewish legal and philosophical literature that men traditionally cover before getting married, dealing with interpersonal dynamics as well as sexual intimacy. The second component was a program of meditation and introspection. By becoming more aware of personal drives and desires, I hoped to be able to clearly communicate my needs to my wife, and to be more sensitive to hers.

A wedding day, we are taught, is like a personal Yom Kippur. In order to enter this new stage of life with a clean slate, it is customary to spend some time that day in intense meditation and confession,[1] to fast, and to immerse in a *mikvah*. No *mikvah* was available nearby. I therefore chose to submerge in the ocean that morning. As on Yom Kippur, the objective is to progress spiritually by eliminating all obstacles and previous debts. Therefore, I had already sought forgiveness from anyone I felt I had hurt or treated wrongly. I also gave some money to a worthy charity, which is a way of arousing God's mercy.[2]

The immersion in a *mikvah*, itself, is for the purpose of entering a state of ritual purity. It was not some magic trick that could erase everything wrong I'd ever done. No true change or accomplishment can come easily or automatically. It was only after long and hard effort; I had worked hard to improve as a person and as a Jew, and to achieve a clear sense of my goals. It is taught that if one sincerely attempts to rectify any damage that he has done in this world, and resolves to improve himself for the future, God Himself repairs everything that one was not able to.[3] Only after all this has been done is *Mikvah* relevant to the process of refinement and self-renewal. It was a restoration of my true potential.

It is difficult to describe something that cannot be seen or touched, but I am certain that when I finally stood under the wedding canopy, I had been stripped down, spiritually, to the real me. For the first time I understood why at a traditional Jewish wedding the groom wears an unadorned, pure white *kittel*.[4]

If my preparations for marriage can be likened to a purification or cleansing, it is in the sense of cleaning a window in order to see in and out more clearly. As opposed to trying to subdue or eliminate my inner drives and desires, it was about achieving a greater awareness of where and who I am so that I can move forward, together with my bride.

Notes

1. In Judaism, confession is between an individual and God; it in no way involves confession to another person. See Maimonides, *Mishneh Torah, Hilchot Teshuvah* 1:1.

2. Rosh Hashanah and Yom Kippur liturgy: "Repentance, prayer, and charity lessen the severity of the decree." *Shulchan Aruch, Yoreh De'ah* 247:3: "The Holy One Blessed be He has mercy on he who has mercy on poor."

3. Rabbi Shneur Zalman of Liady, *Igeret Hateshuvah*, chapter 1.

4. The *kittel* is a white robe which is worn over the clothes by the groom during the marriage service under the *chuppah* (wedding canopy) (*Kitzur* 138:4). The *kittel* is also worn on Yom Kippur (*Kitzur* 131:15).

20
During the Gulf War

Varda Branfman

It was during the first days of the Gulf War, and it wasn't yet clear whether any of the missiles were aimed at Jerusalem. People were playing it safe by staying indoors, close to their sealed rooms and gas masks.

I had mixed feelings about going to the *mikvah* that night, but I had counted the seven days, and it was my time for immersion. I had never missed the designated time and had surmounted many inconveniences: the wedding of a best friend on the same night, parent/teacher meetings scheduled at the same time, and Friday nights when I had to excuse myself to a houseful of *Shabbat* guests, mumbling that I was going to visit a friend, and then returning after my husband had come home from the synagogue with everyone waiting for my appearance so that *Kiddush* could be made and the meal could begin.

But this was different—it was more than inconvenient, it could be dangerous. I made most of my preparations at home before venturing out after nightfall into the quiet streets. The nearest *mikvah* was four long blocks from my house, and I almost ran the whole way. All the time I was thinking of how I would dash back home if there were one of those dreaded sirens.

My heart was pounding when I opened the door to the *mikvah*. The steamy waiting room was bustling with women. They were talking about the war, but clearly it hadn't kept them home.

Here in the *mikvah,* it was business as usual with several dozen women in various stages of preparation for their immersion. I asked the busy *mikvah* attendant what to do if a siren should suddenly go off to signal a missile attack. She seemed nonplussed by the question. There had been two sirens the night before, and those sirens hadn't stopped anyone from proceeding with the precious *mitzvah* of *Mikvah*. Even greater threats to the Jewish people in previous wars hadn't stopped Jewish women from the observance of *Mikvah*.

My question was not an academic one. Several minutes later when I was standing in my private room, I heard a siren go off. I was holding a bar of soap, and my hand stopped in midair.

The wail of the siren was dreamlike and seemed to come from a great distance. More real and immediate were the sounds of water splashing and the voices of the women. Here in the *mikvah*, we focused exclusively on our intense preparations and our heightened anticipation for the moment of immersion.

Saddam Hussein would have been infuriated. His bullying hadn't worked on us, and we weren't following his orders. *Hashem* was running the world, and we were following His directives. As married Jewish women, this was our time to immerse in the *mikvah*, and nothing could stop us.

I didn't rush through my preparations because of those ominous sirens. Somehow, on the contrary, I relished every moment of the *mitzvah*. I was feeling especially proud of myself and those other women who had outsmarted Saddam Hussein, and I was feeling deeply connected to all those women down through Jewish history who had stubbornly kept the *mitzvah* of *Mikvah* under difficult and sometimes dangerous circumstances.

I thought of my friend in the Midwest who traveled six hours each way to the nearest *mikvah*. In Jerusalem there are several *mikvahs* in walking distance from my home. I remember the *mikvah* waters being chilly only one time, and that was due to a broken furnace. I have read of Jewish women living in Siberia who would chop holes in a frozen river in order to observe the *mitzvah* of *Mikvah*.

A woman has three special *mitzvahs:* separating *challah,* lighting *Shabbat* candles, and *Mikvah*. On the surface at least, *Shabbat* candles and *challah* are straightforward and not especially time consuming. *Mikvah,* on the other hand, is brimming with a myriad of actions and intentions. Though a woman may immerse in the *mikvah* hundreds of times, she is always transformed by the experience.

I have come to regard *Mikvah* not only as an obligation but as a distinct privilege conferred by my status as a married woman. There were times I had to pry myself away from my children as I left the house to go to the *mikvah*. I would tell them I was going to a workshop for mommies and would be back in a few hours. Then, furtively, I would pack my overnight bag with towel, robe, soap, toothpaste, etcetera, and breezily say good-bye as I walked out the door without looking back.

All the way to the *mikvah,* I would be haunted by separation anxiety. Leaving them to go to a wedding or *bar mitzvah* never affected me the same way.

I have come up with this explanation: the experience of preparing for immersion and the immersion itself is all-consuming. Nothing else exists for that space of two to three hours. The whole rest of the world recedes into the distance. The woman who walks through the *mikvah* door is not the same woman who leaves through the same door after her immersion. When I go home to my husband and family, I feel as if I have returned from a long journey to a place where I connected to the Eternal and the Infinite.

What happens there in the *mikvah* is compelling and mystical. A woman doesn't even have to be aware of the implications, but someone who has been going to the *mikvah* for many years begins to realize that every time she goes, she is totally transformed. She has cleaned every inch of herself to the extent that she becomes like a new being—all the callouses are removed and every knot combed carefully out of her hair. Over the years, a woman is constantly refining her methods and approach. A little toothbrush becomes an invaluable tool, or she finds that a plastic thread works better for her than dental floss, and she starts to use shampoo instead of soap for the final cleansing because its doesn't leave a film on the skin.

Paradoxically, all this emphasis on the physical leads to greater spiritual awareness. Physically, she has been refined down to her essence. In that state, she can feel herself existing as a soul in eternity.

And then, after all that work and checking to see that every nail is clipped and there are no loose hairs on the skin, only then is she ready to enter the *mikvah* itself. She holds her breath and immerses herself completely in the water. She comes up for air, and she is like a newborn. She says the blessing that is said by all Jewish women, and in her heart she whispers her personal prayers before she enters the waters again.

21

A House of Hopes

Chava Willig Levy

Etymology fascinates me. Take my name, for example. Chava, the biblical name for Eve, means *mother of all living*. As a little girl, I remember learning from my parents that names are very meaningful. Quoting the talmudic sages of long ago, they told me that parents are granted a moment of prophecy when they choose their newborn's name.

I took their words to heart. Not surprisingly, children have always made me weak in the knees. The fact that a 1955 bout with polio made me *very* weak in the knees never deterred me from my dreams of motherhood. My name was prophetic; surely it would contribute to my destiny.

But in spite of my name's all-embracing quality, it looked unlikely that anyone would want to embrace me or, consequently, that I would ever know the joy of embracing a child of my own. So, in spite of my reputation as a disability rights activist, I hardly protested when the entrance to my home town's new *mikvah* boasted a long stairway. *Mikvah* and motherhood: Frankly, I never thought I'd enter either institution. The barriers to the first were architectural; the barriers to the second, attitudinal. Together, they made me feel—not always, but often enough—powerless, insignificant, and isolated.

Chava Willig Levy dedicates this essay to her mother, Ella Willig, of blessed memory, "the first person to immerse me in *mikvah* waters and surely the person who prayed the hardest for that miraculous moment's arrival."

In His infinite mercy, the Master of the Universe felt my pain and, through the subtlest of orchestrations, sent me a wonderful husband. Today, *mikvah* and motherhood are two responsibilities I embrace with infinite joy. And now that the privilege and pleasure of using the *mikvah* is mine, I find myself once again intrigued by etymology.

The word *mikvah* means *a gathering of water,* as stated in Genesis (1:9): "Let the waters be gathered below the heavens to one place." For me, this verse evokes an image of powerless, insignificant, isolated droplets of water converging and ultimately becoming a mighty force. Maybe that is why the *mitzvah* of *Mikvah* is so precious to me: It reminds me that God can transform trouble into triumph in the blink of an eye. It reminds me that having a disability is *not* tragic. What's tragic is the stigma people attach to disability. What's tragic is being isolated, being left out. And *Mikvah* — derived from the concept of gathering — subtly reminds all of us that we must prevent that tragedy by gathering in each member of our community.

Mikvah also is linked to the word *hope*. It is the place where *tikvot,* "hopes," reside. How many of us have come to the *mikvah* to pour out our hopes to God? And isn't it interesting that for our *tevilah,* "immersion," and the *tefillah,* "prayer," accompanying it to be kosher, we have to stand before God just as He made us? *He* cares about our hopes, attaching no stigma to physical imperfections, be they large or small.

My first *mikvah* visit fulfilled a lifelong hope for marriage. On scores of subsequent trips, the *mikvah* renewed my hope that someday my husband and I would be blessed with a child. For six years, the fulfillment of that hope eluded us. I'd pray for other women struggling with infertility — partially, I confess, to hang my hopes on the Talmudic principle that one who prays for a friend is answered first.

One thing I could never hope for was privacy. Like many women, I cherish the anonymity surrounding the *mikvah* experience. But ironically, whenever I have to go to the *mikvah,* sometimes as many as eight women know about it — and who knows how many husbands! — simply because of the help I need getting to and from, and in and out of, the *mikvah,* not to mention my wonderful neighbors' busy schedules.

Before experiencing the miracle of seeing my hopes for a child — indeed, for children — fulfilled, there were many emotional *mikvah* visits. As the seasons turned, I felt like a member of the U.S. Postal Service: "Neither rain, nor snow, nor sleet, nor hail . . ." would deter me from my "appointed rounds." There had been rainy trips and snowy trips. There had been Friday nights and *Seder* nights, Purim nights, Rosh Hashanah nights, and post-Yom Kippur visits. Many were somber, tension-filled experiences. But one visit stands distinctly apart. It occurred on a winter evening, two years before our first child was born. Our *mikvah* lady greeted me with a solemn face.

"You shouldn't have come tonight," she disclosed in her thick European accent. "We have a terrible problem. In fact, you should go straight home."

My heart sank. Preoccupied with infertility, I believed timing was everything; a day lost could mean a month lost.

"What's wrong?" I asked.

She replied, "Our heater broke. The *mikvah* water is ice cold."

I burst out laughing. "Is that all? I thought you were going to tell me that the *mikvah* had no water!"

Needless to say, I took the plunge.

And, time after time, I feel the exhiliration of that plunge. The *mikvah* waters transform me from a woman with four atrophied limbs into—honest to God—a ballerina! For a few glorious moments, my arms extend effortlessly. And as I ascend unassisted the three bottom-most steps, I marvel at the miracle of human grace and motion.

Of course, with one more step, gravity returns. The mood, however, is anything but grave as my helper assists me up to the landing, back to our room, and into my clothing. Our conversation, ranging from the sublime to the ridiculous, flows so easily ("We've got to stop meeting like this," we often tell each other, sotto voce). It is inevitably the end of a long day. I ought to be exhausted; I'm thoroughly energized.

The *mikvah* waters are the primary source of my renewed energy. But coming in a close second is the *mikvah* bulletin board, whose array of business cards and announcements never fails to dazzle me as I head for the blow dryers. Promoting the services of psychiatrists, swimming instructors, social workers, and seamstresses; podiatrists, pianists, and public relations consultants; attorneys, artists, and advertising executives; caterers, cardiologists, and calligraphers, it puts to rest the stereotype some slap on those women committed to the *mitzvah* of *Mikvah:* "victims" of an "archaic, oppressive, offensive ritual." The way I see it, these women resemble the *mikvah* waters: a mighty force to reckon with, even if they enter this house of hopes one by one, with anonymity, without fanfare.

Perhaps that is why many women conclude their *mikvah* immersion with the *Yehi Ratzon* prayer, a plea for the rebuilding of the Temple in Jerusalem. They are busy women, but not too busy to shift their gaze from a tiny, holy house of hopes—where they pour out their personal dreams and dilemmas—to the holiest house of all, whose reconstruction will coincide with a universal dream come true and the resolution of all dilemmas: "Behold, I will bring them from the northern land and gather them from the ends of the earth, among them people who are blind and lame, preg-

nant and childbearing mothers together; a great congregation will return here"
(Jeremiah 31:8).

I believe that glorious gathering will occur because of the women who,
month after month, generation after generation, have whispered this prayer,
relinquishing their claim on God's personal attention for a greater cause.
Surely, in their merit, God will never relinquish His People. Surely, in their
merit, God will rebuild His house of hopes.

22

Honeymoon

Gwenn Drucker Flait

As the DC-10 lifted up and away from Los Angeles International Airport, I breathed a deep sigh of relief. Buildings, and cities, and smog gave way to white clouds, sunlight, and sky, and I was suddenly enveloped in that peace that usually comes only as I light *Shabbat* candles each Friday evening. (You know the feeling—when anything that hasn't been done no longer matters, and you finally just relax.)

Only four weeks earlier, I'd become engaged to a wonderful man. This was to be the second marriage for each of us, and we had numerous friends and relatives in Los Angeles. So we made the only "sane" decision—we would "elope" to Hawaii and be married by the *Chabad* rabbi in Honolulu.

In the course of preparations, I had made arrangements to learn the laws of Family Purity from a woman I respect and admire. The classes went well, but my difficulties had just begun.

I had carefully worked out the perfect wedding date, taking all possibilities regarding my monthly cycle into consideration, and I foresaw no problem. I continued to study the laws as I waited and waited and waited—but no period. To help get things started I tried herbal teas, homeopathic remedies, chiropractic adjustment, tears, and a lot of prayer.

The number of days until our wedding was quickly dwindling, and my body finally decided to cooperate—up to a point. My monthly cycle began, but a new problem arose: it would not end. More tea, more tears, more prayer.

By this time I had made up my mind. *I hated the laws of Family Purity* and all that went with them. I had never spent so much time (it seemed like every waking moment) concerned with my body's monthly functions. I was angry and overwhelmed. I had waited years for the right man to spend eternity with, and now—I felt—I was going to be of no value right from the start. I was convinced that I was at fault for what was happening. It's a feeling that I now believe is shared by many brides in this situation.

My husband-to-be was giving me his total support and being altogether terrific about the situation—so I was mad at him, too.

In the end, I was lucky. I found that I would be able to immerse in the *mikvah* on the evening following our wedding ceremony.

As the DC-10 began its final approach to Honolulu's airport, I had my first view of the tropical rain forests and volcanoes that form the Hawaiian Islands. I also had a clear view of the *mikvah* in which I would be immersing the next evening. It was very blue and very big—the biggest *mikvah* in the world in fact: the Pacific Ocean.

Yes, the Pacific Ocean. Hawaii, which has one Orthodox rabbi and a growing community of observant Jews, had no *mikvah* like the "mini-spas" of *mikvahs* found in Los Angeles or New York. So this certainly was a case of (no pun intended) "sink or swim."

The *chuppah* was beautiful. We were married under my husband's *tallit,* beneath a star-filled Hawaiian sky. The *minyan* consisted of ten Jewish men in varying styles of vacation wear who were brought together by the rabbi.

And there I was, radiantly happy in full makeup, contact lenses, and white wedding outfit.

After the *mazel tovs* were spoken and the miniature Danish eaten, I returned to my room to prepare for my first *mikvah* immersion. Instead of an address, we had received directions that would lead us to a deserted stretch of beach where the rebbetzin would be waiting.

Two hours after my *chuppah,* I found myself walking alongside my new husband in the hotel garage. Gone were the contact lenses, makeup, and new clothes. The bride was now decked out in eye glasses perched on a scrubbed face, an old head scarf, a terry cloth zip-up robe, and a pair of flip-flops. After my husband stopped laughing, we drove off into the Hawaiian night.

Our ride took us about twenty minutes along the Honolulu coast. The evening had turned overcast, and no moon could be seen. We arrived at a parking lot beside a long stretch of beach and waited in the car. My husband helped pass the time until the rebbetzin's arrival by telling me stories about sharks and their eating habits.

Just a few minutes later, the rebbetzin arrived, and she and I set off down the beach. As we walked along the shoreline, I glanced back and watched my husband slowly shrink in the distance. We turned a final bend, and were finally all alone.

It was dark. No, it was pitch-black. The ocean was the color of ink spilled on a sheet of black paper and I was going to walk into it and immerse? I could hear the surf softly hitting the shore as I gulped and moved forward. The rebbetzin waded into the water alongside me in order to explain the procedure and to declare the immersion "kosher." I was happy not to be alone.

Once my apprehension subsided a little, my old sense of adventure returned. I completed the ritual with speed and I hope at least a little *kavvanah* (depth of feeling) for the *mitzvah*. I do recall the rebbetzin saying that as a bride, I had a special closeness to God, and this was the moment for special thoughts and prayers.

"I don't want to have to do this again for a long time," was all I could think of.

I have now been married for eight months filled with much joy and happiness. They have also been filled with one major earthquake, two changes of address, a miscarriage, and several immersions in the *mikvah* (all indoors).

I still hate the separation (my husband is the one who finds it beautiful), hate the checking and the counting, and hate cutting my nails to the proper length. It still feels like an intrusion in my life, and I do it solely out of *Yirat Shamayim* (fear of heaven). Because God so commanded.

But I love the *mikvah* itself. I love that my husband continues to drive me there each month, and I love that he waits by the car for me to return. I love the time and attention the "*mikvah* ladies" always give—as well as their encouragement and counsel. And I love that each month, when I return to the car to go back home, my husband tells me once again that my face has a special glow.

23

Mikvah Dreams

Miriam Sagan

I live on the unfashionable west side of Santa Fe, where the neighborhood is small and funky, adobe houses sitting in well-tended yards of flax and hollyhocks or the neglected ones of dirt and panic grass with a few old car parts thrown in. Old men stand watering the small lawns with garden hoses innocent of nozzles. Every house has a dog, and every dog barks as I pass. This is a neighborhood visited by the moon and by drunks staggering from the liquor store; it is a neighborhood in which no one will win the lottery.

Within the blocks I walk, though, there is a passion of belief. My elderly neighbor Grace C. Baca wears a Virgin of Guadalupe pin; windows are numerous with the statues of saints dressed in rosaries. Down the block is the massage school for holistic healing, the Spanish Pentecostal Church, and turning the corner is my own husband, Robert, driving a Cherokee Jeep with a cracked windshield. He is a Zen Buddhist priest, head shaved, Bodhi beads wrapped around his wrist.

Around the corner, on Franklin Street, is my Hebrew teacher's house. As I walk I can feel prayer rise from the asphalt like mist after rain. My heart beats as I turn up her driveway and knock on her door. In this kitchen, on an old-fashioned lacy oilcloth, I have learned the Hebrew vowels and how to light the *Shabbat* candles; I have worried about Jacob's two wives and my own sister Rachel; I have learned an alphabet that once was forbidden.

I was raised to believe that although I was Jewish, and that this was a vastly superior way to be, religion itself was superstition and ignorance. My father instructed us: God is for children and morons, there is no God, and most important, my father decides what we believe. Without God, rabbi, or synagogue, my father's spiritual authority in the family was absolute. He controlled it all, and he proclaimed: You are an atheist.

I did not even dare to break this injunction until I was almost forty. Gradually I felt the pull. I put a *mezuzah* on my newly built studio. I told my friend Carol I was longing for something Jewish. When she told me there was a chasidic woman who taught Kabbalah literally around the corner from me, I knew I had to go study. When I called Yehudis and told her how surprised I was to find her she said, "When the student is ready, the teacher appears."

As soon as I learn the Hebrew alphabet, I begin to dream. I see the letters, large and dark, rising up like gates over me as I turn in my sleep. I'm reading whatever I can get my hands on about Judaism and feminism, women, spirituality. I'm trying to find a place for myself in a tribe I felt was made of old men wrapped in *tallises,* with no place for me. I keep coming upon the idea of *mikvah,* a pool, water; it has my favorite letter *mem* in it, after all—my name is Miriam with two *mems* in it, and Miriam's Well is a source of water, of inspiration, of healing, that follows me no matter how lost I am.

After Hebrew lessons, Yehudis takes me to her backyard to show me something, but somehow we get sidetracked, and she ends up opening the door to what I always assumed was a greenhouse. Inside it is a *mikvah,* a pool that from the doorway looks like a hot tub. But I'm astonished. It is as if it has appeared just for me. This is the only *mikvah** in New Mexico, perhaps the only one for a thousand miles. And it's right around the corner from me.

I go home thinking, "I have just got to get into it." It's becoming an obsession; I want in even if I don't know why. I start to dream about the *mikvah,* scary dreams of pools hidden in basements, of men chasing me, of blue desire. I can't shake the dreams. Finally I just tell Yehudis, "I want to get into this *mikvah.*" I know there must be lots of rules, and there are. She tells me to read a book on how it's done. I start reading. I knew that I had to wait until after my period, but I didn't quite realize I had to be celibate for at least twelve days.

I plop down next to my husband on the bed. I tell him I won't do this, it's ridiculous. But he is the one to encourage me and insist I do it properly. Here is a man who shaves his head and has a Japanese name, who has sat for seven days cross-legged facing a wall. He believes in ritual. He is also a Jewish boy from New Jersey. He has never been anything but positive about my foray into

---

*For background on how this *mikvah* was built see "Santa Fe," page 221. Chana Katz and her family moved from their home where the *mikvah* was built, and (at the time of this writing) Yehudis lives there.

Judaism. It is as if he believes more than I do that it is right for me. "Twelve days," I tell him, half hoping he'll insist that I'm so irresistible it can't be done. But he tells me it's fine.

I don't like the period of separation, and I didn't learn much from it except for bad things I already knew—I'm dependent and needy and scared of space. I don't think I need this *mikvah* for my marriage. After all, we've been together for a dozen years, we have a daughter, we've withstood sickness and death and mortgage. More important, because Robert has lived off and on in Zen monasteries and because I am writer, there is some solitude built into the relationship, some chosen path.

So I continue—not for my marriage, but for me. At least I have stopped dreaming every night about a *mikvah* I can't get into. When the right night arrives, I take a long bath and scrub with a loofah and fancy face scrub. I lounge. Sunset hits the corner of the bathroom window. I go to a Kabbalah class at the *shul,* come home and get a towel, then drive to the *mikvah* around ten o'clock at night. I don't want to walk in this neighborhood at this hour. I'm singing in my blue Toyota, out of the house, out of time, out under the cover of darkness. I feel the way I did when I rushed to the birth of my friend Debora's son.

The *mikvah* room seems to glow with blue light. I take off my clothes, and Yehudis checks me for stray hairs, dirty toes. I walk backward down the ladder into the pool. After the first immersion I can hardly breathe, my heart is pounding, my lungs seem to want water instead of air, everything is turning blue. I'm full of joy, this is real, I'm in the pool, the pool is in me, this is where I belong. Yehudis holds a scarf over my head, and I repeat the prayer after her. My mind is a blank; I couldn't do it myself. I go under again and again. Now I'm laughing and getting dressed, I'm going home.

It is *Rosh Chodesh* of *Elul,* a month to Rosh Hashanah. There is no moon in the sky. I did this to mark a conversion of sorts, of my own turning. I did this because secretly I hoped, secretly I knew or hoped I knew, that there was a place for me as a woman among Jews. This pool at Yehudis's house, marked with traces of New Mexico rain, was an entry way, a beginning. I went down into the pool, into the letter *mem,* into the moonless sky, into my name.

24
Going to the *Mikvah* (at My Age!)

Sybelle Trigoboff

It started when, on a routine physical examination, my family doctor discovered that an atypical cell had shown up in my pap smear. This could mean that I had some fatal disease or that it was "nothing," something that occurs occasionally to some women for no apparent reason. He retested and checked periodically over the next few months. Fortunately, within a year we knew it was the latter; it did not appear again.

However, upon hearing the good news, my husband's reaction was immediate, spontaneous, and funny. "You and I are going to Israel before it is too late!" This was something we had dreamed of doing in our old age. We simply could not afford it at that time. My reaction was even funnier since I knew we didn't have the funds. I said, "We're not going without the children."

We started trying to figure out how to manage the trip. The last payment was made on our one and only car, and we were about to pay our last bill from the orthodontist. This was surely a sign that we should go to Israel—all of us—before the next set of bills started again and while we were all in good health.

That July, three months before we were to celebrate our twenty-fifth wedding anniversary, all of us went to Israel.

One of the things that impressed me among the myriad things we saw and did was that wherever we went to old digs and sites, in all of the ancient Jewish cities, there was always a *mikvah*. They all seemed to be built alike, and whenever we read about them, they were always stressed as one of the most important priorities for our people.

The trip, the land, the people, the anniversary, the fact that we were all together in Israel and the potential illness and the resulting good health; the whole "package" changed our attitude about a lot of things my husband and I had previously taken for granted.

We realized how easy it was to be Jewish in Israel and how we had to work at being Jewish here in the United States. We started to look again at how we were living here in this Christian country.

I had always thought we were "religious." I lit candles every Friday night (although not always at the proper time), we had a kosher kitchen (but we would eat non-kosher out), and we celebrated all the Jewish holidays. We belonged to a temple and all of our children had been *bar* and *bat mitzvah*ed. But after we returned from our trip, we were determined to do and learn more about our heritage. My husband and I joined a *chavurah* group, and together we started a Jewish coffee house one evening a week. An Orthodox rabbi gave classes at the coffee house to anyone who was interested in learning. I went to every class. It was there that I heard of a class on Family Purity and decided to go. By this time I was menopausal. I went to the class more because I was curious than because I thought it would affect my life. My feeling was that I was too old to go to the *mikvah*. But I went to three classes anyway, one of which was a go-see trip to an active *mikvah* on Long Island.

I was impressed with the detailed care of the physical body and the attention to the spiritual aspects of family relationships, the preparation, the counting of days, the self-examinations, the body, the teeth, the showers, the baths, the blessings, etcetera.

I also had many fears as well. They ran the gamut from would the water be clean, too hot, too cold, would there be privacy, and so on.

I kept telling myself, *I'm too old for this, anyway; I have all my children, and I'm about to complete my menopause.*

And then I heard that *Mikvah's* effect could be retroactive.* My children would still be affected—would be blessed—by my going to the *mikvah*. I knew then that I was a goner. Fears or no fears, I knew I was somehow going to go and get "dunked." I wanted so badly to do this for my grown children and also for my future grandchildren.

When I had what I thought was my last period—I had completed my menopause—I finally got up the nerve and decided to go the *mikvah*. I would go once, and it would cover me and my children forever (or so I thought).

---

*For more on this subject see introduction, page xxxvi, and "A Mother's Gift," page 210.

I had very ambivalent feelings about *Mikvah*. I am an artist trying to stay on the cutting edge of the art world—working on my own paintings and teaching other artists in my studio—in an era of women's lib. Why should I now, at my age, at menopause, go to the *mikvah*?

I had always had this marvelous feeling of connection to all Jews at Passover time. As we sat around the *Seder* table with our family each year, I could imagine that all Jews were doing the same thing at the same time all over the world. When I saw the *mikvahs* in Israel at some of the "dig" cities and realized that they were exactly the same all over the world, and then learned that even today they are built to the same specifications, that same feeling of connection came over me again.

Growing up in Brooklyn, I guess I was like most families there at the time. We had a traditional Jewish home. My parents both came to America as children from Poland and worked hard to raise us children as Americans. Their Jewish traditions stayed with them all of their lives; they observed the Jewish holidays, kept a kosher home, and my mother lit candles every Friday night. They passed them on to us, but with a caveat; they believed it was their responsibility to make us as American as possible. For this reason a lot of observances were left behind and lost to us. Often they would make fun of themselves and other European Jews, now in America, for doing "old-fashioned" things. I got what I now believe to be lots of mixed messages from them: It was good to be Jewish—but not "too" Jewish in America.

My mother used to make *cholent* on Saturday; my father had to work six days a week to make a living and that included working on Saturday, but my mother would not do any work on Saturday. It was the only day of the week that I did not see her working in the house—cooking, cleaning, shopping, washing clothes, and so on. Instead she would relax and read her Yiddish newspaper and listen to the radio. My parents clearly felt that it was all right to be observant in Europe but not possible or desirable to do so in America.

I remember once the subject of *Mikvah* came up in conversation. My parents laughed and said that was what Jews did in the "old country," not here in America.

And now here I was, a grown woman with grown children, contemplating going to the *mikvah* for the first time in my life.

My husband and I talked a lot about this. Fortunately, he was very supportive throughout the entire learning and decision-making process.

I prepared myself scrupulously, as I had been taught. I was sure that this was going to be my one-time-for-life into the *mikvah,* and I would be finished forever.

I went! I did it! I felt wonderful! I was proud of myself for overcoming my fears. I wasn't afraid at all, due to the classes I had attended and the kindness of the "*mikvah* lady." She was most reassuring and helped me through what I thought would be a difficult thing to do. She also helped me overcome my fears and self-consciousness about going for the first time at my age. I felt so good about having accomplished this long overdue responsibility, for me and for the sake of my family. It felt real and right and good and clean, both physically and spiritually.

Then I got my period again—twice more as a matter of fact—and went two more times to the *mikvah* before I was finally finished. To my surprise, I felt just as good each time I went. There is a spiritual cleanness that is hard to describe.

The feeling of overcoming one's fears, the respect with which one has to treat oneself physically, the feeling of "clean" or "new" or "reborn"—these were not words in a book now, they were real emotions that I felt each time I submerged my body in the *mikvah* waters.

I was grateful to be given the opportunity at my age to bless my children, happy to have taken this long overdue step and feel that strong sense of connection to all Jewish women.

25

In the Depths

Liz Rosenberg

You must change your life.
— Rainer Maria Rilke, poet

This is the story of my own experience with *Mikvah*. I realize it is peculiar for two reasons: one, that I was an editorial consultant to this book of essays and, even more important, that I am not an observant Jew. I was not raised as an observant Jew. Religion, in my family, was more of a team sport than a spiritual exercise: you root for the Jews, eat lox and bagels on Sunday mornings, and try not to make too much of a fuss over Christmas. Religiously, I've lived most of my life as a hopeful agnostic, one in whom faith battles it out daily with despair, and despair with stubborn hope.

I can't pretend, either, that I will become a dedicated *mikvah* user. The regimen presents difficulties that I find off-putting. *Mikvah,* above all else, is based on belief, it is a manifest expression of Jewish faith. But I do believe in the power of such rituals, and believe, too, that there are mystical elements at work within them. Like the placement and movement of the stars, like the creation of our original *mikvahs*—the oceans—*Mikvah* touches on the elemental. It has depths beyond what the physical eye can see. Were I to try to become pregnant again, I would return to regular *mikvah* use. I think of it as a special blessing also for any bride, any woman undergoing menopause—

153

indeed, any woman in need of a spiritual transformation. Such ancient rituals have a power beyond what we can know rationally. Medical science has recently discovered, to its own amazement, the efficacy of prayer. *Mikvah* is an especially potent form of prayer; it is a ritual full of wisdom and irrationality, nakedness and power, humility and hope. It touches on the most elemental aspects of human beings and offers, I believe, a conduit between the physical and the divine.

A vast majority of our planet is given over to the brooding waters of the original *mikvah;* a vast majority of our time is devoted to ignoring all that and living on the surface of the land. *Mikvah* is not for the timid, not for the resistant. Yet even I have been transformed by my contact with it. My work on this book has been educational and, thanks to Rivkah Slonim and her family, an amazing joy. Jewish women have the right to know about something so peculiarly and intensely their own. Then they can choose, as they choose in every moment of their lives, whether or not to observe the laws of Torah. This anthology, I hope, is a step toward making this decision about the *mikvah* and finding the courage to enter its depths.

I first heard mention of *Mikvah* when my husband and I considered reaffirming our marriage vows in a Jewish service. Our "first" wedding was a rushed, secular affair that took place in a trailer in early December: the Justice of the Peace came late, and spoke, like Moses, with a heavy stutter. (There the resemblance ended.)

Almost ten years later, my husband consulted a friend, the local Lubavitcher rabbi, about a Jewish wedding service, and came back with news: before we could take part in an observant Jewish ceremony, I would have to take a ritual bath. A bath. That's all I heard. That's all I had to hear. The rabbi's wife—Rivkah—a woman I barely knew, would be with me.

"I'm not letting any strange woman give me a bath," I said. The subject dropped, and it was a long time before "the bath" came up again.

Three or four years later we were at the Lubavitcher rabbi's house, celebrating Sabbath along with a few hundred students from our local university: a typical Friday night at the local *Chabad* house, a surprise to us. Rivkah, the rabbi's wife, and I sat together at one of several long tables; we talked about students we knew in common, about my writing, then about her interest in putting together a book on the subject of Jewish sexuality. I told her that she should certainly go ahead: all I'd ever heard about Orthodox sex had to do with cutting holes in sheets. Rivkah laughed.

We were on our way out of the house—had already stepped out onto the dark driveway, my husband carrying our half-sleeping son—when Rivkah suddenly came rushing after us. I thought we'd left something behind.

"Wait. Please. I want to ask you something," she said to me, out of breath. She put one hand on my arm as if I might otherwise run away. "Please forgive my nerve, but this book—will you help me with it?"

Somehow I said yes. I didn't know this Lubavitcher woman from Eve, but there was something about her I liked: Rivkah was warm, capable, outspoken, devout—as different from me as if we'd been born and raised on separate planets.

It was a few months before she made good on her promise to call. I was busy, she was now four months pregnant with her fifth child. When she called to discuss the book, it was no longer about Jewish sexuality, but about *mikvah,* the ritual bath.

"You don't know what you're getting yourself into here," she warned me, half laughing, half serious.

She was right. I knew nothing about the *mikvah,* very little about Jewish law. And the winter we began to work together on the book was one of the worst in my life. I had been hit—struck down was more like it—by an overwhelming depression, a pit so deep that some days the only thing I *could* do was to look at the newest articles she had gathered, discuss changes, make small editorial suggestions. In exchange for my help, Rivkah was giving me Hebrew lessons, and the *Alef Bet* was one more thing I could manage, on days when I otherwise could barely drag myself out of bed. I would discover only months later that I was suffering from Seasonal Affective Disorder. All I knew then, as we approached the short, darkest days of the winter solstice, was that I was barely hanging on to the edge of some terrible precipice, the last scraps of my sanity.

Those weekly meetings with Rivkah, which may have begun as an act of charity on my part, became a saving grace. Learning calms and uplifts us. It may be our Jewish heritage or, more simply, a human one. As we worked, I learned about the *mikvah.* I came to see its beauty, not in the notion of clean versus unclean, but pure versus impure, which is to say life against death; that it is a ritual of transformation, blessed, guarded and kept by woman, in the province of woman. And I admired a religion that took account of sexual rhythms; the inevitable and sometimes debilitating ebb and flow of passion in long-term relationships. I necessarily learned more about *Halachah* observance—the laws of Torah. I even asked Rivkah to suggest one small *mitzvah* I might do. Without knowing anything about my depression, or its source, she recommended lighting the Sabbath candles on Friday night. Those small lights, coming at the end of the long, dark week, served as beacons that led me through the winter. They not only lit up the house, they marked time, transformed it. Even if only for a few moments in a week, there was a bright spot in life, literally and metaphorically.

I began marking time in other ways as well. In the name of research, I'd promised to go to the *mikvah* before we finished work on the book. My husband was as supportive in this as in everything else. I think he suspected it might actually help me — though he was no more observant than I. It was March — Rivkah and I had been working for months; we had read dozens of articles about *Mikvah,* so I knew something about this ritual's history, its emotional significance, its religious underpinnings.

But I still knew very little about the details of its actual observance. So one afternoon, taking time from the book and our Hebrew studies, Rivkah went through the *Mikvah* regimen with me, going over every detail several times, afraid she might forget something. Depressed and confused as I was, I was terrified that I would make some mistake that would shame us both.

In truth, preparation for *Mikvah* was simple, if too detailed for this brief essay. First I had to be sure my period had ended. Then I waited seven days. The night of the *mikvah,* I cleansed myself down to a bare essence, took a long bath, a short shower. Packed up a toothbrush, slippers, towel, a terry cloth robe for modesty.

Rivkah and I went to the *mikvah* at what seemed like the middle of the night. We worked our arrangements around babysitters, husbands, and one other woman who had reserved the *mikvah* earlier that evening. It was a comedy of near errors, missed phone calls, last minute instructions: Lucy and Ethel in the *shtetl.* It was bitterly cold out, the last lingerings of winter. I was still feeling depressed, anxious, unable to focus. Though I now confided in Rivkah, I tried to keep the worst to myself. Often I was afraid I would infect her with my misery, as if what I had was a bad case of flu. She was eight months pregnant; I was fearful of somehow affecting the sanity of the unborn child.

We had read dozens of articles about family purity and immersion. The *mikvah* pool loomed large in my mind. I pictured the waters of Eden, of totalitarian Russia, of the Holocaust. I remembered tales of women chopping holes in the ice, fleeing to trains with bundles under their arms, secretly digging out *mikvahs* with spoons and knives. Later, that summer, I would be vacationing on Cape Cod and step alone into the Atlantic Ocean at night to immerse in a grand-scale *mikvah* — nothing but the starry sky overhead, the white foam threading the black sea, the pounding of waves, its immensity. One could easily believe that here was the face of the waters over which God himself had hovered, before human beings, before human misery.

But what I saw that first night in March looked like two big bathtubs in a tiny back area of the Orthodox synagogue. The preparation room consisted of a tub, toilet, sink, and shower, neatly laid out with cleansing and beauty supplies, like a well-stocked bathroom in a Holiday Inn. Just past this room lay the *mikvah* itself, with its twin pools of "kissing" waters. It smelled a little like an indoor swimming pool at a high school, but not so chlorinated. Rivkah felt the water;

it was now only lukewarm. I said it didn't matter and went to take my shower. I brushed my teeth, made sure I'd removed all my jewelry. I walked into the *mikvah* area in a pink terry cloth bathrobe, shivering, clutching my towel.

Rivkah said, "You're freezing, and the water isn't even hot." She looked ready to cry. I'm sure I looked worse. I said again that it didn't matter, and it didn't. I took off the bathrobe, more worried that I'd forgotten something—a necklace? a Band-Aid?—than about standing in front of my new friend without clothing. By then we'd bared our souls a few times; a body was nothing compared to that. I stepped down into the *mikvah* pool, which was very clean, small, square, not very warm. My teeth were chattering, though whether from being wet from the shower, the coolish water, the strangeness of the late evening, my own unshakably black depression, I couldn't have said.

Rivkah had once told me that when you're in the *mikvah,* it's a good time for special prayers. Before I went in, I'd had a whole set of requests and blessings in mind. Once I went under the water, everything seemed to wash out of my head but one last thing: I prayed to be returned to sanity.

I ducked under the surface of the *mikvah,* careful not to touch the sides of the pool. I burst back up out of the water, breathless.

"Kosher," Rivkah said. I couldn't hear her from the water in my ears, but I saw her lips move. I put a towel on my head, folded my arms under my breasts, and, repeating the words after Rivkah, said the Hebrew prayer. I immersed twice more. Each time Rivkah was watching, waiting for me, saying "kosher" the instant I emerged.* By the time I got out of the *mikvah,* my whole body was shaking. I was still anxious, still depressed, though trying hard not to show it.

I stumbled into the pink robe that Rivkah held out for me. "You're shaking," she said. "Look at you!"

"I'm fine," I said. In truth, I was no colder than I normally am at home after a bath and shower. I walked back into the little preparation room to change back into my street clothes. I began to think of everything I had intended to pray for: universal peace, my son and husband, friends and family, a special prayer of hope and blessing for Rivkah's unborn child. I felt ashamed. Their images came before me, one by one. I prayed then, anyway, belatedly, in the synagogue bathroom. I thanked God for blessings. It was the first time in months I had been able to think of anything but myself, my depression.

Standing there in the tiny room, it was as if a fog had lifted. A brief respite, a change. I realized it had already begun—almost against my will, certainly without my knowing it, borne along by the tide of something larger than myself, the *mikvah* had already begun to convey its blessings.

---

*When the *shomeret* (woman who accompanies and watches a woman immerse in the *mikvah*) says *kosher,* then in the heavens on high it is pronounced *kosher* and she is blessed (*Arizal*).

26
Renewal

Pamela Steinberg

I don't talk to many people about the *mikvah,* the ritual bath; it's hard to describe the ritual in a word or two. People assume that it's related to a blood taboo and that it implies that women somehow become dirty when they menstruate. I see the *mikvah* ritual on a much higher spiritual level that transcends any notion of "dirty" and "clean."

The first time I went to the *mikvah* was when I was twenty-one, the day before I was married. My mother never went to a *mikvah,* but my husband is religious and he urged me to go. All I remember is cleaning myself totally, and then the *mikvah* attendant insisted that I wipe the polish off my nails and cut them down. I was upset because I wanted to have polished nails for my wedding. People had told me what to do in the *mikvah,* but no one had explained why.

It wasn't until I traveled around with my husband after we were married that I sensed the *mikvah* has greater meaning than simply a thorough physical cleaning. I visited a *mikvah* next to the House of Love and Prayer—a synagogue for hippies—in San Francisco. The *mikvah* attendant there was a beautiful, observant earth mother who was very excited by the *mikvah.* I thought, if a woman like *that* loves the *mikvah,* there has to be something more to it. The second *mikvah* I visited was in Santa Fe, and the woman there was hasidic and also very spiritual. After these two experiences, I studied Jewish texts and learned that the *mikvah* ritual is really an affirmation of a woman's femininity and creative potential.

Jewish women like myself, who weren't brought up with the *mikvah* ritual, are in a unique position. We've taken on the obligation by choice, so we have a fresh outlook on the tradition that we can pass on to our children and to other women.

Basically, when a woman has her menstrual period, she is *tumah.* Some authorities translate this to mean ritually impure: When the Temple existed in Jerusalem, a menstruating woman could not enter it. I believe *tumah* is more closely linked to the fact that a menstruating woman has lost the potential fetus inside her; this loss brings her closer to death, puts death inside of her—she is, then, physically impure. After the *mikvah,* she is *taharah,* ritually pure. She is returned to her creative potential; she is able to conceive again. In a sense, she becomes godly. In the past, some Jews translated these terms as clean and unclean—that's why the *mikvah* ritual was seen as some kind of denigrating procedure, an enforced cleansing.

I'm not concerned with the idea that the Bible tells a man who has sex with a menstruating woman that "he'll be cut off from his people." What does concern me is the chance of damaging the potential offspring. There is a strong belief that a child who is conceived when some sense of death remains on the mother is at a spiritual disadvantage. Who knows why some people have great fortune in life while there are others for whom nothing seems to go right? Just as I don't smoke or drink alcohol when I'm pregnant to nurture my genes *physically,* I go to the *mikvah* to nurture my genes *spiritually.*

I'm always tremendously excited right before I go to the *mikvah.* I feel tingly all over. You remember how it felt when you had a boyfriend and you anticipated what would happen when you were with him? There was a certain sense about you; you even walked differently. Since my husband and I separate from each other physically during my *tumah* days, I feel as if I'm courting a strange man.

Just before the *mikvah,* you're required to soak in a bathtub. I lie in the tub and daydream about being suspended in water. I imagine a blue or gold light coming out from within me, a glowing cocoon around me, like the feeling of the sack in a womb surrounding a baby. Then I rinse my hair, blow my nose, clean my ears, and wash my bellybutton. Sometimes I even giggle.

After soaking in the bathtub and taking a shower, I buzz the *mikvah* lady and she comes with me into the *mikvah* in the adjoining room. Once I'm in the *mikvah*—the bath itself—I want the water to seep into me, into my pores. I dunk three times and say the traditional prayer and then dunk seven more times for the seven days of the week. This is a custom I learned from a friend who studies Jewish mysticism: Seven is the number of God's emanations.

Although I like to concentrate on the spiritual aspects of the ritual, the *mikvah* also provides a powerful way to get in touch with yourself as a woman, to sanctify your body's cycle, as a human being who's part of a universe that has its own cycles. Just as we can celebrate the waxing and waning of the moon, we can celebrate our bodies, not degrade them. I've heard of a *mikvah* where a woman's nails were cut to the quick and filed with Clorox on sandpaper until they became white. I can just picture these crazed ladies with shaved heads concentrating on what's dirty—punishing themselves for being women.

Divine rules are created in totality: They are designed to benefit you, your husband, your offspring. The *mikvah* heightens my physical consciousness and increases my desire for my husband. In fact, I can't think of any drawback to the *mikvah* as I use it—even the part that keeps me away from my husband for twelve days each month. These laws were passed down in a divine way, not written by a group of angry men. Men can be sexists, women can be sexists, but I don't think God is a sexist.

27

A Pilgrim on the Road Less Traveled

Marilyn Wolfe

On a cold, gray, blustery Chicago morning, I wrapped my overcoat around me, fastening the sash securely. The rushing air frantically seeking an outlet was trapped between the skyscrapers. The winds blew steadily all morning. It was weather for endings and beginnings.

Settling into a seat on the 147 Outer Drive Express, I contemplated again with nervousness and excitement the prospect of becoming a Jew. I was riding this bus for the very last time as Marilyn, daughter of Joseph, the son of Joseph, and of Margo, the daughter of Bern. When I returned I would be someone else, I would be Miriam bas Avraham Avinu and Sarah Imainu.[1] In essence, I was traveling to the *mikvah* to attend my imminent birth as a Jew.

When I tell this story to my children, they say in Darth Vader-like voices "You must become a Jew; it is your Destiny!" My destiny? I believe it was. That day my destiny and my destination were intricately tied.

The *mikvah* lady greeted me cheerfully in the vestibule and showed me where to hang my coat. I took a seat on the bench while she grabbed a large and a small towel, brown-paper slippers, and a white sheet with slits in it. *So this is the mikvah,* I thought. It had an interesting-looking interior—austere face-brick walls from floor to ceiling without embellishment save two framed extra-large notices. The first listed *mikvah* hours and fees, the second, a "let the buyer beware" caveat to converts. Before I could finish reading, the *mikvah* lady called, "Come this way, your room is ready and the *Beit Din*[2] has arrived."

I followed the *mikvah* lady behind the reception area to the central hub of the building. Like wheel spokes, four corridors shot off the hub to a dozen identical preparation rooms and a hair-drying room cum library. The face-brick motif gave me the feeling of being in a cave, not an unpleasant feeling at all; rather, it evoked a heightened sense of protection and of history.

I had read about the royal fortress Masada, resting atop a Judean mountain plateau. The fortress and the mountain: hewn stone upon impervious rock. The fortress had two *mikvaot*. These *mikvaot* were carved out of the mountaintop in the fortress floor. There is profound symbolism here: the integrity of the Jewish family is upheld by the *mikvah,* and the Masada *mikvaot* are cut into the mountain upholding the fortress. I was transported. The brick walls and concrete floor enveloped the Chicago *mikvah* as surely as the mountain enclosed Masada.

The *mikvah* lady led me into the preparation room: a large, simple bathroom with the ever-present face bricks, a vanity, a toilet, and a ceramic tiled shower–tub combination. She laid a fresh rug on the floor and placed the towels on the vanity. "Take a shower and comb your hair. Then wrap up in a towel. When you are ready, pull the buzzer string, and I'll be back. Please, take your time." With a warm smile she closed the door behind her. *Well,* I mused to myself, *here you are. This is it.*

I bent over and adjusted the water temperature in the shower and drew the curtain, kicked off my shoes into the "closet," then sat down on the blue-upholstered stool next to the vanity and began to remove my socks, which I hastily stuffed into my shoes. I was putting away the life I had lived until this moment. A sweater. Catholicism. A sock. Christmas. A dress. Today I was leaving behind my old life and how I was living it and joining a new people. My relationship with my family was about to be dramatically altered on a spiritual and cultural level. Slowly, I hung my clothes neatly on the hanger. I moved deliberately, not with remorse, but with respect. These are the people and things that formed my past, and ultimately they enabled me to seek out my Jewish destiny. I stared at my clothes and thought, *Maybe I should have brought new clothes to change into.*

Although my conversion was about to separate me from my family, my family would remain an important part of my life. My mother was very hurt by my decision to convert, but not for religious reasons; she felt I was abandoning her emotionally. I was her firstborn. The depth and the strength of our attachment to each other defies my ability to describe it. That it was painful and frightening to her was the only difficult part for me in converting. I reminded her that she brought me up to choose good things, and this is no different. No matter where I go or what road I follow, I will always love her and she will be a part of my life. The Torah instructs us to honor your mother and father. It was tearful reassurance. No matter how much a parent wants a child to become independent, it is always difficult to let them cross over that bridge.

I was converting after many years of thinking about it. I had read with fascination more than a hundred books on the Jews, on Judaism, the Holocaust, and Jewish history. The more I read, the more I wanted to know. When the topic was the Jews, this was always true. My interest in Judaism was a part of me even in childhood. My mother had grown up in a Jewish neighborhood. My grandfather's dearest friend, although long gone, is still affectionately referred to as "Mr. Kaplan."

My grandfather, an emigrant from the Philippines, lived down the block from a synagogue and a Jewish day school. I loved to visit him so that I could look at the Hebrew letters on the building. The letters were exotic and beautiful. They gave me a feeling of reverence, too; Sister Radagundie in my Catholic school passionately told our class the Bible stories about the Jews. I knew the Bible had been written in Hebrew, just like those signs on the synagogue and school.

When I was a child, it seemed to me that my mother knew a lot about Jewish practices. When I was only six or seven, I asked her many questions about the Sabbath. It was from my mama that I first learned about *cholent*[3] and that Jews don't drive or cook on the Sabbath. I told my mother then that I wanted to be a Jew when I grew up. She told me "Jews don't look for converts, Jews are usually born Jews."

I climbed into the shower and lathered the soap in my hands. Water beaded on my face and sprang rivulets amid the lather. I stepped away from the spray and soaped up from head to toe. How invigorating showers can be. They wash the sleepiness out of us in the morning. After exercising or hard, perspiring work, a shower makes us presentable to the world again. At the end of a long and dead-tiring day, a shower can revive you. It's the water. Water has many properties; water sustains life, it cleanses, it soothes, it refreshes. Water revives.

So essential to life, water can also bring death. Before we are born we are formed and develop in a watery womb. A developing baby would die outside that water world. Ironically, after we are born, we can't survive very long in a water-filled room.

For the convert, the *Bet Din* is both mother and midwife. The *Bet Din* nurtures the convert to a critical level of Jewish development and remains spiritually responsible for the "newborn" for a very long time, fostering observance and encouraging learning. The womb of the *Bet Din* is the *mikvah*. From this womb will emerge not a new physical being but a new spiritual one. It is the same womb that gave spiritual birth to the Jewish people in the Sinai.

After the Jews fled Egypt, on the eve of the giving of the Torah, the entire Jewish people immersed themselves in a *mikvah*. It was not a *mikvah* in a bathhouse, but a natural body of water. The Jews immersed to remove the negative spiritual debris, called *tumah,* (some of them) acquired in Egypt. By immersing in the *mikvah,* they reaffirmed their commitment to the covenant God made with Abraham. A few Egyptians fled with the Jews, like Batya, Pharaoh's daughter who raised Moses. The Egyptian sojourners converted at this time by immersing in the *mikvah,* and they joined with the children of Abraham in saying *Naaseh v'nishmah* ("We will do and we will hear") at *matan Torah.*[4]

"We will do and we will hear." You wouldn't generally want to do business this way: I'll do whatever you say; then I'll sit down and study the contract. *Naaseh v'nishmah* implies absolute trust in God by the Jewish people. Our sages tell us that the Jews were given the Torah on the sole merit that they would accept any commandment God would ask of them without knowing any of the details. God's asking was detail enough.

The *midrash* tells that God searched the entire world for a people who would accept His Torah. God asked the Egyptians, the Greeks, the Romans, and others if they would like Him to be their God and He would give them His Torah. The nations first wanted to know what this Torah would require them to do. God, the *midrash* continues, says, "You shall have no other gods before Me." "Sorry," they said, "it's not our custom." Each in turn rejected God's offer, finding fault with one or another of the *mitzvot.*[5] When God came to the Jewish people, they said *Naaseh v'nishmah:*[6] "We will do and we will hear." No questions asked. With that, God embraced and blessed the Jewish people and gave them the Torah at Mount Sinai.

Reb Avraham *ger tzaddik*[7] (righteous convert) of Vilna, a Polish prince who converted to Judaism, explained that this *midrash* has particular significance for the convert. The other nations did not respond "no" unanimously. There were a few individuals who wanted to accept the Torah, but their voices were drowned out by the unaccepting masses. Reb Avraham writes that it is the descendants of those unheard individuals who have merited to become Jews through conversion.

A convert is converted in the *mikvah* because the *mikvah* water represents a life–death nexus. Since human life cannot be sustained underwater, the *submerging* in the *mikvah* water represents the death of the old life. At the same time a human being begins its life by *emerging* from water. Life always emerges from death: it is the way God ordered the universe.

There are two ways to view life — as either a process of living or as a process of dying. The two processes come together in the *mikvah* water during conversion. The Torah states: *V'chai bahem*[8] — "and you shall live by them." "Them" refers to the *mitzvot*. The passage has twofold meaning. First, you shall live according to the *mitzvot* in this life. Second, the verse infers that the *mitzvot* will not only sustain your life in this world, but adherence to the *mitzvot* will merit you life in the world to come. A convert is accompanied to the *mikvah* by the sins of the past life. When the convert submerges in the water, that past life is killed off (symbolically speaking). When the person emerges she or he is a new and unblemished soul.[9]

I turned off the shower and grabbed the towel. As I dried myself, the lucite-covered conversion notice posted on the wall caught my eye. I read it as I combed out my hair.

Statement of the Rabbinic Committee Concerning Conversions[10]

Use of the Mikvah for conversion ceremonies should in no way be construed as a sign of approval or recognition of the validity of these procedures by the Rabbinic Committee or by any other recognized Halachic authority.

Use of a Kosher Mikvah does not guarantee the Kashrus of the conversion.

The Rabbinic Committee hereby states that it in no way countenances any conversion that does not meet the time honored requirements of Halacha [Jewish Law] as codified in Shulchan Aruch and as practiced throughout the generations.

Conversion is not just an immersion ceremony during which the candidate gives the right answers to certain prescribed questions. In order for the conversion to be valid, the prospective convert must unequivocally and without reservation accept and sincerely intend to observe all the mitzvos of the Torah and all Rabbinic laws as codified in Shulchan Aruch and formulated by the accepted Halachic authorities.

To cite some examples:

Shabbos must be observed in all its halachic details as it has been practiced throughout the ages.

Kashrus dietary laws must be carefully observed in all its halachic details as it has been practiced throughout the ages.

Taharas Hamishpacha the laws of Jewish Family purity which include abstinence from marital relations during the menstrual period and the prescribed period thereafter and use of the mikvah prescribed in Shulchan Aruch and observed throughout the generations.

It was like the poster was inquiring, "Are you sure you are ready to say you will live like a Jew? It is the Torah that makes Jews—Jews. Will you live by its laws no matter which way the world goes?" I thought the rabbinic statement was a bit strong, but on the other hand it had to be. The poster was the final warning light to alert you to the enormous significance of what you were about to do. Conversion is a commitment on the level of marriage. My eyes were open. My heart quickened with eager anticipation. I was ready to fully embrace the life they were describing.

I wanted to be able to say, "Blessed are You our Lord, King of the Universe who has commanded *us*," and know that I was a member of *us* the commanded by God. I believed in God my whole life and wanted to be a part of His people. I rang for the *mikvah* lady. I was ready.

Notes

1. Daughter of Abraham our father and Sarah our mother.
2. A Jewish ecclesiastical court of three judges.
3. The traditional Sabbath stew, eaten at lunch time on the Sabbath.
4. The giving of the Torah at Mount Sinai.
5. Commandments.
6. Exodus 24:7.
7. Reb Avraham forsook his title and family to embrace Judaism. Later, he was burned at the stake for his renunciation of Catholicism.
8. Leviticus 18:5
9. From a discussion I had with Rabbi Moshe Soloveichik, *shlita.*
10. Excerpted from the actual statement of the Chicago Rabbinical Council.

28

The Woman on the Podium

Ellin Ronee Pollachek

Let's say you've decided to go to a lecture. I don't know what your specific interests are, but let's pretend that it's a lecture on the arts. Or perhaps there's a special scholar speaking in a nearby university, and a friend asks you to go and you accept.

In actuality, the lecture you are attending is more about *why* the slide on the screen is a photograph of a work of "art" than it is about any single work. You don't necessarily agree with the woman giving the explanation, but you like listening to her. And you can identify with her. She's a contemporary of yours, attractive, modern. She talks. You listen. You realize she's an artist and her work is . . . well, it's transgressive, unconventional, committed to subverting a system that she believes needs subverting.

Afterward at the wine and cheese party, you start talking to her. That's when you find out she's married; she has no kids and she's Jewish. In retrospect, you're not sure how the topic came up, but she tells you that she goes to the *mikvah*. It's a rather personal bit of information, and you're not quite sure what to do with it. The information is somehow unsettling. It doesn't make *sense*. In other words, you would never associate a woman like this going to a *mikvah*, immersing herself in a holy bath every month after her period. You wouldn't

---

The author wants to thank Rabbi Shlomo Carlebach for his wisdom and his insights into the *mikvah* and, of course, Rabbi Ephraim Buchwald, who made it all possible.

think a woman that smart would buy that "women are dirty" stuff. So what's the scoop?

The scoop, which isn't a scoop at all, is the duality of this woman's life. The duality of many women's lives. Sure, there are the "obvious" *mikvah* goers: the typically heavyset Jewish woman with a wig that's never quite straight; or maybe she's not heavy, maybe she's quite attractive but she *never* wears pants, always looks "ladylike" in that Eisenhower sort of way. Her pride and joy are her children and if, God forbid, she doesn't have them, she's in agony every day. Every day. Whether she has children or not she generally has another job as well. Perhaps teaching at a girls' *yeshivah,* perhaps working as a secretary or a freelance artist. You're not going to find her on the Alps with Ivana Trump. Or so you think.

In truth, what we have here are assumptions. Assumptions about women we rarely get to "know." Those of us in the secular world, like the secular world in general, base our knowledge of others on appearances. So what's with the woman at the lectern? In fact, what's the point altogether?

The point is that I'm the woman on the podium, and while I certainly don't walk around with a sign on my back saying that I go to the *mikvah,* my attendance there seems pretty inconsistent with who I am. So much so that when I'm traveling and go to *mikvahs* I've never before attended, it becomes clear from the attendant's questions of me that she thinks it's my husband who is "the religious one," and I'm just going along for the ride.

Nothing could be further from the truth.

What is it about the *mikvah* that seems wrong, out of date—offensive to us as modern women? Is it something intuitive that says we shouldn't go, or is it something external to us? It's something external, isn't it? It's similar to what Adam and Eve took in when they took a bite from the fruit of the tree of knowledge of good and evil. The problem wasn't *just* that they disobeyed God but rather that, in their disobedience, humankind internalized something we've been trying to rid ourselves of ever since: duality. By eating of the tree of knowledge of good and evil we incorporated into our bodies knowledge of good and knowledge of evil. Prior to that everything was one. Our nakedness was neither good nor evil—it *was.* Dominion over the animals was again neither good nor evil—it *was.* By eating the fruit, we incorporated within ourselves what linguists now refer to as the *binary discourse system*—the either/or, black or white, good or bad, young or old, ugly or beautiful sense about things. We lost the unity of creation and moved into a *this or that* way of thinking.

So what has this got to do with the *mikvah?* The *mikvah* is water. Water not only represents unity—it *is* unity. Even a droplet is a body—always connected to itself, always unified, following itself downstream until it reaches a larger body of water. We can live far longer without food than water. We accept that because we know it's true. If we fast, it's thirst that gets us long before hunger. Cola won't do. Nor will wine or milk. Water is what we want.

So why is it that we can acknowledge our physical need for water but not our spiritual one? In large part it's because as products of a culture focused on the physical, we also focus on the physical. Our diets. Our cholesterol levels. Our skin tone. Our laugh lines. We *live* in our bodies.

But what of our souls. Don't they exist?

If knowledge is our only true test (like knowing how thirsty we get), then at what age did we learn how to make our blood pump, our menstrual cycles begin, our hair turn gray, our breasts develop? If knowledge is all, and we really are in charge, why is it that we spend so much time correcting ourselves with braces on our teeth, nose jobs, liposuction, and heaven knows what else? If we're in charge, then how come one family gives birth to a Mozart or a Cezanne and another to a Forrest Gump? Before you get excited and think I have the answer, let me tell you that, joyfully, I don't. I say "joyfully" because if I did, I'd never have time for myself—what with all those talk shows I'd be invited to.

But what isn't a mystery is that there are aspects of our being we will never understand, aspects that provoked Walt Whitman to write, "Do I contradict myself? / Very well then I contradict myself / (I am large, I contain multitudes)." The experience is universal.

So what's so offensive about the *mikvah?* We're not offended by having to drink water, knowing that if we don't, we die. What's so offensive about immersing oneself in a pool of water? We swim in heavily chlorinated pools—or at least cool off in them. What's so offensive?

Well, there's that passage that says that because a woman is dirty after her menstrual cycle she needs to be cleansed before she can unite sexually with her husband. That's pretty offensive, isn't it? Especially since "dirty" means you've been rolling around in the mud too long. Or it means you smell. Or you've been standing over a hot stove. But you're not dirty, you say. You shower daily, powder and pamper yourself, get a bikini wax, have your nails done. You even douche. So you're not dirty.

The Bible doesn't say "dirty." Actually it says pure and impure. It says the woman is *impure* after her menstrual cycle. So what's the difference?

All the difference in the world.

Pure means open to receive. Open to receive what? The depth of her oneness, her connection with her husband, herself, her God. The word that is used is *tumah. Tumah* is related to the word *satoom,* which means "to be stuffed up." When a woman is *tameh* she is not available to receive. Not physically—obviously she can have sex with whomever she wants and receive the physicality of the act—but what she cannot receive is the spiritual unity that comes from God, her husband, and her self. And only she—you—can provide that. It is the woman who brings the ability to receive to the equation. It is the woman who brings her husband to that level.

We are the earth, the soil, in which life grows—and, granted, plenty of women give birth without every going to the *mikvah*. Maybe you don't want to give birth. Well, let me tell you a secret. Neither do I. But I still go to the *mikvah*.

Immersing myself in the waters is walking off the podium, closing all the books, putting that fight I had with my husband or boss or mother or daughter (if I had one) on the outside where it belongs. Immersing oneself in the holy waters is acknowledging *my* humanity, *my* creation, *my* participation in the creative process. Immersion is acknowledging *my* composition, *my* blood, *my* God. In a world in which I am, as are most of us, rendered helpless by people officiating over concerns that are as foreign to me as Aramaic, once a month I get to do something holy, something beautiful, something that ties me to my foremother, Sarah, and all of her descendents who were willing to risk their lives to immerse themselves in a *mikvah*. In America, it is all so easy. And yet very complicated.

So if you think immersing yourself in a *mikvah* is demeaning, may I ask you to ask yourself where that idea came from. Was it from someone you know and love and honor? Was it from someone who wanted only the best for you? Or was it from a magazine or a book? Or worse, was it from a woman on a podium who knew all about art and science and literature and math but didn't know a thing about you?

III

Memories and Tales

29

The Magid's Wife

Adapted and Translated by

Rivkah Slonim

On a bitter cold night in the city of Mezritch, in White Russia, the rebbetzin, wife of the renowned Magid, made her way to the *mikvah*. Reb Dov Ber the Magid was known far and wide for his scholarship, piety, and above all else, his supernatural vision. Unfortunately, the great Magid's fame was matched only by his poverty. The couple lived as humbly as the poorest peasants. The rebbetzin had no money with her that evening, not even the nominal fee necessary to pay for entrance to the *mikvah,* nor did she want to worry her husband, since he had no money either. She hoped that the *mikvah* attendant would permit her entry without the requisite payment.

Alas, upon her arrival, the woman on duty proved to be a jaded and heartless type. She cruelly forbade the rebbetzin entry to the *mikvah*.

Her heart heavy with disappointment, the rebbetzin retraced her steps along the dark, icy road to her home.

Suddenly, to her great surprise, a carriage drew up alongside her. Within it she saw four women, obviously wealthy and of extraordinarily regal bearing. They asked her what she was doing on the road alone at that hour. Weeping, she related how she had been turned away from the *mikvah*.

"How lucky!" they exclaimed. "We are on the way to the *mikvah* ourselves. Come along with us, and we'll be happy to pay for you as well." Trembling with gratitude at this unexpected reversal, the rebbetzin accepted their kind offer and climbed into the carriage.

The women did indeed pay for her entry. The rebbetzin thanked them profusely, and with an uplifted spirit she used the *mikvah,* then made her own way home.

There, her saintly husband detected something about his wife, for there was almost an aura about her. When he questioned her about her evening, she recounted her initial heartbreak at the *mikvah* and then the elation brought on by the kindness of total strangers.

"Ah," said the Magid, smiling. "Your benefactors are *not* unknown to you after all. They were our Matriarchs, Sarah, Rebecca, Rachel, and Leah. You brought them down to earth through your tears. They heard your plea and came to take you to the *mikvah.*"

30

The Sweet Scent of a
Mitzvah

Menashe Miller

It was in the winter of the year 1724 that Reb Baruch, a simple innkeeper, received a blessing for children from the Baal Shem Tov, a man he knew only as a *tzaddik* cloaked in the obscurity of poverty and anonymity.

Just a few weeks later, on the first night of Chanukah, Reb Baruch's wife set out for the neighboring town of Uman. It was the night when the monthly period of separation was over. She was traveling to Uman in order to immerse in the *mikvah*, to purify herself so that she could reunite with her husband.

The forces of evil had roused themselves in strength to try and prevent Reb Baruch's wife from accomplishing her task. They knew that a very great soul was waiting to descend into the world, and that this woman was the vessel through whom this soul would be born.

The water was supposed to have been heated for her, as her health was fragile and delicate. But as she lowered herself downward, she noticed that the water was icy cold. Still, she did not hesitate. She immersed herself in the icy *mikvah*. After she emerged from the *mikvah,* she got dressed and stepped out,*

---

*"When a woman emerges from the *mikvah,* she should encounter another woman before any other living being, and that woman should touch her so that the first living being she encounters after immersion should not be an impure entity—e.g., a dog, a donkey, a pig, a horse. . . . When the first living being she encounters is one of the above, if she is a God-fearing woman, she should return and immerse herself again" (*Kitzur Shulchan Oruch,* Code of Jewish Law 162:10).

shivering, into the night air. Suddenly a black cat jumped out screeching in front of her. Back she went into the *mikvah* a second time.

This time Reb Baruch's wife managed to walk several steps toward the waiting coach before a huge, fat pig ran from behind the back of a barn, grunting, honking, and scaring her half to death. Back she went, into the freezing waters of the *mikvah*.

She was almost in the coach a third time when a ferocious-looking black dog leapt out of nowhere, barking and gnashing his teeth and snapping at her feet. The servant girl who had accompanied her begged her not to go into the waters again. "That would be too much even if your health were good," the servant girl argued. "We'll come back tomorrow night and try again."

But her mistress insisted. "More than meets the eye is going on here," she replied. "I've never had so much happen to try to stop me from immersing in purity all of my life as on this one night. It must be a test from on high. And if that is the case—back into the water I go."

And she did. Leaning on her servant girl's arm, breathing with great difficulty because of the cold, Reb Baruch's wife entered the water for the fourth time.

And this time a miracle occurred. The ice-cold water suddenly was warm to the touch. A sweet delicate fragrance of spice and tropical flowers—the scent of Eden—wafted upward from the surface of the *mikvah* waters. As the inn-keeper's wife immersed in the warm fragrant waters, she could feel the aches and pains she had suffered for so long melting away. Strength returned to her fragile limbs; she felt her body wholly renewed.

As she pulled herself out of the water, an idea, a strategy for evading the evil one's traps, occurred to her. She held on to her maidservant's waist, closed her eyes, and allowed the young girl to guide her through the street to where the carriage was waiting.

The servant girl was the first person to notice that the delightful scent that had risen up from the *mikvah* waters now emanated from her mistress.

As they arrived home, Reb Baruch also smelled the lush, sweet fragrance that had suddenly filled the room. Though he didn't say anything, his wife could sense that he was displeased. Her sharp intuition told her something was wrong.

"Baruch," she said, "what's the matter? What have I done to upset you?"

"My dear wife," answered the innkeeper, "how can I fail to be upset? Do we not see with our own eyes how many of our brothers and sisters are impov-erished and downtrodden and don't know where their next meal will come from—let alone their next suit of clothes? Don't you think it would be better to spend our money to help them eat, to help them live, than to spend it on perfume? And one so expensive at that!"

Reb Baruch's wife listened to her husband's outburst without interrupting him. But after he fell silent, she asked him with a smile playing on her lips, "Baruch, since the two of us were married, have you ever known me to be extravagant and seek luxury? You must admit, this is not a trait of mine. Perhaps there is more here than meets the eye—or the nose, as the case may be. If you are interested, I will tell you exactly what happened to me at the *mikvah*—something wonderful, something miraculous.

She told her husband everything that had happened to her, all the obstacles she had encountered as she attempted to complete her immersion in purity, and her final triumph after which the *mikvah* turned from icy cold to a warm spring of sweet and healing waters.

As he listened to his wife tell her story Reb Baruch realized that the blessing they had received from the Baal Shem Tov was beginning to be fulfilled.

Chasidim say that until the day she died, this wonderful fragrance surrounded this righteous and holy woman who was to become the mother of the saintly and famed sage, the Shpoler Zeide.

31
Shreiber the Jew

Abraham Boyarsky

In May 1934, a young doctor by the name of Menachem Shreiber completed his studies in Warsaw and returned to Byalestok. With the help of his father, a well-to-do farmer who some years earlier had moved his family to the city, he set up a small office in view of the town clock. As the months sped by, his reputation grew and with it the size of the crowd in his waiting room. Handsome and amiable, he was at ease in the social circles of Byalestok, quickly becoming the toast of the secular Jewish community. Wealthy industrialists vied for the opportunity to introduce their daughters to him and the intellectual elite was constantly after him to address their groups and attend their social gatherings. More often than not he declined their invitations, unimpressed by the glitter of their parties and by the all-too-familiar topics of their conversations. He devoted his time to his practice; his leisure hours he spent strolling through the streets and parks of the city.

Between patients, he often glanced across the room at the graduation photograph of his elementary school class, dated 1922. Time was passing quickly. He was a doctor, respected, almost famous in Byalestok, but he was not happy with his accomplishments — something was missing. The life around him lacked purpose and consistency. Even his work depressed him at times.

"Shreiber the Jew," while excerpted from a work of fiction, is based on an actual story told to the author.

The death of a young patient, as he looked helplessly on, touched him deeply. What was the meaning of his life, he asked in his heart. Why did it have to happen?

Six months after his return to Byalestok, he met Freda, the beautiful daughter of the manufacturer and philanthropist, Leon Metreger. He did not love her, but he was resigned to a life with her. She respected him and often came to the office to help out. It was enough of a base, he thought, on which to build a marriage. And so it would have been had not the Assistant Mayor of Byalestok, a tall educated Pole, called on Menachem one day late in October.

A year earlier, the city administration had hired a new District Attorney, Andrei Maritus, who immediately set in motion a number of projects. The unabashed purpose of one of them was to close down all the *mikvahs* in Byalestok. On the second day of Rosh Hashana, after hundreds of Jews had immersed themselves in the *mikvah* of the Main Synagogue, Andrei Maritus, accompanied by the City Health Inspector and three policemen, collected two samples from the water that had become dark and turbid. A day later all the *mikvahs* in the city were ordered closed, pending a hearing to be held two weeks hence. Late that same afternoon, the Assistant Mayor paid Dr. Menachem Shreiber a visit.

"It's simply a matter of health," said the Assistant Mayor, a tall, square-shouldered Pole with a rim of reddish hair around his bald scalp, smiling genially. "The community must be protected from an outbreak of typhoid fever. Why, only last month six cases were discovered in Olsztyn, another four in Siedlce." Menachem stared expressionlessly across the table. The Pole met his gaze and grinned affectedly. "This is a sample taken from the *mikvah*," he said, placing the vial on the table. "We want you to examine it and report to us in three days."

"I see," Menachem said. Now the purpose of the visit was clear to him: he, a respected member of the Jewish community, was to provide the conclusive evidence.

Sensing a hint of indecision in the Doctor's eyes, the Assistant Mayor said:

"It is a simple matter of health, Dr. Shreiber—the water is clearly polluted. We want your confirmation. Needless to say, you will be handsomely rewarded for your time."

"How do I know this is a true sample?" asked Menachem.

"Ha!" laughed the Pole with a gesture of dismissal, but he could not conceal his sudden annoyance. "Dear Dr. Shreiber, that sample has not left the hands of the authorities for a moment. You must understand, Doctor, that Poland has no place for medieval practices," declared the Administrator, deftly changing the subject. "We are forging a modern Poland! Nothing less! We do not ask you to pass judgment or to lie, heaven forbid. We request only that you present your findings truthfully! Nothing more! After all, you are a scientist!" The Assistant Mayor stood up and extended his cold, sweaty hand across the table to Menachem, who took it dutifully. "By the way," said the Pole as he was about to open the door, "we may have to ask you to testify at the hearing."

Menachem sat for a long time at his desk. From the street below came the sounds of children playing. He went to the window and looked down. Squeezed between shadows the roseate sunlight of evening blanched the faces of the children. For the first time since he had taken occupancy in this office, he wondered if they were Jewish. At length, he turned around and picked up the sample. He placed a drop on a slide, then slipped it under the eyepiece of the microscope. One glance showed him that it was full of bacteria—he did not bother trying to analyze it further.

He apologized to the patients waiting outside his office and hurried down the stairs into the street. He walked through the main square with the pedestrian traffic, then strolled pensively through the Gardens to the commercial center of Byalestok. From there he headed toward the Main Synagogue. The enormous, domed structure dominated the surroundings for many blocks. Here and there, Jewish children played in the dusty streets, dressed in rags, their earlocks drifting in the breeze. Menachem had never made real contact with the observant Jews of Byalestok; in his social circle they were regarded with disdain, as one thinks of a distant relative who is squandering his life, but at whom one can only shrug one's shoulders in helpless disapproval. He never understood their ways—then again, he never tried. His university days came to mind; there had been more than a trace of anti-semitism in the air but, somehow, absorbed as he was in his studies, he made little of it, attributing it to the ignorance of a few misguided individuals in the faculty.

Suddenly, a five- or six-year-old boy came out of a lane carrying a pail of water, and stood directly in front of Menachem. A brown cap with a narrow visor extending over his brow covered his head, while a torn black coat concealed the little man's body from neck to ankles.

"Where is your skull cap?" he demanded with a nuance of contempt, jutting his chin upward.

"I don't wear one," said Menachem, smiling.

"Every Jew must wear a skull cap!" asserted the boy, hot with anger.

"Not every Jew".

"Yes, every Jew!" he insisted stubbornly, pursed his lips, and shook his head reproachfully like an adult. "You wear glasses, don't you, but glasses are heavier than a skull cap," he said, with a Talmudic thrust of the thumb.

The following week two elderly Jews came to Menachem's office. One was the Chief Rabbi of Byalestok, the other Leib Orenstein, President of the Main Synagogue. They had learned that Menachem was scheduled to testify at the upcoming hearing.

"The *mikvah* is not a place to wash ourselves," said the aged Rabbi through the slit in his long, white beard. The axe-like handle of his cane leaned against his breast; he clasped it tremulously and went on, his narrow eyes set deeply between the swollen lids: "The *mikvah* is life; it is like the waters of the placentae in which the foetus lives and develops—when the infant breaks through the waters, it is alive. And so it is with a Jew when he comes out of the *mikvah* in the morning; he is rejuvenated, eager to serve the Creator."*

The wan cheeks of the Rabbi merged into his beard and all one saw was the dark, patient eyes and the serrated outline of his beard against the backdrop of his black coat. Menachem nodded respectfully.

"Even if you do not understand what a *mikvah* means," said Leib Orenstein, a clean-shaven man of sixty, in a voice straining to be calm, "you must respect the fact that it is of the greatest importance to thousands of Jews in Byalestok. When a woman goes to the *mikvah,* she feels assured of a healthy child. This is not a detail in our lives; it is everything!" Unable to contain his emotion, he went on: "And do not deceive yourself into believing that this is an isolated event and that it will end here. Should they, God forbid, force the *mikvahs* to close it will encourage them to attempt more; soon they will want to destroy our slaughterhouses—cruelty to animals they will charge! Then our schools will be attacked, and then, Dr. Shreiber—I ask you—what will be left?"

Menachem gazed somberly at his visitors.

"The water is full of bacteria," he said frankly. "It is a health hazard."

"No Jew has ever become sick from a *mikvah,*" stated Mr. Orenstein, his lips trembling at the Doctor's misconception.

"That may be so, but nevertheless the water does pose a danger to the health of the community," he said, weighing his words carefully.

"Science and logic are not everything, Dr. Shreiber," said the Rabbi. "The history of the Jews is ample evidence of that."

The visitors stood up to leave. Menachem accompanied them to the corridor. He expected them to plead with him, to evoke in him a sense of guilt. But they said no more, and he respected them for it. Menachem extended his hand to them; the Rabbi held it lightly between both his hands as if to transmit a final message through it.

Menachem sought advice from those closest to him. Freda listened to his arguments, but showed no real interest in his conflict. Secretly annoyed by this

---

See introduction, page xxvi.

unexpected snag in their blossoming relationship, her eyes stirred restively when he spoke. More than once he saw her scrabbling absently at the nail polish that lay hardened around her fingernails. He soon realized that it was hopeless trying to commune with her. He began wandering through the streets alone, a deeply troubled look on his face. In the religious district he imbibed the hum of Torah talk seeping out of windows and the smell of challeh baking for *Shabbos*. He was touched by the simplicity and devotion of their activity, admiring with envy the consistency of it all. But in the Jewish secular districts he reverted to his concern for truth, his intellectual desire to defend it wherever it might be threatened.

"What is truth, after all?" asked Efraim, accompanying him home one evening. "What is true for the Pole is probably a lie for us."

"I needed to hear that, thank you," Menachem said with gratitude. They walked on together, then Menachem turned to him with sudden urgency.

"What shall I do, Efraim?" he pleaded helplessly. "Tell me what to do!"

"I cannot tell you anything, my dear brother."

"Do I listen to my brain or to my heart?" he asked, staring into Efraim's honest, open face.

"Listen to both. There's still time. When the moment comes, you'll have reached a decision."

"I hope so," Menachem muttered under his breath.

The highly publicized hearing attracted officials and journalists from all over Poland. The hall was crowded. In the front row to the left, sat three Rabbis, the Chief Rabbi in the middle, his trembling fingers dovetailed over the handle of his cane. The stage was set. The District Attorney, a tall bespectacled Pole with a grape-sized growth in the middle of his right cheek, veritably bursting with confidence, strutted back and forth between his colleagues, adding the final touches. The judge, a towering man distinguished by his flowing gray hair and an involuntary smile, called the hearing to order. Andrei Maritus wasted no time. First on the witness stand was a former janitor of the main synagogue, a drunkard named Babules. Anyone who was even vaguely acquainted with Babules knew that for a swig of whiskey he would testify that grass was blue. Today, however, he was a different man. Dressed in a new suit and tie, his pitch black hair slicked down, he indeed had the appearance of a decent, law-abiding citizen. Only his eyes betokened the real Babules; bloodshot, they strove in vain to follow the District Attorney as he paced back and forth in front of him a little too quickly. With a coherence that surprised many of the onlookers, Babules described conditions at the *mikvah* as he claimed to know them. Using adjectives and superlatives utterly alien to him, his description of the squalid conditions brought the hostile audience to shouts of outrage.

"How often I pleaded with the Rabbis to permit me to change the water daily!" he testified bitterly.

"And did they let you?" prompted the District Attorney, radiant with anticipation of victory.

"No! Never!"

"Why?"

"Money! What else?"

"You should have offered to do it for free," suggested Andrei Maritus magnanimously.

"I did! Out of the goodness of my heart," Babules offered! "I could not endure the odor, Sir! You see—I should have mentioned this earlier—but the older men were not reluctant to sneeze into the water."

"That's all for now, Mr. Babules," said the District Attorney, smiling unrestrainedly as he fondled the growth on his cheek. He glanced meaningfully at the judge, who lowered his eyes to the notepad on his desk.

Six witnesses followed. The testimony of each was increasingly more devastating. However, it was clear that the prosecutor's case rested on statements of questionable witnesses. There was no hard evidence, no scientific facts. For that, he called on Dr. Menachem Shreiber, who was seated in the back row of the hall.

"Now, Dr. Shreiber," began the District Attorney, slowly and deliberately, "you were given a sample of water from the *mikvah* and asked to analyze it. I presume you have had an opportunity to do so."

"Yes, Sir," Menachem answered politely, his stern gaze wrinkling the corners of his eyes into a tiny staircase of furrows.

"What are your findings, Doctor?" asked Andrei Maritus, pointing to the glass of blackened water which a court officer had placed on the ledge of the witness stand.

"The water is dirty," said Menachem without a trace of hesitation, meeting the Attorney's eyes with a hard stare.

"How dirty, Doctor?" he continued with confidence, glancing discreetly at the judge.

"Very dirty," answered Menachem in the same resolute tone. A wave of silence rippled through the room.

Feeling the firm ground of his case, Andrei Maritus glanced at the crowd with a slight inclination of the head. He could barely collect himself to pose the decisive question. Meanwhile the visitors had become noisy with excitement. The District Attorney beckoned the crowd to be silent. At length, he turned to Menachem, straining to control his every muscle.

"Would you say, then, that the water is hazardous to health?" he asked in a tone that permitted only one answer.

"The health of whom, Sir?" Menachem asked with exaggerated politeness.

A sudden hum of voices coursed through the hall, blending with squeals and shouts into a market day cacophony.

"Silence!" the Judge ordered.

"Humans, of course!" the District Attorney enunciated haltingly, a shocked look of outrage on his face. Then he grinned nervously at the judges and pinched his cheek.

Menachem lifted the glass to his eyes as if to ponder the question. He had no idea what they had put in it.

"For humans?" Menachem asked reflectively, paused for one final glance at the water, and then uttered a firm, "No!" Before the stunned eyes of the crowd he brought the glass to his lips and drank it down in one gulp. Showing no sign of discomfort he placed it back on the ledge in front of him. "Are there any more questions, Sir?"

32

In Nazi-Occupied Europe

Shimon Huberband

Before the war, there were nine functioning *mikvehs* in Warsaw. Two societies named The Purity of the Daughters of Israel paid for those indigent women who went to bathe themselves in the *mikvehs*. The societies issued special slips, without charge, to all women who turned to them for help. These slips were accepted by the *mikveh* owners as admission tickets. Women bearing slips from The Purity of the Daughters of Israel were treated no worse than those who purchased their admission tickets from the owners.

In addition to the *mikvehs* in Warsaw, which were under private ownership, there was also a communal *mikveh* in the suburb of Praga, luxuriously built and exquisitely maintained. Almost all the wealthy women of Warsaw who went to the *mikveh* would travel to Praga.

During the bombing of Warsaw none of the *mikvehs* were operational, since they served at that time as bomb-shelters. When the bombing ended and Warsaw's water supply was restored, the *mikvehs* immediately resumed service. Attendance was very high, and it was a time of great prosperity for *mikveh* owners. . . .

The happy days for *mikveh* owners, and perhaps also for the Jewish population at large, lasted until December 1939. The director of the Warsaw Department of

"In Nazi-Occupied Europe" and "*Erev* Yom Kippur" are chronicles of actual events. See Contributors and Credits sections for details.

Health, the well-known anti-Semite, Dr. Schrempf, then began to take an active interest in the *mikvehs*. He and his cronies inspected all the *mikvehs,* and on the day immediately after his inspection, Dr. Schrempf published an article in the German-language *Krakauer Zeitung* about the Jewish ritual baths in Warsaw. In this article, he wrote that the *mikvehs* were breeding grounds for epidemic diseases, because the pools could be replenished only once every three months according to the Jewish religion. He claimed that the Jews bathed in these pools while clothed. He depicted the filthiness and uncleanliness of the *mikvehs* in horrifying terms.

All the *mikveh* pools were subsequently closed. In certain *mikvehs,* the baths and showers were allowed to remain open. Dr. Schrempf demanded that in return for keeping the baths and showers open, these institutions destroy their ritual *mikveh* pools, by filling them with sand, demolishing their steps, and so forth. Since the *mikveh* owners refused to meet this demand, the entire institutions, including the baths and showers, were locked up.

The owner of the *mikveh* at 22 Dzielna Street, Mr. Leybl Rozenfarb, was the person who spoke out most forcefully against destroying the ritual pools. Schrempf was infuriated by Rozenfarb's statements and once turned to him with the following question: "Does this mean that you believe the political situation will change and that there will be a different regime in this land? Are you holding on to your stinking pools for such a time?" Rozenfarb replied that he knew the current regime would remain forever. He refused to destroy the ritual pools because he intended to intercede with the central authorities and request permission for the pools to resume their activity. He hoped the authorities would accede to his request. Schrempf answered with the words: "That will never be!"

All the institutions whose ritual pools had been ordered destroyed were sealed, including their baths and showers. Notices were posted on the entrances, stamped with the swastika, declaring that the use of the *mikveh* would be treated as an act of sabotage and would be punished by anywhere between ten years in prison and death. Two weeks later, the baths and showers of these *mikvehs* whose ritual pools alone had been sealed beforehand were locked up.

During the closing of the *mikveh* at 22 Smocza Street, Dr. Schrempf took his revolver out of his holster and said to the owner, Mr. Goldman: "Whoever bathes in this *mikveh* will be shot immediately, and the *mikveh* owner will be shot as well."

Jewish Warsaw was left without any *mikvehs,* and the problem of the purity of the daughters of Israel became as serious as it was in the days of the ancient Roman edicts against Judaism. Well-to-do women and pious men began to travel to the towns near Warsaw, such as Otwock, Falenica, Rembertow, Grodzisk, and Pruszkow. They would immerse themselves in the local *mikvehs* and return to Warsaw. The evil decree fell most heavily upon the truly needy women.

In the beginning of the winter of 1940, a law was issued forbidding Jews to travel by train without special "lice passes."* Soon afterwards, Jews were forbidden to travel by train altogether, even with such passes. Following the pronouncement of the travel ban, a whole series of cities could no longer be reached by Jewish women. The latter began to concentrate their journeys on three cities: Rembertow, Pruszkow, Piaseczno.

Primarily poor women traveled to Rembertow. A group of women would get together, hire a coachman, and travel there by wagon. They would leave Warsaw in the middle of the day in order to return before the nighttime curfew. The cost of such a group excursion was relatively low.

The greatest number of women traveled to Pruszkow, which was the most convenient town for women to reach. The trolley ran regularly to Pruszkow, and one did not need to present "lice passes" to travel by trolley. Each and every day one could witness the identical scene—Jewish women filling the trolleys to Pruszkow in the afternoon hours. The scene attracted particular attention because each woman carried a little bag underneath her arm.

When the trolley reached Pruszkow, a great panic would erupt among the women. Each one sought to leave the trolley first, so as to reach the *mikveh* earlier, catch a spot on line, complete the ritual procedure, and return to Warsaw before the curfew. When the afternoon trolley arrived in Pruszkow, the town was thrown into a tulmult by the hundreds of Jewish women running in the direction of the local *mikveh*. The Gentiles, who learned from their Jewish neighbors the meaning of the daily arrival of the Jewish women from Warsaw, would burst into laughter as they watched the women race through the streets of the town. The conductors of the trolleys would smile broadly as the Jewish women emptied out into the Pruszkow station.

The trip to Piaseczno by commuter railway was also very convenient for women. But the local *mikveh* was heated only once a week. Under the initiative of the Piaseczno Rebbe, Rabbi Yitskhok Shapiro, and Mr. Meshulam Kaminer, funds were raised among the pious Jews of Warsaw and given to the Piaseczno *Kehilah* to enable it to heat the local *mikveh* daily.

The Jewish community then published a railroad schedule in Yiddish and Polish, listing the departure times of commuter trains leaving for Piaseczno and returning to Warsaw. Since "lice passes" were required for travel by commuter railroad, the community purchased a large number of passes from the various offices which issued them. The passes were given over to a group of

---

*Passes issued by the local German authorities permitting Jews to travel by train. They certified that its holder had been vaccinated against lice. Such passes were an additional means of humiliating the Jewish population. (YV)

Warsaw rabbis: Any women who desired such a pass in order to travel to the *mikveh* could acquire one, free of charge, from any of the designated rabbis. The pass was issued in her name.

It thus happened that Piaseczno drew many women away from the Pruszkow *mikveh*. This trend increased after an incident in which two policemen patrolling the streets of Pruszkow noticed a large crowd of women from Warsaw running in a certain direction with packages under their arms. The policemen followed the women, suspecting that they were smuggling illegal merchandise, and barged into the *mikveh*.

During the summer of 1940, Rabbi Yitskhok Shapiro along with one Meshulam Kaminer rented a number of bathing areas along the Vistula River and hired two *mikveh* ladies to supervise the women's immersions in the Vistula. They also rented the bathhouse at 14 Muranowska Street, where the women cleansed themselves in preparation for the immersion. They would then proceed to one of the bathing areas along the river, and immerse themselves under the supervision of the *mikveh* ladies. All this without charge. Men would simply immerse themselves in the open river. This arrangement, however, did not go on for very long because many women, unaccustomed to the cold waters of the Vistula, caught cold, contracted inflammation of the lungs, or otherwise fell ill. There also occurred a mishap in which a student of the Gerer *shtibl* at 9 Mila Street, Berish Fileger of 36 Nowolipie Street, drowned while immersing himself in the Vistula. The popularity of the *mikvehs* in Piaseczno, Rembertow, and Pruszkow grew once more.

In the beginning of October 1940, an ordinance was issued banning Jews from riding the public trolley cars and instituting separate trolleys for Jews. The ordinance made it more difficult to travel to Rembertow and Piaseczo. Traveling to Pruszkow was now out of the question, because Jewish trolleys left from Pruszkow only once every four or five hours, making it simply impossible to leave Warsaw and return on the same day before curfew.

The season of the High Holidays arrived. It was by then impossible to immerse oneself in the Vistula. It was no longer possible to travel to the abovementioned towns. The problems of the *mikvehs* became a pressing one for men as well.

The owner of the *mikveh* at 14 Grzybowska Street then had a clever idea. He contacted the local police precinct and negotiated a monthly payment for which the police agreed "not to see or hear anything." He also reached an agreement with the Polish police, and proceeded to open a hole in the wall of a nearby basement which led into the *mikveh*. The owner heated the *mikveh* and let men enter through the basement hole in the daytime and women in the evening. Due to the fear of detection, they heated the *mikveh* only once a week. At night, the hole in the basement wall was sealed. "Business" was conducted this way for endless weeks. The official entrance to the *mikveh* was pasted over with a notice stating that bathing in the *mikveh* would be punished by anywhere between ten years in prison and death. Meanwhile, Jews bathed and immersed themselves in the *mikveh* undisturbed, scoffing at the notice.

The system employed by the *mikveh* at 14 Grzybowska was soon learned by other *mikveh* owners. Before long there were four clandestine *mikvehs* functioning in Warsaw — 14 Grzybowska Street, 1 Grzybowska Street, 38 Dzielna Street, and 22 Smocza Street.

Needless to say, the bathing was conducted in total secrecy. The *mikvehs* were heated once a week or once in two weeks, due to fear of detection by Christian neighbors, who lived alongside Jews until the institution of the ghetto.

In late November 1940, the ghetto was sealed off. There were no longer any Christian residents in the area of the ghetto, and there was, hence, no longer any danger of Christian neighbors detecting the *mikvehs*. The *mikveh* owners then began to heat the pools three times a week and later on a full six days a week. There were specified hours for men and for women. The attendance at the *mikvehs* was very high. The *mikvehs* were thus able to function secretly in this fashion the entire winter of 1940–41 and the early summer of 1941.

In the meantime, Schrempf left his position. He was succeeded by Hagen and Koblenski. For a certain sum of money, it appeared that it would be possible to obtain the legalized opening of the *mikvehs*. The *mikveh* owners began to negotiate with various ghetto officials in this regard. A fund of over ten thousand zlotys was created. Dr. Sukhatin demanded twenty-five thousand zlotys for arranging the legalization of the *mikvehs;* Gantsvaykh demanded forty-eight hundred zlotys.* In the end it became clear that both these officials were bluffing. The *mikveh* owners interceded directly with the authorities for the legalized opening of the mikvehs. Finally, in August 1941, they were granted permission to open the four above-mentioned *mikvehs,* as well as the *mikveh* at 26 Franciszkanska Street.

In the beginning of the winter of 1941, the attendance at the *mikvehs* fell sharply. The reasons for this were the raging typhus epidemic, and the shortage of fuel, which caused the price of a visit to the *mikveh* to reach more than ten zlotys. Under current conditions, in the closed ghetto, this is considered to be an enormously high price. Three of the five *mikvehs* have therefore closed. Currently functioning are the two *mikvehs* at 26 Franciszkanska Street and 38 Dzielna Street.

---

*Avrom Gantsvaykh headed the ghetto's Office of Price Supervision, which was ostensibly empowered to control and combat high prices, usury, and smuggling. In fact, this office was an arm of the Gestapo. (YV)

33
Erev Yom Kippur, October 1940

Shimon Huberband

Among all the evil decrees issued by the Kingdom of Wickedness, there was also a decree forbidding Jews to immerse themselves in *mikvehs*. The *mikvehs* were locked up and a notice was hung on their doors that "opening the *mikvehs* or employing it will be punished as sabotage, and will be subject to between ten years in prison and death."

The Rebbe* made a decision, an iron-clad decision, that he must immerse himself in the *mikveh* before Yom Kippur. All the arguments put forth by his intimates that this would endanger his life were of no avail. The mere walk to the *mikveh* was dangerous, especially for such a person as the Rebbe. But the Rebbe did not alter his decision, and we made plans to implement it. But how? As mentioned, all the *mikvehs* were locked, and their use was subject to such dangerous consequences. Finally, after a number of secret consultations between the Rebbe and a *mikveh* owner, the matter was arranged.

At dawn of the day on which the Thirteen Divine Attributes are recited,† at exactly 5:00 A.M., the hour when Jews are first permitted to be outdoors, a small group of people headed by the Rebbe assembled and began the dangerous journey to the *mikveh*. It was still dark outside. We prayed the darkness would thicken even more and last even longer. We hoped that we would be able to hide

---

*The Piaseczno Rebbe, Rabbi Kalonimus Shapiro. (YV)
†Yom Kippur

in the darkness, remain unnoticed, and carry out the dangerous journey successfully.

The distance between the Rebbe's home and the *mikveh* was quite long. The wagon which we had ordered did not arrive. By ten minutes past five o'clock, the group was getting nervous because everything had been planned according to the exact minute. We decided to begin walking by foot, in the hope that the wagon would meet us en route. It was rather difficult to find another wagon at that hour of day. One also couldn't trust just any wagon, since all the arrangements had been made in secret and the coachman we had hired knew all the strategic information—how to travel, which streets to take, and where to stop. Apparently, he had encountered some sort of difficulty, as is so often the case.

Quietly, on our tiptoes, we descended the steps. But then, there was a new, unanticipated problem. The janitor didn't feel like getting up so early to open the gate. He was eager to know why Jews needed to go outside so early. A pretty penny "softened" his heart, and he agreed to let us out of the gate.

With silent footsteps, we walked in pairs, each pair a certain distance behind the preceding one. Our hearts beat like hammers. Our eyes strained to look into the depths of the night at each approaching silhouette, to see whether it wasn't one of "them." When we detected the echo of heavy footsteps ahead of us or behind us, our limbs numbed with fear. Suddenly, we heard the ring of an approaching night-trolley. We ran quickly to the station to take the trolley, since it followed the same route we needed. But as we drew nearer we saw that it was an Aryan trolley—off-limits to Jews. It would be a long time until a Jewish trolley arrived, since "Jewish" trolleys did not run so early in the morning.

We walked from street to street, when suddenly we heard the sound of an approaching automobile. Its headlights cast a blinding light in our eyes. We stood paralyzed in place because in these times it isn't good luck to meet an automobile on the street. In most cases, one is "invited" to a place from which there is no return. There was no gateway in which to hide; the gates were all still locked, due to the early hour. But we were graced with a stroke of luck. The automobile passed us by and neglected to spot us. Holding our breath, we walked past the more dangerous points and reached the gateway in which the *mikveh* was situated.

The courtyard of the *mikveh* was pitch-black. Mysterious shadows crept about the walls and disappeared into an adjacent cellar. A secret emissary awaited us. Silently, without words, but with a lone wave of his arm, he began to lead us. We descended into a deep, dark cellar. We groped in the darkness. We had instructions to walk straight and then to turn left. We reached a chiseled hole in the wall. With great difficulty, we pushed ourselves through the wall. We found ourselves standing on a platform of wooden boards, and after a successful jump we entered a corridor which led to the steps of the *mikveh*.

Despite the great danger in which we found ourselves, we were fascinated by the whole event. We imagined vividly the sight of our forefathers in Spain— how they rescued Torah scrolls, how they prayed with a *minyan* in secret cellars, due to fear of the Inquisition. They certainly never imagined that their descendants would find themselves, four hundred years later, in a much worse situation, and that in order to immerse themselves in honor of a festival, they would be forced to follow the same kinds of dangerous procedures. In the *mikveh* we found a sizable number of people who had received secret word that the *mikveh* would be open for an hour. Silently and in great haste we undressed and immersed ourselves in honor of the festival. A few minutes later, we repeated the same procedure we had used to enter. By the time we reached the courtyard, day was beginning to break, and we could see on the lock and bolt on the entrance gate to the *mikveh* the well-known notice: "Opening the *mikveh* or employing it will be punished as sabotage and will be subject to between ten years in prison and death."

34
The Remaining Sign

Sterna Citron

A friend of mine from Berkeley, Sophie Trupin, who wrote *Dakota Diaspora,* told me about her early years growing up in North Dakota. Her parents had emigrated here from Russia at the turn of the century. Sophie's father felt that the Jewish laws belonged to the "old country" and didn't have a place in their new world. Life was challenging enough on the farm in the harsh climate of North Dakota without having to worry about outdated rituals. Sophie's mother, however, remained true to her faith and to the ways of her forefathers. North Dakota or not, she would keep the rituals taught her by her parents and observed by Jews from time immemorial. She was determined that her husband build her a *mikvah,* a ritual bathhouse, where she would immerse herself once a month and thus observe the law of marital purity.

To please her, he did. Sophie describes the *mikvah* in her book.

> The bathhouse was a wooden structure built close to the windmill. The floor was made of cement, and there were a couple of steps leading downward to the *mikvah,* which might be compared to a miniature swimming pool. There was a circular enclosure of cement in the middle of which stood a potbellied stove which heated water for the bath.

The *mikvah* stood there for many years, a testimony that Judaism could be practiced even in the forbidding country of North Dakota. In fact, many years after the farm had been abandoned, Sophie's brother returned to the old homestead to see what still remained. In an almost mystical account, Sophie relates what her brother saw.

> The house and barn and windmill were gone without a trace. There was no sign that anyone had [ever] lived and worked there. None of the dwellings of our three neighbors were there. . . .
>
> My brother searched for some sign—some little token of his first home in this new land. As he walked about on the rise of the hill where our house with its sod roof had stood, he found, in the prairie grass, the cement outline of the old *mikvah.*

It was the only thing that had withstood the fierce winds, snows, and rain of that hostile land.

While the farm on which Sophie's father had toiled disappeared without a trace, the foundation of the *mikvah,* which had been built on the insistence of Sophie's mother, had survived. In the endless argument between Sophie's parents, God had proven her mother right. The only eternal things in this world are God, His Torah, and His precepts.

35

Mikvah Swedish Style

Yaffa Zager

When I was a child, the members of our family were practically the only ones who kept kosher in Boras, Sweden. There were no certified kosher provisions, so my mother had to make everything herself, from rye bread and flaky cakes to ice cream and blueberry jelly made from berries she had picked in the forest. We could never eat at anyone's home, not even our Jewish friends'. At the time we felt very limited, but in retrospect this proved to be a powerful tool against assimilation. When a synagogue was purchased, it was located close to our home because my father was the only one concerned with living within walking distance of *Shabbat* services.

Although I was unaware of it at the time, my mother was one of the very few women in Sweden who kept the laws of Family Purity. There was no kosher *mikvah* in Sweden when we lived there, but the Jewish women were allowed to utilize some particularly Swedish facilities.

In our town there was a lake that was surrounded by beautiful pine trees and was visited by swans and pheasants. The lake was divided into three sections, two separate enclosed areas for men and women respectively and an open area for mixed swimming. In the two enclosed areas people went swimming Swedish style, in their natural garb. This accommodated my mother's *mikvah*

Yaffa Zager lived in Boras, Sweden, from 1947 to 1966.

purpose perfectly. She would go into the women's section and immerse herself three times without anyone noticing.

When we went on vacation in the summer, my mother sometimes took a dip in the ocean at night, when the beach was empty. We children did not pay much attention to this.

Winter posed more of a problem, because all of the lakes were frozen over. Here again, Swedish sporting life came to my mother's rescue. Many Swedes enjoyed the following sport: they cut a hole in the ice with an ax, jumped into the icy water with nothing on, got up, rolled in the deep snow, and finished off by sweating in a sauna. We children always thought our mother loved this kind of recreation. She used to go at night and return home with a radiant face.

Years later, when she joined us in America, she confirmed the true motive for her involvement in these sports. She told us that on occasion the winter ice was so thick that for months they could not make a hole in it. She therefore had no choice but to wait until the spring to go to the *mikvah*. "I used to get a headache from the waiting and anticipation," she admitted.

36

Alaska!

Adapted and Translated by

Rivkah Slonim

They looked like an all-American young couple, but outward appearances belied the Habers' devotion to Judaism and their strict adherence to Jewish law. Yisroel was the administrator of a Jewish day school in Dallas, Texas, in 1972–1973 and was completing his doctorate in psychology. Miriam was pursuing an advanced degree in special education and speech pathology. Both had a burning desire to help Jews; to guide, to teach, to inspire, to make a unique contribution. But where to find their niche?

For some reason the Air Force beckoned. A career as a chaplain with the United States Air Force would present the young rabbi and his wife with a wide-open vista. There was much to be done, they reasoned, both within an air force base and with the civilian population of any given location. It would be a five year experience.

The Habers began to take the necessary steps. Yisroel applied for and completed the requisite courses with the Air Force in Alabama. Next he received his acceptance; he became a chaplain, captain in the United States Air Force. Now the Habers awaited placement. They were hoping for a location close to their families.

Nothing prepared them for the call from Washington in the fall of 1972. Within a minute Miriam understood that the call was from the Air Force, but to her great alarm, she watched her husband's face drain of all color and his body stiffen in fear. And then she heard her husband say Alaska. A chill ran through Miriam. What a frightening notion—they were being sent to Alaska!

Everyone knows that you can't choose a location—you go where the Air Force sends you. But in that desperate moment Miriam couldn't think rationally. "Tell them your wife won't go with you to Alaska," Miriam whispered urgently. "Just tell them straight! Don't they have any military bases that are closer than godforsaken Alaska?

Stammering—trancelike—Yisroel repeated Miriam's words. For a moment it seemed there might be hope. The Air Force was hiring another rabbi, he was told, and perhaps they could switch assignments. Yes, certainly it could be arranged!

With bated breath the Habers waited to hear about the alternate location. "The other rabbi is poised to accept a position in Bangkok," he was told. "Rabbi, your choice is Alaska or Bangkok." Alaska it was.

Once the shock wore off, the Habers began to make extensive preparations for their new position as rabbi and rebbetzin to both the military and civilian Jewish population of the forty-ninth state. Alaska was home to some 800 Jews spread across the 586,000-mile territory. Haber was expected to travel around the state ministering to his people's needs, and he wanted to be ready.

There were a million and one concerns for this young, observant couple who were being stationed in a spiritual wasteland. But chief among them—the most serious by far—was the issue of a *mikvah*. There are many location where there is no *mikvah;* in a pinch one can always use the ocean or a river. But they were moving to Alaska where there are no safe, accessible, natural waters—certainly not for most of the year.

They began to deal with this problem immediately. They contacted the Pentagon offices where U.S. Senator Mike Gravel from Alaska alerted the Air Force and urged them to deal with this concern seriously and promptly.

But that wasn't enough to assuage the Habers' fears. One day, in desperation, Yisroel decided to contact the Pentagon himself and explain the hardships involved in moving so far from an organized center of Jewish life. Much to his surprise, he had a very productive conversation with the powers that be. In fact, he was successful in procuring a promise that they would accommodate all of his religious needs. "We'll give you whatever you deem necessary," they said. "Please state your specific needs."

"A *mikvah,*" Yisroel replied.

In a subsequent telegram from the Pentagon to Haber, officials conveyed their utter confusion regarding his request. We simply can not find the word *mikvah* in a dictionary, they wrote.

But he had their promise. The United States Air Force was on his side. They would fund a *mikvah,* but who would come build it in Alaska? And what would he and Miriam do in the interim? Yisroel called many Jewish organizations, and all expressed sympathy but none could offer him the on-site physical assistance he required.

Divine providence works in mysterious ways. En route to their new home, the Habers made a stop in St. Paul, Minnesota, to say their good-byes to some relatives. That very week a *Chabad* House had opened its doors in St. Paul, and the Habers made their way there to get kosher provisions. They got to talking with the program directors, Rabbis Moshe Feller and Gershon Grossbaum, about their impending move and their concern about a *mikvah*. By the time they left, Rabbi Grossbaum had pledged his unqualified assistance and encouraged them to stand firm in their convictions.

From St. Paul, the Habers flew to Seattle, and from there they flew to Anchorage with trepidation in their hearts and a six-month supply of kosher meat.

Immediately upon their arrival at Elmendorf Air Force Base, due to strict orders from the Pentagon, plans were set into motion for the construction of a *mikvah.* Over the ensuing months, members of the 21st Civil Engineering Squadron were in constant phone conversation and correspondence with Rabbi Grossbaum concerning this most peculiar "engineering" job. Grossbaum developed plans and provided details for the *mikvah,* which would be built in Chapel Number 2.

In the meantime, Miriam made use of the closest *mikvah,* which was 1800 miles away in Seattle—a five hour plane trip each way! Air Force regulations did not allow a woman to fly on a military plane without her husband, but the highest-ranking general on the base issued an emergency order granting Miriam Haber special permission to be flown on a Hercules C-130 to the *mikvah.* "If this isn't an emergency, I don't what is," the general quipped. Initially, Miriam was strapped into the belly of the plane's cargo section. After a while the crew took pity on her and invited her to don headset earphones and sit in the cockpit with them. Miriam made these trips to Seattle monthly for six months until the *mikvah* on the base was completed.

In the winter of 1974, the Pentagon flew Rabbi Grossbaum to Anchorage to inspect the construction site. Due to the intricacies of *Mikvah,* many changes had to be made, and Grossbaum stayed for over a month to personally supervise every nuance of the project. Day after day he worked with the engineers and construction crew, constantly surprising them with his ingenious ideas and mechanical ability. When the pool was ready, the *mikvah* was filled with melted snow. At last, Rabbi Hendel of Montreal, Canada, a noted halachic expert in the field of *mikvahs,* was called in to do a final inspection and in March of 1974 the *mikvah* was dedicated.

After three years, the Habers finished their stint in Anchorage, Alaska, and moved on for two more years to Travis Air Force base in California. But their legacy lives on. As of this writing, the first and only *mikvah* to be constructed on any U.S. Army installation is still used by a small core of women. During the summer season it is used with greater frequency by tourists to the region.

What follows is a copy of the (heretofore unpublished) letter sent by Rabbi Menachem M. Schneerson, the Lubavitcher Rebbe, to Yisroel Haber upon being informed that the *mikvah* on Elmendorf Air Force Base was completed.

RABBI MENACHEM M. SCHNEERSON

Lubavitch

770 Eastern Parkway

Brooklyn, N. Y. 11213

———

Hyacinth 3-9250

By the Grace of G-d

Rosh Chodesh Sivan,

5734. Brooklyn, N.Y.

Chaplain Israel Haber

Elmendorf Air Force Base

Alaska.

Greeting and Blessing:

Due to a very crowded schedule, this is my first opportunity of congratulating you on your extraordinary Zechus of initiating the project of the first Mikveh in Anchorage for the Alaskan Jewish community, which you accomplished, with G-d's help, as I am informed by our mutual friends, the Rabbonim who flew in to participate in this great event.

As for the importance of this matter, I need hardly emphasize it to you, since your own initiative is best proof of being fully aware of it.

However, on the basis of the dictum of our Sages, "Encourage the energetic," I wish to express my confident hope that you are doing all you can to make the Mikveh a busy place, frequented regularly not only by the women who directly benefit from your good influence, but also by their friends and acquaintances who will be induced by them to follow their example. And while this kind of religious inspiration is a "must" wherever Jews live, it is even more so in the City and State where the Mikveh has just been established for the first time. It is well to bear in mind that a "Jewish heart is always awake" and responsive to Torah and Mitzvoth.

It is significant in this case that the one who merited the great Zechus of establishing the Mikveh is a person in military service. For, military service, by definition and practice, very aptly illustrates the basic principle of commitment to Torah and Mitzvoth, namely, *naaseh* ("we will do", and then) *v'nishma* ("we will understand").

Moreover, the soldier's duty to carry out the orders of a commanding officer, and carry them out promptly and to the best of his ability, is in no way inhibited by the fact that in civilian life the soldier may be vastly superior to his commanding officer in many respects. Nor does such a circumstance diminish in the least the soldier's self-esteem in obeying the order. On the contrary, by not allowing any personal views to interfere with his military duties, he demonstrates his strength of character and integrity.

The same is true in the area of Torah and Mitzvoth. One may be a very rich man—in the ordinary sense, or rich in knowledge of the sciences, or in other achievements in public life. Yet, when it comes to Halachah, the Law of Torah conduct, he accepts it with complete obedience and dedication, on the authority of a fellow-Jew who had consecrated all his life to Torah study and Torah living and is eminently qualified to transmit the "Word of G-d—the Halachah."

A further point which characterizes military discipline also has a bearing on the subject of Torah and Mitzvoth. In the military, no soldier can claim that his conduct is his personal affair; nor can he take the attitude that there are many other soldiers to carry out military assignments, but he will do as he pleases. For it has often been demonstrated in military history how one action of a single soldier could have far-reaching consequences for an entire army and country.

Every Jew is a soldier in the "Army of G-d," as is often emphasized in this week's Sedra—*kol yotze tzovo,* "everyone going forth as a soldier." And he is bound by the same two basic rules: To carry out G-d's commandments promptly and fully, without question (*naaseh* before *v'nishma*), and to recognize his responsibility to his people ("All Jews are responsible for one another"), hence the consequences of one good deed. To quote the Rambam: "Every person should always consider himself and the whole world as equi-balanced. Hence, when he does one Mitzva, he tips the scale in favor of himself and of the whole world" (see it at length in Hil. Teshuvah, 3 hal. 4).

May you go from strength to strength in all that has been said above, in all aspects of Yiddishkeit, which includes also influence to promote

among non-Jews the observance of the basic Seven Mitzvoth, with all
their numerous ramifications, which are incumbent upon all mankind
and the foundation of human society.

At this time before Shovuos, I wish you and all our brethren at the
Base as well as the community, a happy and inspiring Festival of Receiv-
ing Our Torah, with the traditional Chasidic blessing—to receive the
Torah with joy and inwardness.

With esteem and blessing,

/signed/ M. Schneerson

37
Dipping in Aruba

Helene Storch

We had amazing food, luxurious accommodations, exciting water sports, enchanted evenings, tropical breezes, and technicolor days surrounded by turquoise, crystal waters.

We snorkeled. We watercycled. We climbed rock cliffs. We toured the ocean floor in a submarine.

It was a fantasy-come-true family get-together. My parents had treated us to this dream vacation at the Americana in Aruba, a five-star hotel. There was my brother, a sister, their spouses, and my nieces and nephews. This was a big departure from our usual journey to the Catskill Mountains in New York State.

We had everything—but a *mikvah*. Owing to a glitch in my menstrual cycle, the absence of a *mikvah* presented a challenge.

What to do? To me it seemed obvious. My husband was incredulous—no, astonished—when I told him that I would turn the Caribbean into a *mikvah*.

"Helene," he said, "I think you're nuts! Do you want to risk a shark attack or pneumonia, just so we can make love?! Wait a few days until we get home and use our community *mikvah*."

I know my husband. There is no way he would want me to take any risks just so that we could resume marital relations. But here we were in a romantic setting out of a travel brochure, enjoying an almost perfect vacation—surrounded by water!

My husband, a logical M.D., Ph.D. scientist, tried to discourage me, but my older sister conspired in my plot. She was to be my willing accomplice. My sister would watch as I dipped three times under cover of darkness.

My husband finally agreed to my wild plan and offered to keep a sharp eye out for "peeping Toms" from his post 250 feet up the dry side of the beach.

Way back there, past the darkness of the wide beach, my husband would stand in ear shot—someone to hear our screams if disaster struck.

It was late in the evening when my sister and I slunk through the hotel's public rooms. Wearing fluffy white robes and carrying towels, we could have been headed for the hotel pool. But we crossed the patio and made straight for the sea.

Couples strolled the beach. Their paths were lit only by a sliver of moon and the fuzzy lights of the hotel set back on the beach. We waited until the coast was clear, literally. After half an hour, at about 11 P.M., the last of the strollers faded into the hotels.

My husband was in place, and my sister and I made our move.

As we approached the water we tried to calm our fears and convince each other that this was a well-tended resort beach that was cleared of debris each day; that the walk into the sea was smooth and graded; that the water was clean and clear; and that sharks were unlikely in the area—especially at night.

But no matter how logical we tried to be, darkness was not our friend, and every scary thought surfaced in our minds. We wondered if there would be broken sea shells or glass underfoot, sharks and other sea creatures, sudden drops in the ocean floor, and murky waters bearing globs of algae—or worse yet, a night swimmer!

Sparkling white, hot sand had turned gray and damp. Clear water was now black, hiding who knew what. And without the Caribbean sun, the water was cold—really cold. And I hate cold. My body is averse to cold. I wear thermal underwear all winter long and sleep with three blankets.

After I had undressed, my sister screened my dash for the water with my robe and I paddled through the breakers. My goal was to reach the chest-high water about a city block out; my sister, the watcher, trailed behind. She had to go into the water to see me fulfill the halachic requirement of submerging completely three times.

Once in the water I tried to think of God and the *mitzvah*. But it took all I could muster just to fight the discomfort and fear. I said my blessing in record time. You could call it speed dunking or express *mikvah*. And I dashed out of the water as fast as my flailing limbs could carry me. But I did it.

As the soles of my feet hit dry land it dawned on me that my *mikvah* experience could have been worse. What if we had been vacationing at a desert resort or an arctic lodge?

Walking up the beach, the first sounds I heard were the strains of calypso music from the hotel patio where a midnight make-your-own ice cream sundae party was under way. The thought of ice cream had a chilling effect on our already half-frozen, soggy bodies.

Looking like two drowned rats with purple lips, we dripped our triumphant way through the lobby. Bypassing the ice cream kegs, the maraschino cherries and hot fudge, we headed straight for our rooms.

The following evening good, warm feelings flowed through me. I was dolled up and strolling with my husband on the promenade, looking out at the beach that had been so fearsome the night before.

"My dear," he said, "you are a brave woman."

Under his loving gaze and the starlit sky, I didn't feel like the same wife anymore.

38

No Sacrifice Too Great

Naomi Futerfas

When the Communists were attempting to destroy the Jewish way of life in Russia, the previous Lubavitcher Rebbe chose a handful of his most trusted and loyal *chasidim* to travel around the country and ensure that Jews were given as much help as possible to enable them to observe the *mitzvot*.

One *chasid* was assigned the task of building *mikvahs*. Whenever the authorities closed one down, he would try to build another. He was daring, ingenious, and successful. Sometimes the *mikvahs* he built didn't last more than a few days because they were discovered. This work placed his life in constant danger, and the previous Lubavitcher Rebbe was asked how he could allow someone to endanger his life in this manner. The rebbe at that time indicated that no sacrifice is too great if it ensures that even one Jewish soul is born pure.

* * * * *

In London, not long ago, there lived a Russian woman whose life was a testimony to contemporary fortitude. She frequently related a particular experience with the *mikvah:*

> My husband was exiled to Siberia by the Stalinist government for defying Communist decrees forbidding Jewish education of children, which he uncom-

Excerpted from an address at the Second European Convention of Neshei uBnos Chabad, January 1979.

promisingly and vigorously perpetuated. Consequently, he was arrested, tried, and sent to Siberia. Because this occurred just prior to our marriage, I went also, and in this cold, miserable place, so void of love or human compassion, we married. The night before our marriage, when I first fulfilled the laws of *Mikvah*, there was only one alternative — to break the frozen surface of a lake and immerse in the ice-water beneath. I was determined to keep God's *mitzvah* that my mother and grandmother and all my ancestors had observed for thousands of years. I went to a lake, chopped a hole through the thick ice, and immersed. It was so cold, you cannot imagine it.

39

A Little Girl's Promise

Paysach J. Krohn

. . . I was one of the *Yaldei Teheran,* the refugee children gathered from the concentration camp survivors who were transported through the Balkans and Turkey on the way to Teheran, from where they were eventually brought to Israel. I was placed in a kibbutz and there I spent my days and nights, thinking that I would be there forever. I met a girl who had come from Germany and we became friendly. After a while our relationship became serious and I asked her to marry me. It was then that she told me she had a secret of great importance to tell me.

We walked out into a field, and there she told me of her last emotional moments with her mother. The Germans had burst into her home and the Jews knew they were going to be carted away. Rumors abounded about parents being separated from their children, never to be reunited again. The desperate mother took her seven-year-old daughter, held her tightly, and said to her, "My dear child, they will soon take us away and who knows if we will ever be together again. I want you to promise me one thing. There is something called *Taharas Hamishpachah* (Family Purity). You're too young to understand what it is, and there is no way that I can explain it to you today. When you get older go to a *rav* and he will explain what it means. Promise me that you will abide by those laws." The little girl was bewildered but saw the seriousness in her mother's face and promised to obey her wishes.

Mother and daughter were torn apart and never saw each other again. But she remembered. Years later, after being freed, she went to a *rav* and learned the significance of her promise. Although she was not an observant Jewess, she resolved to observe the laws of *Taharas Hamishpachah*.

As we walked in the field, she told me that she could only consent to marry me if I would agree to her commitment. The fact that we would be living on a kibbutz where no one else observed these laws would make matters very difficult. But the young woman was determined to uphold these laws. I told her I would need time to think about it and asked for three days.

After much thought I told her that I would agree to her condition. All the years that we lived on the kibbutz, we had to make extra efforts, usually in secret, and often go to the nearby town to use the *mikvah*. Nevertheless, we were very serious about the promise. . . .

40

A Mother's Gift

Devori Paul

It all began with the children. I had never encountered a family with so many children! Six kids! Each child was sweeter and more beautiful than the next one! And their parents were the most observant Jews I had ever met.

I had to know how they got this way because I wanted kids just like them. So I looked into Judaism to see what it's really all about. But that's another story.

Four years later, long after I had moved on to another city, I took a leave of absence from my job with Unijax Inc., a division of Alco Standard, to study and live Judaism at the Machon Chana Women's Institute in New York City. I loved the new world I discovered—the tastes, the smells, the answers, the intensity, the mysticism, the Divine. I became religious.

In the course of my studies I came across an exhortation regarding the education of one's children:

> Just as wearing *tefillin* every day is a *mitzvah* commanded by the Torah to every man . . . so too it is an absolute duty for every parent to spend a half hour every day thinking about the Torah education of his child/ren and to do everything in his power—and beyond his power—to inspire children to follow the path along which they are guided. (Rabbi Sholom Dov Ber of Lubavitch as cited in *Hayom Yom*)

For some reason I couldn't get these words out of my mind. How beautiful, I thought. If parents took this seriously, they could impact their children's lives in a wondrous fashion. Parents spend a lifetime responding to their children's needs and to situations that affect their precious charges. But how many set aside time to seriously contemplate the educational and emotional needs of their child on a daily basis?

While I didn't have children of my own, this thought resonated deep within me, and I put the concept to work in my own way. I began thinking about the *mikvah* in relation to my own family. This was something I desperately wanted my own mother to do. I had learned a great deal about the importance of immersion in *mikvah* and its deep spiritual affect on a woman and her family. And so, I spent a lot of time over the next four years thinking about how I could ask my mother to immerse in the *mikvah*. It meant so much to me that she do so before I myself got married.*

A word about my mother is in order. When I was just tentatively discovering traditional Judaism and debating the merits of studying in a *yeshivah,* I sought my mother's counsel. Both she and I knew that this could possibly jeopardize my career with a prestigious Fortune Five Hundred company.

Her advice to me was as follows: "Go. You must go. See that it's not for you, and then go on with your life. If you don't go, then for the rest of your life you'll say, 'If only I had gone. . . .' " I took her advice, but I found out that it *was* for me.

When I began dating, my mother asked, "Why can't you just be Jewish on the Sabbath? Why does your future husband have to look so obviously Jewish [with a *yarmulke, tzitzit,* etc.]?" And of course she said, "Don't *ever* try to make *me* religious!"

Well, eventually it happened. I got engaged, and my mother came up from Florida to attend to the details of my special day. She agonized over the menu, the colors, the gown, the flowers. This was her baby's wedding. And all I could think of midst the prewedding madness was: How am I going to find the right words to ask?

But the perfect time finally arrived. It was 2:00 A.M. and we were having one of those incredibly warm and intimate mother/daughter discussions, and the words came out.

"Mom," I said calmly with my heart pounding, "I have something to ask of you that would make me happier than anything else, and no one else in the world can do this for me—except you."

She was listening.

"Mom," I said, "I would like you to do me the greatest favor a mother can do for her child . . . go to the *mikvah.*" I spoke to her with all my heart. "It affects the spiritual purity of myself, my children, and their children, all the way down

---

*For more on this subject see introduction, page xxxvi, and "Going to the *Mikvah* (at My Age!)," page 149.

the line. Jewish mysticism teaches that even if the mother goes after the child is born, the effect of *Mikvah* is retroactive. And besides, since you've already been through menopause, you only have to visit the *mikvah* once, and it will benefit you for the rest of your life. Think about your children whom you love so much," I rushed on, "especially me. After all, I am your only baby and maybe even your favorite. (I must admit, in my desperation, I really did say this.) Will you go in for me?" And then I shut my mouth.

My mother was quiet for a moment and then said, "Yes." I couldn't believe I had heard what I heard, but I certainly wasn't going to repeat the question and risk everything, so I said nothing. A few days later she left, and I didn't say another word about it. But I was so excited.

A few weeks before the wedding I called my mother. I knew we had to discuss preparations for visiting the *mikvah* and that I could no longer procrastinate. I half expected her to have changed her mind, but she hadn't. She listened to the instructions intently and even wrote notes to herself so she would remember each detail. She made me promise that I wouldn't tell my father what we were planning.

My parents flew up several days before my wedding. The night before, my mom told my dad that we had a few last-minute errands to run. We got to the *mikvah* promptly at our scheduled appointment. Luckily I had arranged for my very close married friend, Dobra, to act as a helper/go-between since my mother and I would both be in separate bathrooms doing our preparations simultaneously. The bathrooms at the *mikvah* were gorgeous, and they had a helpful reminder list to go through to make sure you didn't forget anything.

Dobra ran between our rooms, keeping the humor high and the nervousness down. My mother was great. After all, the last thing she expected was a long hot bath in a beautiful spa!

My mother went into the *mikvah* first, and she was a real trooper. She doesn't know how to swim, yet she willingly and patiently went under the *mikvah's* waters seven or eight times until she was completely submerged and the *mikvah* attendant could say, "Kosher." We all gave her a big cheer! Then it was my turn.

Later, as we drove home, I was feeling overwhelmed with gratitude and unable to properly express what this had meant to me.

As we got out of the car, she said something I'll never forget: "Just remember, I did this for you."

41

Counting the Days:
Wise Advice from
the Rebbe

Elizabeth Applebaum

All my life, more than just about anything in the world, I wanted children.

I always was fortunate in my professional life. When I was in my twenties I wished I could find a job in New Orleans, which seemed like a fascinating place to live. I got one. Then I hoped to become a full-time journalist, and I found work at the *Kansas City Jewish Chronicle*.

But I didn't meet my beloved until I was thirty, after I had moved to a city I never thought I would be living in: Detroit. I was set to take a job in Boston when the publisher of *The Detroit Jewish News* called and asked me to take a position with the paper. Initially I said no, but he was so persuasive, I changed my mind. Soon afterward a colleague introduced me to my future husband, Phillip. I knew right away he was just what I wanted. Not only was he kind and thoughtful, he was brilliant.

We were married at Young Israel of Oak-Woods in 1989.

While I was working in Kansas City, a gentile acquaintance of mine had asked me about the *mikvah*. Being *shomer Shabbat* she thought would be difficult, and keeping kosher next to impossible. But the idea of the *mikvah* appealed to her.

"I wish we Christians had something like that," she said. "It sounds so nice, to be able to come like a bride each month to your husband."

After I married, I always liked going to the *mikvah*. Each month I would buy myself some treat—a new shampoo, a little bottle of perfume—to use after my visit. But I eagerly awaited the time when my *mikvah* trips would be put on hold, when I would become pregnant.

My husband and I had hoped for children right away. But more than a year after our marriage, I still wasn't pregnant. I felt such despair each time I bought one of those home pregnancy-test kits, and the result was negative.

I began trying everything, from avoiding caffeine to sleeping on my left side (I'm still not certain what any of this had to do with conception, but if there was even a single rumor that it helped, I would try it). A friend suggested I ask for a blessing from the Lubavitcher Rebbe.

"Miriam, I'm not even Lubavitch," I reminded her.

"Just try it, anyway," she said, handing me the Rebbe's fax number.

So I did—and received no response.

After I had been trying, unsuccessfully, to get pregnant for about fourteen months, my physician, Dr. Weinberg, recommended a D & C and laparoscopy. Perhaps, he suggested, my problem was a physical one.

I went in for the surgery early in the morning and woke up several hours later.

"Everything looks fine now," Dr. Weinberg said. "You had some endometriosis, which likely accounts for your inability to get pregnant. We cleared it all up."

I was so excited I could hardly stand it. I called my mother and told her the news. I called my sister and told her, too. As far as I was concerned, I should be pregnant in any minute.

My surgery was in December, and by March I still wasn't pregnant. I was, in a word, miserable. By chance I was speaking with Miriam again and told her my situation. She encouraged me to send another request to the Rebbe.

"I just don't see the purpose," I said.

"Just try!" she insisted.

So I did (it's hard to argue with Miriam). The response came hours later, a phone call from one of the Rebbe's assistants. "The Rebbe," he told me, "says you should carefully review the laws of *Taharat Hamishpachah.*"

I was both troubled and surprised to receive this message. Why should the Rebbe encourage me to review a practice I was convinced I already knew so well? I had been going to the *mikvah* for more than a year. I went on the exact day I was supposed to be going. Surely he had made a mistake.

I called Miriam and discussed my schedule. That's when I caught my error.

"You're going a day early," she explained. "You're not waiting enough time after your period has ended before going to the *mikvah.*"

All this time I was so certain I had been properly doing *Taharah.* I felt miserable.

Of course, I set about to immediately correct my mistake and counted the correct number of days the very next month, which was April. The first time I did so—literally, the first time—I became pregnant. Our daughter, Adina Elisheva, was born January 15, 1991.

I think often of this unusual occurrence. By nature and because of my work as a journalist, I readily admit to being a skeptic, especially about mystical kinds of experiences. But I can find no easy, logical answer for what happened to me. Two things about this incident strike me as particularly curious. First, how could the Rebbe, whom I never even met, know that I needed to examine my practice of *Taharat Hamishpachah?* Second, in retrospect it is completely understandable that I did not hear back from the Rebbe upon my first request. It wouldn't have made any difference what blessing he gave me or what he said about *Taharat Hamishpachah*. I had a physical problem and could not have become pregnant until it was cleared up. But how could the Rebbe have known that?

Today, my husband and I have two children, Adina and Yitzhak Natan, thirteen months. And despite labor (it took twelve hours for Adina), I can't wait for more.

One of my closest friends is my sister Rebecca, who lives in Chicago. An educator, Rebecca often gives talks about why she loves going to the *mikvah.* "It's part of the cycle of our family and integral to our Jewish life," she says. "It's also an important aspect to my partnership with my husband. We eagerly anticipate the time I go to the *mikvah,* then we both look forward to preparing for the evening (my husband's job is fixing a nice dinner)."

Recently Rebecca called, though, with news that she would no longer be going to the *mikvah.* For the next nine months, that is. She and her husband are expecting their first child in April. "Soon you'll understand exactly why Mother always insisted we wear our seat belts and get plenty of sleep," I tell her. "You just won't believe how much you're capable of loving someone until you have a child."

42

In Scandinavia: The Cruise

Chana Sharfstein

It happened in August of 1994. According to the calendar it was summer, but in this part of the world one could feel the emergence of fall. The long summer days were gradually growing shorter; the light summer nights were steadily growing darker; the heat of the sun's rays were decreasing in intensity, and an autumn chill was in the evening air. The beaches and outdoor pools were becoming increasingly deserted, and a midnight swim was definitely not on most people's agenda. Yet here I was finalizing plans to facilitate *mikvah* immersion—minus the formal *mikvah*—"au naturel."

In discussions preceding the fifteen-day tour I lead through Scandinavia, one couple had expressed concern regarding the feasibility of *mikvah* immersion, and I had assured them that there would be no problem. As it happened, there were actually two women who needed to immerse in the *mikvah* around the same time. On the overnight cruise approaching a large harbor city, this issue was brought to the forefront. After breakfast aboard ship, we enjoyed a guided city tour, and immediately upon arrival at the hotel we began to make specific plans. Everything went according to Murphy's Law—one problem leading to another. An entire afternoon of attempting to reach the woman in charge of the local *mikvah* proved futile. In the late afternoon we finally learned that this woman was a top executive. By the time we reached her office, business hours were over. Apparently she had plans for the evening, and there was no answering machine on which to leave a message. The local rabbi was on vacation—understandably so, since almost all of his congregants had deserted town for their vacations in the mountains or nearby islands. It became obvious that, unlike in large metropolises, in small cities such as this one, arrangements for *mikvah* use had to be made at least several days in advance. There was a possibility of postponing the immersion for the following evening; however, there was no certainty that we would succeed in contacting the local *mikvah* personnel the next day, either. Without hesitation, each woman in turn expressed with firmness her desire not to postpone this timely *mitzvah*. They decided to use the ocean. The husbands were hesitant, somewhat fearful of the situation, but the courageous attitude of their young wives was very convincing.

As a seasoned tour director I have encountered numerous unexpected and unusual situations, but this one surpassed them all. Furtively I glanced at the two young women sitting beside me in the taxi. They were lovely, charming young women, yet I wondered if they were equal to the task that lay ahead. Raised in America, in comfort, they had chosen to fulfill the *mitzvah* of ritual immersion in an overwhelmingly difficult and dangerous situation. For me this was an entirely new experience, and the bravery of the young women inspired me.

The preparations for immersion had been accomplished in the hotel rooms—all cosmetics and nail polish carefully removed, nails cut, hair carefully brushed . . . so far everything was in order. The next hurdle to overcome was extricating ourselves from the rest of our tightly knit group; after all, *mikvah* is an intimate and private ritual. Knowing the situation could be hazardous, I had requested that the husbands accompany us. After dinner, as the group congregated in the hotel lobby to discuss plans for the evening, each of the two couples left separately, unobtrusively making their way to the taxi that was waiting. The greatest difficulty, however, was my own departure from the group. Everyone wanted to join me or at least be informed of my destination. There was no choice. I had to fabricate a story about an invitation from local friends for a short get-together. This was at least partially true.

Allowing five people in a taxi was against regulations, but after some arm twisting, the driver agreed, so here we all were. I wasn't sure of our exact destination, but it was essential to maintain an air of confidence and calm. Speaking to the driver in his native language, I quickly invented a story. The American men had made a bet with the young women about going swimming in the harbor, I said. This comment was then followed by an essential question: What spot would he suggest for this activity? Somberly the cab driver shook his head. He had never attempted to swim in the harbor, but perhaps it could be done. I was disheartened by his response, and it was only the calm and courage of the young women that inspired me to face the unknown.

We drove to a forestlike park area on the outskirts of the harbor. I asked the driver to stop in a brightly lit area where a narrow path joined the asphalted city road. Hopefully this path would lead straight to the water, to a place that would be accessible for immersion. During the day, in all seasons, this part of town was a popular recreation area for nature lovers. On this dark August evening, however, the place was deserted. I suggested that one of the men remain in the car with the driver. This suggestion was heartily approved, for his glum, confused expression made us all aware that he might want to drive away to safer grounds, leaving us stranded. The second husband accompanied us.

Without flashlights, without the benefit of prior exploration, the walk down this path was cumbersome. Within moments we were enveloped in almost total darkness. It was an eerie feeling, walking in single file down the narrow path, stumbling on large pebbles and fallen twigs. Branches and thorny bushes had to be pushed aside to clear the way. A few turns on the curvy path, and the light from the street could no longer be seen. Fortunately there was a bright moon in the clear sky that peeked through the leafy branches to illuminate our way. And to add to my sense of uneasiness, I was not even certain that this path would ultimately lead us to the proper destination.

When we reached the edge of land, I was overwhelmed by the beauty of the scene in front of us. The dark sky was splattered with thousands of bright, shining stars, and the light of the full moon illuminated the entire setting. Across the water one could see the city with its modern, tall buildings amid historical places and sturdy pre-World War II edifices. Immediately in front of us were scores of pleasure boats safely anchored in the harbor. The larger yachts and sight-seeing cruise ships made me uncomfortable, however. A ship that could hold fifty passengers is quite large, and I did not think it could be anchored in shallow water. I began to feel a chill spread through me. How deep were these waters? Would a safe immersion by these women be possible?

I walked to the very edge of the land and glanced down into the water. Entrance into the water would be extremely difficult. There was a sharp incline of about four feet of huge, jagged rocks; just reaching the water under these conditions would be a most hazardous feat. Everywhere I looked, there was more of the same. The two women, however, were intent on fulfilling the *mitzvah* and had already begun to remove their sneakers and socks. I was amazed at the calmness of my voice when I requested that they pause momentarily. I suggested that we double-check the depth of the waters. The husband quickly removed his shoes and socks, rolled up his pants, and proceeded to walk down to the water. He used his hands to balance his descent. Once he appeared to almost lose his balance and nearly slipped, while I watched in tense silence. He planted himself firmly on a rock lying halfway in the water and then, using great force, he pushed a huge nearby rock into the water. From the sound of the splash we understood that the waters were not too deep and that immersion would be possible.

The husband stayed firm in his position with his back toward us, while the women in complete silence removed their outer garments, placing them neatly near the plastic bags. The most private garments were discarded near the rocks. They shivered slightly as they began their dangerous descent—in reality, a spiritual ascent—their goose pimples a combination of the cool night air and fear. They seemed so delicate and vulnerable as they gingerly moved from rock to rock. They crouched to keep their balance among the sharp, cold, hard rocks. These young women who were used to soft leather shoes and comfortable slippers uttered not a word of complaint as they bruised their legs and feet in this inhospitable environment. My heart was beating loudly, and I felt frozen in fear. One wrong step, God forbid, could be disastrous. I looked up into the sky for reassurance. *God, please watch these women. Look how eagerly they rush to fulfill this* mitzvah. *Protect them and keep them safe.* Over and over again I inwardly recited these thoughts. I felt comforted, too, by the husband who, feet firmly planted on a huge rock, served as a safety anchor. Slowly the women walked into the water. When they were halfway immersed, I told them to submerge themselves completely. With each step they had taken into the water, I was greatly concerned about the increasing depth of the water.

Down they went. And up. And again. And again. My voice rang out loud and clear. "Kosher! Kosher! Kosher!"* Wordlessly, I watched them walk back to shore. Their nude bodies glistened in the moonlight, against the setting of the harbor scene and the majestic trees of the park. I followed their climb up that sharp incline—and then let out a sigh of relief as they quickly wrapped themselves into the huge, fluffy hotel towels.

It was reminiscent of an Ingmar Bergman film, a combination of the harshness of nature and the innocence and delicacy of women. It was a scene to inspire poets, artists, composers. There was an added dimension, however, that was less obvious but of greater and deeper significance, an intangible something that could be discerned only by the initiated. The most delicate strokes of a brush, the most highly sensitive film, the most finely tuned instrument would find it difficult to capture that special *tzniut* (modesty) of the women as they performed this ancient ritual.

There was an aura of holiness surrounding them; their faces radiated with a pureness of intent and joy. They had successfully fulfilled the *mitzvah* that forms the foundation of a Jewish home.

The following day, the entire group returned to this very area as part of the sightseeing tour, to visit a very famous ship museum. Viewing the scene in

*When the *shomeret* (woman who accompanies and watches a woman immerse in the *mikvah*) says *Kosher,* then in the heavens on high it is pronounced *Kosher* and she is blessed (Arizal).

broad daylight, the young women were quite overwhelmed at their courage of the preceding night. They looked at each other and shook their heads in bewilderment, finding it hard to believe that they had overcome all the obstacles to perform the immersion.

Brave, courageous women are familiar to us all from our Torah. Our history—starting with the Matriarchs, Sarah, Rebecca, Rachel and Leah—is filled with illustrious women who risked their lives to assure the continuity of Judaism. To discover in 1994 that there are American-born, American-raised, young Jewish women as brave and courageous as our role models of yesteryear is indeed an inspiration and renewal of faith in the future of Judaism in our modern world.

43
Santa Fe

Chana Katz

Santa Fe has grown in many ways in the last ten years, but the one that has been most important to me is the growth of a Torah community. When my husband and I were married, a "traditional" service began in Santa Fe. We liked the service and began going every *Shabbat*. There were five couples and a few singles involved. We also began to study Bible together once a week with a rabbi from out of town who would speak to us all over a speaker phone.

We studied like that for almost a year. Around January, one woman mentioned that she wanted a *mikvah* in town. She had used the *mikvah* in Albuquerque, but when it closed down, she began using rivers and hot springs around Santa Fe. She was tired of lakes and rivers, she told us. We decided to help her.

We began a fund and found Rabbi Gershon Grossbaum of St. Paul, Minnesota, to help us. (In those days our group was very small, and we used to joke that everyone is doing a different *mitzvah,* put us all together and you'll get one observant Jew.)

Rabbi Grossbaum was very helpful. He came up with a unique design for the *mikvah* that would cost us only three thousand dollars. By May we had about seven hundred dollars in the fund. Rabbi Grossbaum decided to build the *mikvah* even though we didn't have all the money. "Why wait on the *mitzvah?* The money would come," he assured us. Still we were unsure.

A few days later, Rabbi Grossbaum called. He was coming, no matter what. It was Friday; he had two *challot,* and he'd gladly spend *Shabbat* at the airport if we didn't come to get him. We were now on our way to building a *mikvah* and bringing Torah into our lives and community.

That *Shabbat* changed our lives forever. Rabbi Grossbaum spoke to us late into the night. He showed us how to view the world and our lives from a uniquely Jewish perspective. Most people left by one in the morning, but there were three couples, including me and my husband, who remained.

"Sooo," Rabbi Grossbaum said, "where should we put the *mikvah?*" And my husband raised both his arms and said, "Let's put it at our house." I looked at him in shock, and the great *mikvah* adventure began.

The next day, at 9 A.M., we began to build, or more precisely, to break, ground. Rabbi Grossbaum had figured out a clever circular design for our *mikvah,* with the smallest halachically acceptable dimensions. He drew a circle on the ground with *matzah* meal (really!), and we began to dig.

The first day everyone took turns—men, women, and children. There was even one three-year-old who helped out. We were quite a sight. Shovels going, dirt flying, buckets heaving ho! Soon it came down to the men. They dug and dug. At first they could throw the dirt out. Then it got too deep, and they had to haul buckets of dirt out and empty them. It was slow and tedious. They had to keep checking to be sure they were digging straight up and down, not angling in or out. That was one of the main reasons we had to dig by hand. To keep the costs down, the *mikvah* was designed to be a certain size. A backhoe or any other piece of construction equipment would have made the hole too large.

Looking out of my window, I'd see different people digging there at all hours of the day and night—someone would find a half hour here, twenty minutes there. . . .

It was during this time that I decided to begin observing the laws of Family Purity. I studied with two rebbetzins by phone. However, our *mikvah* was not ready, so I had to use lakes or rivers.

In New Mexico, even in the summer, it can get very cold at night; temperatures sometime drop to as low as 30°. The first two times I used the Pecos River. I got lost going, so it was almost 11 P.M. before I got there. The bottom felt squishy with rocks and mud, the water was flowing swiftly. My friend who served as the *mikvah* attendant helped and encouraged me. Still it was so cold, I cried all the way in and out.

In subsequent months I went to Lake Cochiti. The first time was two days before Yom Kippur, during a major blizzard. By the time I got there, the park service had closed the lake. When I went back three days later, I had to park the car ten minutes from the lake. The parking lots were closed due to the snow.

I had been told by my friend that there were large boulders near a remote part of the lake that I could use to provide me some privacy as I undressed. But with eight inches of fresh snow on the ground this was totally unnecessary. The lake was completely deserted. An icy wind was blowing as I went in to the water. Again, I cried the whole time, but thank God I did it. I was so cold after that *mikvah* that on the way back to the car, try as I might, I couldn't even remember the names of all four Matriarchs—only three. I had brought a huge thermos of hot broth, and I drank it all on the way home. At home I had to spend an hour in a hot bath to chase away the chills. Then it came to me, the name of Leah, our matriarch known for her eyes "weakened from weeping."

All of this time, work on the *mikvah* was progressing. We sought rabbinic counsel every step of the way, so that our *mikvah* would be one hundred percent "kosher."

The next month, Arel, a friend of mine who had also been using lakes, wrote a check for one hundred and twenty dollars. She said she was either going to fly to Phoenix to use the *mikvah* there or donate the money to our *mikvah* fund if the *mikvah* could be finished on time.

Well, everyone worked hard and finished the *mikvah*—except for the last two things: no heat and no cover. The *mikvah* is now enclosed in a double layer of plastic-covered greenhouse, but at that time the plastic cover was not up.

I was actually the first woman to use the *mikvah*. It was mid-November, and a light snow was falling. Arel had to hold up sheets around me for privacy. The water was cold, cold, cold. Yet I was so grateful that I was only ten feet from home. I remember, as I immersed, thinking of how blessed I was in so many ways—the least of which was that this would be my last icy *mikvah*.

I admit I cried this time, too, from the cold, but I felt that my tears were somehow a down payment on my desire for a beautiful family.

Thank God, I now have four lovely children, and our *mikvah* has been serving New Mexico for over seven years. The men use the *mikvah* before *Shabbat* and holidays. Women come regularly from Taos and Albuquerque, and visitors to our city use our facilities, as well. Best of all, our "sisterhood" of *mikvah* users includes women from all segments of the Jewish community. The *mikvah* has brought our community together in a very beautiful and profound way.

44

To Return in Purity

Yaffa Eliach

An *aktion* took place in the Bochnia Ghetto. Among the people caught that day was an especially large number of young women. The women knew full well what would happen to them. They discussed something among themselves and selected a spokeswoman. She was a very attractive young woman in her early twenties. She walked over to the German officer in charge of the *Aktion* and said: "We know the inevitable. You will murder us as you murdered the other innocent Jews before us. We demand that you grant us our last wish." "Granted," snapped the German as his hand lovingly caressed his pistol. "And what is it, may I ask?" he said in a derisive tone. "We demand that the ritual bath house, closed since your occupation of our town, be reopened, heated, and cleaned, and that we be permitted to take our ritual bath of purification," said the young woman.

For more than half a day the women cleaned the ritual bath house and filled it with water. Then they cleaned themselves and immeresed themselves in water as prescribed in the Laws of Purification.

As they were led off to be shot, the German officer asked for the young lady who had approached him earlier in the day. When she stood before him, he said: "You are a filthy race, the source of all disease and vermin in Europe.

Based on the author's conversation with Rebbetzin Bronia Spira, June 1976.

Suddenly, before your death, you wish to be clean. What spell did you cast in that ritual bath house of yours?" "Cleanliness and purity of body and mind are part of our tradition and way of life. God has brought our pure souls into this world in the pure homes of our parents, and we wish to return in purity to our Father in Heaven."*

The German officer took out his pistol from his holster and at close range shot the woman between the eyes. Most of the other women were also killed that day.

---

*See introduction, page xxvi.

45

Under the Kitchen Table

S. Z. Sonnenfeld

Before the Communist Revolution, Kiev had hundreds of synagogues and dozens of *mikvahs* to serve its huge Jewish population. In my time, nothing had survived except the *shul*[1] on Shakovitzkaya Street, near our house, and a few small *shtibelach*.[2] I don't know how the *shtibelach* kept going—our *shul,* the "big one," had a bare *minyan* of ten on weekdays and only about fifty on *Shabbos.* Most of them were elderly; younger people knew better than to risk being seen going to *shul.*

As for *mikvahs,* since they weren't needed to show to tourists, Stalin had them all closed down. In Kiev, however, *Tatteh*[3] wasn't about to let the Communists get away with it. Since our apartment was in the basement, we dug a hole under the table, big enough to be a kosher *mikvah.* We lined it with waterproof cement and made a cement lid for it, and it was ready to be filled. How to fill it in accordance with the *Halachah* might have proved a problem in other parts of the world, but not in Russia, where, for most of the year, snow lies on the ground. All we had to do was to fill sacks with snow and dump them in, and once it had melted, we had a perfectly kosher *mikvah.* Of course, it was still ice cold, but we found a way to lower a samovar loaded with glowing coals down into the pool. At any rate it took the chill off.

Sometimes a woman would travel hundreds of miles by train just to use our *mikvah,* and that would have to be the day that the samovar was out of order. You wouldn't think that anyone would be eager to stand in ice-cold water over her head in the middle of the Russian winter, but these women did. Mama used to say of them, "If a woman immerses herself in the ice, her children will never be burned in the fire of *Gehinnom.*"[4]

The *mikvah's* lid was heavy and had to be pulled up with an iron ring *Tatteh* had set in it. Mama always gave this *mitzvah* to the woman who had come to use the *mikvah.* As she bent down to grab the ring, Mama would deliver this little speech—from the bottom of her heart, as always with her:

> Jewish daughter, this iron ring is actually a link of the golden chain that binds you and me to our holy Mothers—Sarah, Rivkah, Rachel, and Leah—and all the pious women in every generation. Remember! A chain is only as strong as every link in it. If, God forbid, this link should snap, then the whole chain is ruined, from start to finish. So grasp it tightly, this link of yours, and be proud that you are upholding the golden chain of holiness that spans four thousand years unbroken.

Notes

1. *Shul*—synagogue (Yiddish).
2. *Shtibelach*—small informal synagogues (Yiddish); literally, small homes.
3. *Tatteh*—father (Yiddish).
4. *Gehinnom*—purgatory (Hebrew/Yiddish).

46

Reb Leibeh
the *Mikvah* Attendant

S.Z. Sonnenfeld

After Stalin's death, some of the persecution against religion was lifted. We even received permission to build a public *mikvah* next to the *shul* on Shakovitzkaya Street. But although the Communists were a bit easier on us, they were still Communists, and life was far from easy. For example, following Stalin's lead, *mikvaos* were permitted only in the few cities that had a tourist office. That alone was enough to tell us that all the "liberalism" was just a publicity maneuver.

Then again, there was a catch about the *mikvah*. We were allowed to build it, yes, but there were no daily hours; it was open only by appointment. And when the attendant went to get wood from the government warehouse to heat the building, he had to fill out a form stating for whom he was opening the *mikvah*: name, address, and all the other details. This, of course, had nothing to do with religion; oh no, it was purely an administrative procedure (if you were fool enough to believe that). Needless to say, it was enough to scare away most of the women. Life was difficult enough as it was; to become known to the government as someone overtly practicing religion was simply asking for trouble.

Something had to be done about this, but everyone was too scared to do it— except *Tatteh*. He agreed to take on the job of *mikvah* attendant, and under his care the women didn't have to fear any longer. Later on he said, half laughing and half serious, "I have been through many stages in my life. When I was young, I was a *yeshivah bochur;*[1] afterwards I traded in skins; then I was a guard on a *kolkhoz;*[2] then I ran a carpentry shop for Sabbath observers; then I was a mattress repairman. The height of my career came only in my old age, when people called me by the heroic title of 'Reb Leibeh the *mikvah* attendant.' "

How did he manage? Well, if a woman was already known to the government as overtly religious, she usually didn't mind if they knew a bit more about her. So very often *Tatteh* would put down that he was opening the *mikvah* for Mama. And since there were other elderly women who did the *mitzvah* of accompanying the younger women to the *mikvah,* it was no problem to write down the older woman's name instead of the younger woman's. And as I said, these women didn't care if the government had one more thing to write down about them. In for a penny, in for a pound, they said. Of course there was always a good chance that the KGB was watching to see who came, but the young women simply dressed in old, torn clothes and pulled their *babushkeh*[3] down over their face, and then no one could tell that it wasn't an old woman coming.

Then there were working women who arranged with a sympathetic doctor to be "sick" just so they could make the twenty-hour train ride to go to the *mikvah* in Kiev. Woe to them if their name appeared on a *mikvah* list when they were supposed to be home sick! But once again *Tatteh* would find some older woman willing to have her name on the list.

He himself never saw the women who came. Wrapped in his Jewish modesty, he would finish filling and warming the pool, and then go sit by the exit and study Torah while either Mama or one of the other older women assisted by the pool. He never looked up to see who it was coming out. He sat there so that they could see him as they left, as the Torah says: the first thing a woman sees as she leaves the *mikvah* should be something pure.

Notes

1. *Yeshivah bochur* — a student in a *yeshivah* (*bochur,* Hebrew/Yiddish).
2. *Kolkhoz* — farm (Russian).
3. *Babushkeh* — head covering or kerchief (Russian).

47

Sossonko: Out of the Depths

Freida Sossonko

My dear ladies, when I visit a *mikvah* here in Brooklyn, I see and I feel the comfort and luxury of the *mikvah,* and the bath and the bathing room and all of the surroundings. And when I finish, I want to be a little bit more in the *mikvah.* I close my eyes, and in my mind I feel another *mikvah* that we Jewish women used about thirty years ago in Tashkent. . . .

In the Second World War, we evacuated from the Ukraine via Samarkand, and we came to Tashkent, the capital of Uzbakistan in middle Asia. Thousands of other Jews who were forced to run from different countries also made their way there, to Tashkent. There was only one *mikvah* in the backyard of the *shul,* and all of us used it. That *mikvah* became an international *mikvah.* Suddenly, in the summer of 1962, the communist government closed it, the only *mikvah* in Tashkent, a city with so many Jews.

After a few weeks, I heard a rumor that there was a *mikvah* available for women. I asked my friend, and she told me that it was true, there is a *mikvah.* She went there, and if I needed it, she would go with me. But it is a secret.

On the day that I was to go, I prepared myself and we went to the *mikvah* together. Sure enough, we came to the same backyard of the *shul.* She called out to the woman who used to work in the *mikvah* and also lived in the same

Transcribed from an address at an evening to benefit Mikvah Yisroel in the Flatbush section of Brooklyn, New York, in the winter of 1992.

yard. The woman came out and went to the side of the *mikvah* that was closed and sealed. And she took off a cover on the earth, and there appeared a well. The well had been dug many years before near the *mikvah*.

A *mikvah* is kosher only when the water is connected with *mayim chaim,* living (natural) waters. Because of this, the original builders built another *mikvah,* near the first, much deeper, and filled it with rainwater. In Tashkent it doesn't rain very often, so the builders also dug a well right near the *mikvah*. Since Tashkent is in the mountains, they had to dig the well very, very deep.

It was decided that until we could build another secret *mikvah* for women, we would use this well. Well water, since it comes from a natural source, is one hundred percent kosher for immersion.

They put a table at the bottom of the well, and they bound two long ladders one on top of the other, and they put that long ladder on the table in the well. The woman who was in charge of the *mikvah* took a pail of hot water and poured it into the well, and it seemed to me like a drop in the ocean. When I took the first step on the ladder, ice-cold air came up from the well. I looked down, and it was dark and so deep I could hardly see the water. When I began to go down, it took a while for my toes to touch the water, and when they did, I immediately drew out my foot because it felt like needles. I put the other foot, but it was the same. I washed my lips, my arms, my face. . . . And again, I closed my eyes and put my foot deep, and I felt fire. I had never experienced such cold. I tried this way and that way and saw that I couldn't take this water. So I decided to go without immersing myself, thinking I would wait until, with *Hashem's* help, we could build a *mikvah*.

But at the same moment, I heard two women enter the yard to use this *mikvah*. One of them was my friend. She talked and I recognized her voice. She was younger than I, and a mother of seven children. And here I began to think differently. What will happen when I go out now from this *mikvah* well? The women will even not try! They will turn back and go home. If they had come a little bit later, nobody would tell them I didn't take the *mikvah*. But now I am a live example for them, a real example, that it is impossible. And that could be a very bad thing.

We lived in Russia, where the government, the communist regime destroyed all the religious life. The *rabbonim,* the *shochtim,* the teachers, all were sent to Siberia. Many didn't come back. And still there were people who did study Torah and perform *mitzvahs* but did this with the greatest self-sacrifice. And *Hashem* put us to live in that country. So He gave us strength to live there and to perform the *mitzvahs* and study Torah. Here we are three women, three Jews, preparing to immerse ourselves. And because it's cold, is that a reason that we shouldn't go?

And here I thought that Satan would come in the picture, and we didn't have to teach Satan how to work. My friend's husband used to work at night in the factory. My friend would come home disappointed and tired from the day's work; she would wait for her husband to inform him that she didn't immerse herself, and waiting, she might fall asleep. You would think that she could leave a note, but how many times have you wanted to do something very important and you forget? Or the husband wouldn't find this note. Satan would see to that. That's the way Satan works. The husband would come, and there would be no chance to inform him that she didn't take the *mikvah*. And a disaster could occur. . . . And with the other woman, Satan also would do his work. And it would be another disaster. And the fault would be on my soul. Could I stand that? No. And I decided no matter what, I must immerse myself in this well.

I began to try again and again, the same thing. The water was cold like . . . impossible. And I began to think that I have to put something in my head that would take away the feelings of my body; only then could I immerse myself. In the Talmud it is related that someone once saw the great sage Ravah studying Torah. He was so immersed in study that he was biting his fingers. Blood came out but he didn't even notice, he didn't feel it. . . . So when you think of something very, you know, powerful, you don't feel where you are and what is with you. And I began to think about one day in my life.

It was in the beginning of February 1951. My husband, as a religious Jew, was arrested by the KGB on May 26, 1950. At that time the KGB had all the power of that communist country, and they used it to the fullest. They arrested many people, many religious Jews—especially religious Jews.

They arrested him when he went to *shul* on a Friday, in the morning. And in that one month when he was taken to Tashkent, I could bring for him kosher food once in ten days. When I came the next month, they told me they had sent him away to another city. I asked them where, but they claimed they didn't know. I explained that I had to send him food; he would not eat the food there. I talked to the wall. For eight more months I didn't know where he was and I wasn't sure if he was alive.

When they arrested him, it was only a few years after our marriage. We had two small children. Eight months after they took him, on one terrible day, *Hashem* decided to take away from me my two small children. They both died in one day. I never . . . I try not to think about that. But at this time my whole body and my whole feelings and what I am doing, it is with this feeling. And I sank deeper and deeper into the memory of what happened that day. And when I felt that I was out of myself and out of my feelings I jumped into the well, and I didn't feel cold at all. I could swim and I wanted to come out to the surface of the well, but I couldn't. There was no strength in my bones. There was no air in my lungs. I tried and I couldn't. I became afraid. I prayed to *Hashem* to spare my life. My husband had returned in 1956. In 1957, *Hashem* had given us a son. And I prayed at that moment, to save my life for my family. It took a while and finally, *Hashem* . . . it was a miracle, I don't know how I came out from that well. I came to the table. I rested a little bit. I finished immersing myself, and then I began to come out from the well. In the middle of the way, it was a long way up, I felt hot inside my body. The circulation of the blood began to work. I touched my body; it was cold like ice. But it was a wonderful feeling, the heat inside.

When I came out, the women approached me. "How did you do it?" "How did you make out?" "It's very cold there?" I couldn't talk to them; I didn't want to tell them a lie, and I couldn't tell them the truth. I showed them three fingers. Usually when we go from the *mikvah,* we put on three things, then we talk. I went to get my clothes and my friend went down. And my thoughts were with her, how she would take it. And suddenly a scream came out from the well. "It's too cold! I can't stand it! I'm going out! It's so cold!" She began to cry, and I began to cry with her. But she immersed herself. She finished and she came out. The second woman was much younger. She saw and heard what was going on here. And she went down quietly; she immersed, and quietly she came out.

My heart was full of joy, and thanks to *Hashem* that He gave us the strength to do it. And now Satan had nothing left to do around us. The result of that night was that my friend offered to build a *mikvah* in her backyard for women, a secret *mikvah*. And with *Hashem's* help, we built a *mikvah* in our kitchen, also for women. Because it wasn't safe for too many women to use the same place.

In 1964, with *Hashem's* help, we received permission to go out from Russia, but we wanted the *mikvah* to remain open. We found a family, and we gave over the *mikvah*. They promised us that the *mikvah* would stay open. We gave over also our home. We didn't take a penny. And the *mikvah* stayed open.

So, my dear friends, the communist regime closed the only *mikvah* in Tashkent. With *Hashem's* help, we opened two *mikvahs*. This was our answer to that regime.

Appendix A
Suggested Reading and Resources

Selected Titles on *Mikvah* and Marriage

Abramov, Tehilla. *The Secret of Jewish Femininity.* New York: Targum/ Feldheim, 1988. A practical and detailed guide to the observance of *Taharat Hamishpachah*/Family Purity.

Bulka, Reuven P. *Jewish Marriage: A Halakhic Ethic.* Hoboken, NJ: Ktav Publishing House, 1986.

Friedman, Manis. *Doesn't Anyone Blush Anymore: Reclaiming Intimacy, Modesty and Sexuality.* San Fransisco: HarperSan Fransisco, 1990.

Kahana, Kalman. *Daughter of Israel.* Trans. Rabbi L. Oschry. Jerusalem: Feldheim, 1970. A practical and detailed guide to the observance of *Taharat Hamishpachah*/Family Purity.

Kaplan, Aryeh. *Made in Heaven: A Jewish Wedding Guide.* New York/ Jerusalem: Moznaim Publishing, 1983.

Kaplan, Aryeh. *Waters of Eden: The Mystery of the Mikvah.* New York: NCSY/ Union of Orthodox Jewish Congregations of America, 1976.

Kaufman, Michael. *Love, Marriage, and Family in Jewish Law and Tradition.* Northvale, NJ: Jason Aronson, 1992.

Kitov, A. Eliyahu. *The Jew and His Home.* New York: Shengold, 1963.

Lamm, Maurice. *The Jewish Way in Love and Marriage.* Middle Village, NY: Jonathan David Publishers, 1980.

Lamm, Norman. *A Hedge of Roses: Jewish Insights into Marriage and Married Life.* New York: Philipp Feldheim, 1966.

The Modern Jewish Woman: A Unique Perspective. New York: Lubavitch Educational Foundation for Jewish Marriage Enrichment, 1981.

Tendler, Moshe David. *Pardes Rimonim: A Marriage Manual for the Jewish Family.* Hoboken, NJ: Ktav Publishing House, 1988.

Educational Audio- and Videotapes

Enhancing Intimacy. Taharas Hamishpochah: A Channel to Enrich Sensitivity, Love and Communication. Audio. Six talks (three cassettes) by Malka Touger. Available through Lubavitch Educational Foundation for Jewish Marriage Enrichment, 824 Eastern Parkway, Brooklyn, NY 11213. (718) 756–5720 or 778–1070. Fax: 735–4455.

The Sanctity of Jewish Marriage: Insights into the Mitzvah of Taharat Hamishpacha. Video, 48 minutes. Available through Mikveh Israel of Montreal, 7015 Kildare Rd., Montreal, Quebec H4W 1C1. (514) 487–5581.

Still Waters Run Deep. Video, 34 minutes. Available from Higher Authorities Productions, 9500 Collins Ave., Bal Harbour, FL 33154. (305) 867–1414 or 1 (800) TORAH-18.

Mikvah Directories

A directory of *mikvahs* in the United States is available through the Union of Orthodox Congregations of America, Synagogue Services, 333 Seventh Avenue, New York, NY 10001. (212) 563–4000.

A directory of *mikvahs* built and maintained by Chabad Lubavitch around the world is available through Lubavitch World Headquarters. Send for World-wide Directory of Chabad Lubavitch Institutions by contacting Machne Israel, 770 Eastern Parkway, Brooklyn, NY 11213. (718) 774–4000.

See pages 239–240 in this volume for a listing of *mikvahs* accessible to the handicapped.

Outreach

To obtain brochures, audio- and videotapes and other educational materials, and for assistance in arranging a speaker or *mikvah* tour call your local *mikvah* office, Orthodox synagogue, or Chabad House.

In the United States, an organization dedicated to disseminating information on *Mikvah* is Lubavitch Educational Foundation for Jewish Marriage Enrichment, 824 Eastern Parkway, Brooklyn, NY 11213. (718) 756-5720 or 778-1070.

In Canada you can contact Mikveh Israel, 7015 Kildare Rd., Montreal, Quebec H4W 1C1. (514) 487-5581.

For Further Information or Assistance

If you wish to study more about *Mikvah* or have questions or concerns about *Mikvah* usage or *Taharat Hamishpachah*/Family Purity, contact your local Orthodox rabbi or rebbetzin or the Chabad House in your area.

If you do not have a local resource, if you think you might need special assistance due to some medical condition, or if you have questions or comments regarding *Total Immersion* please write to the editor:

Total Immersion
Rivkah Slonim
420 Murray Hill Road
Vestal, NY 13850

Appendix B
Mikvahs in the United States Accessible to the Handicapped

This listing* was compiled with the assistance of Dr. Mark Young of TODA, Torah Organization for Disability Access. For more information about this organization contact Dr. Mark Young at (410) 764–6132.

CALIFORNIA

Mikvah Yisroel
3847 Atlantic Boulevard
Long Beach, CA 90807
(310) 427–1360

Mikvah Chabad
18211 Burbank Boulevard
Tarzana, CA 91356
(818) 881–2352

ILLINOIS

Chicago Mikvah
3110 Touhy Avenue
Chicago, IL 60645
(312) 274–7425

NEW YORK

Mikvah Yisroel of Flatbush
1690 Ocean Avenue
Corner of Avenue L and Ocean
Avenue
Brooklyn, NY 11230
(718) 253–8302

Mikvah Congregation Yetev Lev
(Williamsburg)
212 Williamsburg Street East
(between Lee and Marcy Avenues)
Brooklyn, NY 11204
(718) 387–9388

* As of June 1995.

NEW JERSEY

Mikvah Association (Teaneck)
1726 Windsor Road
(Next door to Temple Emet)
Teaneck, NJ 07666
(201) 837–8220
(This location is approximately ten
miles from midtown Manhattan.)

PENNSYLVANIA

Jewish Women's League
for Taharas Hamishpocho Mikvah
2336 Shady Avenue
Pittsburgh, PA 15217
(412) 422–7110

Editor's note: Despite numerous and diverse attempts to create a comprehensive listing of *mikvahs* accessible to the handicapped and disabled, I do not believe the above information is exhaustive. Please note: some establishments are fully accessible and equipped (have hoyer lifts to facilitate immersion, etc.); other establishments may offer accessibility into the building, bathrooms, and showers but may not be suitable for the severely disabled. The personnel at any *mikvah* will extend the maximum assistance and courtesy. It is always best to call ahead, explain the situation and arrange an appointment. There is, thankfully, a heightened sensitivity to this important issue in Jewish communities today, and I think we can expect to see many more accessible *mikvahs* built in the future.

Contributors

Elizabeth Applebaum was born in Columbus, Ohio, and raised in Missouri. She attended Stephens College and went to graduate school at Hebrew University in Jerusalem. Since 1987, she has served as assistant editor of the *Detroit Jewish News*. She and her family live in Oak Park, Michigan.

Gila Berkowitz is a novelist and magazine writer. Her latest book is the forthcoming novel *The Diet*. She also lectures widely on Judaism and sexuality.

Abraham Boyarsky, Ph.D., is a professor of mathematics at Concordia University and the founder and director of Bais Menachem Seminary in Montreal, Canada. He has published a number of historical novels. His *Shreiber* (Ontario: General Publishing, 1981) received the Award for the Best First Novel in Canada in 1982. He has had more than one hundred articles in the fields of mathematics, engineering, cancer research, and physics published in scientific journals.

Varda Branfman was the director of Maine's Poetry-in-the-School program. She now lives in Jerusalem with her husband and children.

Reuven P. Bulka, rabbi of Congregation Machzikei Hadas in Ottawa, Canada, is a highly regarded author and editor. He was ordained at the Rabbi Jacob Joseph Rabbinical Seminary in 1965 and received his Ph.D. in logotherapy from the University of Ottawa in 1971. Founder of the Center for the Study of Psychology and Judaism, Rabbi Bulka is the author of eighteen books and scores of articles.

Sterna Citron is a teacher at Bais Yaakov High School for Girls in Los Angeles, California, as well as the editor of *The Jewish Reader,* a magazine for children. She is the author of *Why the Baal Shem Tov Laughed: Fifty Two Stories about Our Great Chasidic Rabbis* (Jason Aronson, 1993).

Aidel Dubin was a reputed educator in pre–World War II Europe. She was the daughter-in-law of the renowned statesman Rabbi Mordechai Dubin, who headed a political party in the Latvian House of Representatives and also was the chairman of the Jewish Community of Latvia from 1920 to 1940.

Yaffa Eliach, Ph.D., was born in Vilna and is Broeklundian Professor of History and Literature at Brooklyn College, where she is also the founding director of the Center for Holocaust Studies. She lectures widely both in the United States and abroad and has served as a member of the Holocaust Commission. In 1987 she received the Yavner Teaching Award for distinguished contributions related to Holocaust and human rights teaching from the Regents of the New York State Education Department. In the same year she also received a Guggenheim Fellowship for her study of an Eastern European shtetl through its nine-hundred-year history. Her book *Hasidic Tales of the Holocaust* (Oxford University Press, 1982) won the Christopher Award for affirmation of the highest values of the human spirit and artistic excellence. Her *Tower of Faces,* a photo exhibit of European Jewish life as it existed before the Holocaust, is part of the United States Holocaust Memorial Museum in Washington, D.C.

Gwenn Drucker Flait lives in Los Angeles, California, where she is the program coordinator at Martyrs Memorial and Museum of the Holocaust in Los Angeles.

Tamar Frankiel, Ph.D, is a scholar of comparative religion and American religious history who currently teaches at the School of Theology at Clairmont, California. She is the author of *The Voice of Sarah: Feminine Spirituality and Traditional Judaism* (HarperSan Francisco, 1990) and three academic books including the *Christianity* volume in HarperSan Francisco's *Religious Traditions of the World* series and *California's Spiritual Frontiers.* Her numerous scholarly articles have been published in *Tikkun, Commentary,* and *Wellsprings.* She writes and does research in Los Angeles, where she lives with her husband and their five children.

Manis Friedman is rabbi and dean of Bais Chana Institute in St. Paul, Minnesota. He is in wide demand as a speaker and counselor and hosts his own critically acclaimed television series, "Torah Forum with Manis Friedman."

Naomi Futerfas is a well-known teacher and lecturer who resides in London.

Susan Handelman, Ph.D., is a professor of English at the University of Maryland, College Park. She is the author of *Slayers of Moses: The Emergence of Rabbinic Interpretation in Modern Literary Theory.* (State University of New York Press, 1982) and *Fragments of Redemption: Jewish Thoughts and Literary Theory in Scholem, Benjamin and Levinas* (Indiana University Press, 1991).

Lis Harris has been a reporter for *The New Yorker* magazine since the 1970s. She is a visiting professor at Wesleyan University in Middletown, Connecticut, and a two-time recipient of a Woodrow Wilson Fellowship. She lives in New York City with her two sons.

Joshua Hoffman is a member of the Gruss Kollel Elyon of Yeshiva University. He received his rabbinic ordination from Rabbi Aaron Soloveitchik at the Brisk Rabbinical College of Chicago and an M.A. in modern Jewish history at Yeshiva University's Bernard Revel Graduate School. His master's thesis, "The American Rabbinic Career of Rabbi Gavriel Zev Margolis," has been cited in scholarly journals, including the Hebrew journal *Zion.* He has served as associate editor of the *Orot* newsletter and is currently collaborating with Rabbi Dr. Moshe Sherman of Rutgers University on a dictionary of American Orthodox rabbis. His essay *The Institution of the Mikvah in America,* written for this volume, won first prize in the 1994 *Imrei Shefer* essay competition coordinated through the Rabbi Isaac Elchanan Seminary of Yeshiva University.

Shimon Huberband was born in Checiny, Poland, in 1909. He received his rabbinic ordination from his grandfather, Rabbi Chaim Shmuel-Halevi Hurvitz, the Checiny Rebbe. A versatile and prolific scholar, he published articles on a myriad of Judaic disciplines as well as poems and short stories in Yiddish and Hebrew. He was the founder and chairman of Tseirei Emunei Yisroel (the original name of Tseirei Agudas Yisroel, the youth movement affiliated with the religious-political organization Agudath Israel). During World War II, Huberband became the chief chronicler of the tragic events surrounding the Jews in Poland, his main focus being their religious life. As a member of *Oneg Shabbos,* the clandestine Warsaw ghetto archives, he recorded events from everyday life and assembled all the historical materials in the responsa literature written by rabbinic luminaries of Poland. At the age of thirty-three, Huberband was tortured to death by the Nazis in the Treblinka death camp.

Sara Hyamson was married to Rabbi Moses Hyamson, rabbi of the Orach Chaim Congregation in New York (1913–1949), where she was the beloved rebbetzin and active in community affairs. Rabbi Hyamson was also professor of codes at the Jewish Theological Seminary.

Shaindy Jacobson is a teacher of Judaic Studies at the Bais Rivkah High School and Seminary in the Crown Heights section of Brooklyn, New York.

Chana Katz was raised and educated in Texas. She received her Masters in psychology/dance therapy from New York University. She lives with her husband, Asher, and their four children in Santa Fe, New Mexico.

Debra Renee Kaufman, Ph.D., is the Matthews Distinguished Professor in the Department of Sociology and Anthropology at Northeastern University. She is the author of *Achievements and Women: Challenging the Assumptions* (The Free Press, 1982) and the award-winning *Rachel's Daughters* and the editor of *Public/Private Spheres: Women Past and Present* (Northeastern University Customs Textbooks, 1989).

Andrew Klafter graduated from the State University of New York, Binghamton, in 1991. He has studied in Jerusalem at the Hebrew University, Yeshivat Torat Chaim, and Yeshivat Darche Noam/David Shapell College of Jewish Studies. He is currently a medical student and resides with his wife in Buffalo, New York.

Paysach J. Krohn is a fifth generation *mohel* and a well-known lecturer and writer. Rabbi Krohn's published works include *Bris Milah* (Mesorah Publications, 1985), a widely acclaimed compendium of the laws and customs surrounding birth and circumcision, *The Maggid Speaks* (Mesorah Publications, 1987), and *Around the Maggid's Table* (Mesorah Publications, 1989).

Maurice Lamm occupies an endowed chair on professional rabbinics at Yeshiva University's Rabbinical Seminary and is the president of the National Institute for Jewish Hospice. Rabbi Lamm is the author of *The Jewish Way in Death and Mourning* (Jonathan David Publishers, 1969), *The Jewish Way in Love and Marriage* (Jonathan David Publishers, 1980) and *Becoming A Jew* (Jonathan David Publishers, 1991).

Daniel Lapin was born in South Africa and was educated and received his rabbinic ordination from the Gateshead Yeshivah in England and Yeshivat Kfar Chassidim in Israel. Rabbi Lapin came to the United States in 1974 and cofounded Kerem Yeshivah in Northern California. In 1978 he cofounded the Pacific Jewish Center in Los Angeles, which became nationally known as a center of Jewish outreach. In 1991, Rabbi Lapin established Toward Tradition, a political and grass-roots effort to change the way in which the organized Jewish community is commonly perceived by propagating the close alignment of traditional Jewish and politically conservativevalues. His articles have appeared in the *Wall Street Journal, Crisis* magazine, and other periodicals. Rabbi Lapin lives in Mercer Island, Washington, with his wife, Susan, and their seven children, who are all home schooled.

Chava Willig Levy is a freelance writer, editor, and lecturer living in New York City.

Menashe Miller is an Israel-based writer. He is one of a circle of scholars who worked for the Zecher Naftoli Institute. The institute was founded by the late Rabbi Eli Chaim Carlebach for the purpose of researching and recording the lives and teachings of great chasidic rebbes.

Devori Paul is the controller of her family-owned, nationwide business, Continental Company, and is the mother of two active boys. She and her husband make their home in Morristown, New Jersey.

Ellin Ronee Pollachek is a New York City–based writer and thinker. *Seasons* was her first novel and *Midnight Sins* her second. She is completing a doctorate in humanities at New York University.

Roni Loeb Richter grew up in Salt Lake City, Utah, and attended the State University of New York, Binghamton. She received her M.S.W. from the Wurzweiler School of Social Work in Manhattan. She married her husband, Mark, in June 1994.

Liz Rosenberg is an award-winning poet who has published four books of poetry, most recently, *Children of Paradise* (University of Pittsburgh Press). She has also published six books for children, including *Monster Mama,* which won a Parent's Best Book Award, a Children's Choice Award, and Pick of the Lists from Booklist. She writes reviews and essays for *The New York Times, The New Yorker,* the *Boston Globe,* and the *Chicago Tribune,* and is a book-review columnist at *Parents Magazine.* She is associate professor of English at the State University of New York, Binghamton, and lives with her husband and son in Binghamton. She recently edited an anthology of great contemporary American poems for young readers, *A Light in the Mind* (Henry Holt).

Miriam Sagan teaches writing at the Aspen Writer's Conference and Taos Institute of Arts in Santa Fe, New Mexico. She is the author of a dozen books, among them a poetry collection *Pocahontas Discovers America* (Adastra, 1993) and a nonfiction work for children, *Origins: Tracing our Jewish Roots* (John Muir, 1994). She is the recipient of a grant from the Barbara Deming Foundation/Money for Women, based in Brooklyn, and has had many poems published in Harvard's Judaica magazine, *Mosaic.*

Chana Sharfstein spent her childhood in Stockholm, Sweden, where her father, Rabbi J. I. Zuber, was the head of the Orthodox community. She has been in the field of education for many years, both as a teacher and administrator and presently is an English-as-a-second-language teacher for the Board of Education of New York City. She lectures frequently and leads workshops for student teachers. She has authored three children's books and numerous articles. For the past fifteen years Chana has been leading kosher Jewish tours to Scandinavia and enjoys taking tourists to the land of her childhood on a truly Jewish experience. She resides in Crown Heights, Brooklyn, with her husband, Mottel.

Janet Shmaryahu is a Ph.D. candidate in English literature at Cornell University. She lives in Israel with her husband and four children and teaches English literature at Bar-Ilan University.

Chana Silberstein is the administrator of the Chai School in Ithaca, New York, and programming director of the Chabad House of Ithaca. She is currently a National Science Foundation fellow, completing a doctorate in cognitive psychology.

Rivkah Slonim, a nationally known teacher, lecturer, and activist, is the educational director of the Chabad House Jewish Student Center in Binghamton, New York. The student center, which she cofounded with her husband, Aaron, in 1985, has gained recognition as one of the most successful campus outreach programs in the nation.

Shlomo Zalman Sonnenfeld is a rabbi and author. He lives with his family in Jerusalem, where he is active in community affairs.

Freida Sossonko is a well-known and respected figure in the Lubavitch community of Crown Heights in Brooklyn, NY, where she has been living since the 1960s. Rebbetzin Sossonko is actively involved in outreach and teaching and has been organizing and administrating Torah classes for women for the last three decades. Her adherence to Torah law, with enormous self-sacrifice and yet unmitigated pride and joy, under the communist regime in the Soviet Union is legend and serves as a source of inspiration to all who know her.

Helene Storch (née Sauerhoff) was raised in Woodmere, Long Island. A graduate of Stony Brook University and Hunter College, she has a master's degree in gerontological nursing. She lives in Hillside, New Jersey, with her husband and children.

Sybelle Trigoboff studied at the Brooklyn Museum Art School, the Paul Margin advanced workshop, and completed an independent-study-program seminar with artists at the Whitney Museum of American Art. She has extensive experience in teaching art to audiences of all ages. Currently she conducts drawing, painting, and life workshops and lectures on aesthetics in art to intermediate and advanced artists.

Chava Weissler is associate professor of religion studies at Lehigh University and holds the Philip and Muriel Berman Chair of Jewish Civilization. She has published numerous articles on the religious lives of Ashkenazic women and *tkhines,* women's prayers in Yiddish.

Marilyn Wolfe is the mother of six wonderful children and the wife of a wonderful family practitioner, husband, father, musician, and inventor (but not necessarily in that order). She is a frequent traveler on the information superhighway. In her spare time she is a full-time student at Northwestern University and is the chief research associate at the Family Studies Laboratory in the department of psychology. She is the coauthor of two published research studies in the area of human sexuality. Her plans for the future include applying to doctoral programs in clinical psychology and subsequent practice at a women's health clinic.

Yaffa Zager was born and raised in Sweden. She did her undergraduate work at Bar-Ilan University in Israel and received her master's in English from William Paterson College in New Jersey. She is the coordinator of college and developmental English at a branch of Touro College in Spring Valley, New York. She lives with her husband and their seven children in Monsey, New York.

Dov Zlotnick is a professor of Talmud at the Jewish Theological Seminary in New York.

Credits

The author gratefully acknowledges permission from the following sources to reprint previously published material. Every effort has been made to ascertain the owners of copyrights for selections in this volume and to obtain permission to reprint copyrighted passages. The author will be pleased, in subsequent editions, to correct any inadvertent error or omission that may be pointed out.

Alaska Adapted and translated by Rivkah Slonim from the Hebrew in *Kfar Chabad* magazine, no. 306, with kind assistance from Rabbi Yisroel Haber. The letter from the Lubavitcher Rebbe was given to the editor for publication in this volume by Rabbi Haber. A full account of Yisroel and Miriam Haber's adventures in Alaska appears in the forthcoming book *A Rabbi's Northern Adventures—From Alaska's Heights to the Golan Heights* (Kfar Chabad: Uforatzto Publishers).

A Little Girl's Promise Excerpt from *The Maggid Speaks: Favorite Stories and Parables of Rabbi Sholom Schwadron, shlita, Maggid of Jerusalem,* by Rabbi Paysach J. Krohn. Copyright © 1987 by Mesorah Publications, Ltd. Reprinted by permission of the publisher, Mesorah Publications, Ltd.

***Erev* Yom Kippur 1940** From *Kiddush Hashem: Jewish Religious and Cultural Life in Poland During the Holocaust,* by Rabbi Shimon Huberband, translated by David E. Fishman, edited by Jeffrey S. Gurock and Robert S. Hirt.

In the Merit of Righteous Women   By Rebbetzin Aidel Dubin; excerpted and translated by Rivkah Slonim from a speech given in Yiddish, as transcribed in *Der Haint,* Riga, May 8, 1938. Furnished to the editor by Rabbi Moshe Kolodney of Agudath Israel Archives.

The *Magid's* Wife   Translated by Rivkah Slonim from the original Hebrew in *Sefer Bais Ruzhin.* Special thanks to Rabbi Dovid Dubov, Princeton, New Jersey, for researching the source of the story.

The *Mikvah*   Excerpted from the chapter "The Mikvah (Ritual Bath)" in *Holy Days* by Lis Harris. Copyright © 1985 by Lis Harris. Reprinted by permission of the publisher, Simon & Schuster, Inc., and Georges Borchardt, Inc., for the author.

In Nazi-Occupied Europe   From *Kiddush Hashem: Jewish Religious and Cultural Life in Poland During the Holocaust,* by Rabbi Shimon Huberband, translated by David E. Fishman, edited by Jeffrey S. Gurock and Robert S. Hirt. Copyright © 1987 by Yeshiva University Press. Published by Ktav Publishing House and Yeshiva University Press. Used by permission of the publisher.

No Sacrifice Too Great   From a speech given by Naomi Futerfas in London at the Second European Convention of N'shei uBenos Chabad.

Reb Leibeh the *Mikvah* Attendant   From *Voices in the Silence,* by S. Z. Sonnenfeld, translated into English by Yaakov Lavon. Copyright © 1992 by Basya Berg. Published by Philipp Feldheim. Used by permission of the author.

Renewal   From *The Invisible Thread: A Portrait of Jewish American Women* by Pamela Steinberg; interviews by Diana Bletter, photographs by Lori Grinker. Text copyright © 1989 by Diana Bletter and Roundtable Press, Inc. Used by permission of the publisher, The Jewish Publication Society.

The Sexual and the Sacred: Newly Observant Women Speak   Excerpted from the chapter "Practicing Family Purity Laws," in *Rachel's Daughters: Newly Orthodox Jewish Women,* by Dr. Debra Kaufman. Copyright © 1991 by Debra Renee Kaufman. Used by permission of the publisher, Rutgers University Press. Introduction written for this volume by Dr. Debra Kaufman.

The Sexual Component in Love and Marriage   Excerpted from the chapter "The Sexual Component in Love and Marriage," pp. 24–34, in *The Jewish Way in Love and Marriage,* by Maurice Lamm. Copyright © 1980 by Maurice Lamm. Used by permission of the publisher, Jonathan David Publishers.

Shreiber the Jew   Excerpted from the historical novel *Shreiber,* by Abraham Boyarsky. Copyright © 1981 by Abraham Boyarsky. Published by General Publishing Company, Ontario, Canada. Used by permission of the author.

Sossonko: Out of the Depths Transcribed from an address by Rebbetzin Freida Sossonko delivered in the winter of 1992 at a fund-raiser to benefit Mikvah Yisroel, located in the Flatbush section of Brooklyn, New York. Used by permission of Rebbetzin Sossonko.

The Sweet Scent of a *Mitzvah* Excerpted from *Ish Hapeleh* by Menashe Miller, Machon Zecher Naftoli, translated by Micha Odenheimer. Furnished to the editor by Sterna Citron.

Techinot Courtesy of the Library of the Jewish Theological Seminary of America. Translated by permission of Professor Mayer Rabinowitz, librarian, from *Tefillos Lenoshim,* an anonymous, undated manuscript found in the collection of the Jewish Theological Seminary Library. Special thanks to Rabbi Jerry Schwartzbard of the library's rare-book room for his assistance and to Rabbi Nissen Mangel for reviewing and editing the English translation. English translation of Psalm 121 and *V'hi Noam,* from *Siddur Tehillat Hashem,* translated by Rabbi Nissen Mangel (Merkos L'Inyonai Chinuch, 1988). Instructions from old Italian into English translated by Rabbi Levi Garelik.

Thinking Like a Jew Excerpted from "Purity of the Family . . . Survival of the Nation," by Chanoch Shuster, *Uforatzto Journal* 4:1 (Winter 1976). Copyright © 1976 by Lubavitch Youth Organization. Used by permission of the Lubavitch Youth Organization.

Today's *Met Mitzvah* Sermon by Rabbi Dov Zlotnick, delivered on Rosh Hashanah at the Jewish Theological Seminary of America and published in *Best Jewish Sermons of 5727–5728.* Copyright © 1968 by Jonathan David Publishers. Used by permission of the author and Jonathan David Publishers.

To Return in Purity "The Ritual Bath," in *Hasidic Tales of the Holocaust,* by Yaffa Eliach. Copyright © 1982 by Yaffa Eliach. Published by Oxford University Press. Used by permission of the author and Oxford University Press, Inc.

***Tumah and Taharah:* Mystical Insights** Originally published in *Di Yiddishe Heim* and later reprinted in *Wellsprings.* Used by permission of the author.

Under the Kitchen Table From *Voices in the Silence,* by S. Z. Sonnenfeld, translated into English by Yaakov Lavon. Copyright © 1992 by Basya Barg. Published by Philipp Feldheim. Used by permission of the author.

We Must Act By Mrs. Moses Hyamson; reprinted from the *Jewish Forum,* January 1927, "Ritual Baths *(Mikvaoth),*" pp. 22–24. Furnished to the editor by Zalmen Alpert of Yeshiva University Library.

Your Honeymoon Should Never End From *Doesn't Anyone Blush Anymore? Reclaiming Intimacy, Modesty and Sexuality,* by Manis Friedman. Published by HarperSan Francisco. Copyright © 1990 by Bais Chana Education Association. Used by permission of Bais Chana Tapes.

Index

About the Editor

Rivkah Slonim is the education director at the Chabad House Jewish Student Center in Binghamton, New York, and a nationally known teacher, lecturer, and activist. She travels widely, addressing the intersection of traditional Jewish observance and contemporary life, with a special focus on Jewish women in Jewish law and life. During the last decade she has lectured throughout the United States and abroad, counseled individuals, and served as a consultant to educators and outreach professionals on the subject of *Mikvah* and the observance of *Taharat Hamishpachah,* Family Purity. She and her husband are the parents of five children.